Gettin' by

Gettin' by

GIL ANDREWS

Deeds Publishing | Atlanta

Published by Deeds Publishing in Athens, GA
www.deedspublishing.com

Printed in The United States of America

Cover design by Mark Babcock

ISBN 978-1-947309-36-4

Books are available in quantity for promotional or premium use. For information, email info@deedspublishing.com.

First Edition, 2018

10 9 8 7 6 5 4 3 2 1

This book is dedicated to those that serve—law enforcement, firefighters, first responders, the military, and especially to the "war fighters"—and to Don Ware, my partner. Those that serve honorably DESERVE honor, respect, and thanks.

"In today's even more urban world, the cowboy retains his anti-urban allure."

—Lawrence Clayton in *The Cowboy Way*

Introduction

For more than ten years, I have contemplated writing this book. I have told some of these stories to friends over the many years. Many times, friends have told me, "You should write a book." But I could never convince myself that anyone would be interested in reading a book about my life. I am someone that has never achieved a measure of fame or fortune. I am not even sure my story is unique, or that my story is worth telling. After much convincing by a close friend, I finally decided that I would sit down and memorialize these stories. In 2009, I was diagnosed with chronic lymphocytic leukemia. In 2012, I was diagnosed with prostate cancer, prompting me to rethink my life. I began to take one year at a time. I also figured it was time to start working on my bucket list. I am not writing this book to elicit any measure of sympathy from the reader. I do not have the victim mentality that is so prevalent today. Surely there are many whom have had it tougher than I have.

I mainly decided to write this book to give the reader a raw, gritty (the way it was lived) glimpse into someone's lifestyle, someone who was not raised in a privileged environment, who had to struggle to achieve a measure of the American dream and then had to struggle to hold onto that dream. At a minimum, I want to provide a history for my only son. I never knew the history of my own father. I knew little of the life of the man that raised me, from his birth in 1904 until 1946, and I did not want my son to be missing such a big part of his family history. To a lesser degree, it may be an old man's attempt at self-reflection. It is a story about the contrast between 1950-60s culture and the current culture. It is an attempt to paint a not-so-pleasant picture of the lives of a family that struggled to survive in much less fortunate circumstances and in a different time in America, when Americans were proud to be Americans. It is the story of the struggle of one of the family members to break out of that life and the subsequent interactions with many other people who never quite succeeded in such an escape.

Today, more than back in the 1950s and 1960s when I was growing up, America has become a divided society. One of the growing segments of today's society is the entitlement culture. I grew up envying, maybe even resenting, those who could just ask for things they wanted. I grew up with the mindset that if you wanted something ,you had to get it yourself because your parents were not capable of giving you many of the things you wanted. Often, we were told, "No, we can't afford it." We finally learned to stop asking. Due to a fretting personality trait, I did not have the temperament to think I could get what I wanted by taking it from others illegally, and I was not the type to befriend someone solely to get what I wanted. I found ingratiating myself to others for help was humiliating. Even when I could have asked for help, I would not.

Raising six children on welfare, my parents were only able to provide for our basic needs—food, clothing, and shelter, maybe an occasional treat. Welfare aid to dependent children back in the 1950s and 1960s was not something that people were proud to have to resort to. For many years, I would lie to my friends about what my father did for a living. I did not want my friends and classmates to know that we were on welfare and were just "gettin' by" on it.

So many of today's citizens seem to think that they are entitled to have the things that they see on TV, in the movies, or that their friends have. All they must do is ask, and they should receive it. They seem to think they are entitled to a college education. No one in my family thought about asking for something other than the basics. No one in my family even thought about going to college. We were conditioned by our mother at an early age that, at eighteen years old, or if you dropped out of high school before eighteen, welfare would cut off benefits to the family for you. If you stayed in the family household, you would be expected to contribute the amount that welfare had provided for you. If you did not contribute to the household, then you were expected to move out.

The mother-bird mentality is a hard lesson for a child to accept. For the girls in the family, the options were few—get married, get a minimum wage job, or in a few cases, join the military. With the boys, the options were also few—get a job working in minimum wage seasonal agriculture or at a gas station, or get drafted, or enlist in the military. After graduating from high school in 1964, during the buildup for the Vietnam War, knowing that I was looking at few prospects and the draft, I enlisted in the United States Air Force. It was the wisest decision I would ever make. I probably would have ended up in prison if I had stayed in the Colusa County, California, area. The constant struggle just to get by lends itself to taking the wrong path.

I never did know what I wanted to be, nor did I have any real aspirations. All I knew was that I did not want to get trapped in a seasonal agricultural lifestyle, supporting a wife and several children on minimum wage, and then drawing unemployment in the off-seasons. I did not want to be poor or just gettin' by. I hated being poor. In my senior year of high school, I expressed interest to the school counselor about becoming a helicopter pilot. She immediately dashed that idea by suggesting that I did not have what it took. I wanted to rise above my raising, but I did not anticipate that my family would think later I was a snob for doing so.

By a stroke of monumental good luck, I found myself in a 29-year-long law enforcement career, and at times struggling to hang on to that career. The need to avoid poverty drove me most of my life. It drove me to be frugal, which did not make me popular with my ex-wives and children. As I have discovered over the years, there is a thin line between cheap and frugal. It is all a matter of who is spending who's money. If a spouse expects you to expend your money to make a purchase and you say, "No," then you are labeled cheap. If you suggest she expend her money for the purchase and she says, "No," she is being frugal.

The stories in this book are true, though some details have been blurred by time and memory. The names of many of the people have been changed to protect their privacy. These stories are a look into the lifestyles of the underprivileged/undereducated "white trash"—society's underbelly in a different time and culture in the United States, an America with different values, and an America that had not yet acquired an entitlement mentality. It is a story of someone struggling to dig himself out of an impoverished life, shed the victim mentality, and achieve some measure of the American dream... and the struggles to maintain that dream once it was realized. It is a story about constantly struggling to overcome adversities. Part of that American Dream was to be "married with children," but my career choices would often conflict with that role. I found that the responsibility of "making another person happy" did not come easy to me.

One of the individuals mentioned in this book, after reading the manuscript, suggested that it took "Big Balls" to reveal some of these stories. Writing this book has been very personal for me, but it had to be done. Exposing the skeletons in the family closet and baring your soul to the world can be both humbling and frightening. It is also cleansing and therapeutic. I am sure there are those who will judge me negatively, but they never walked in my shoes.

Any resemblance between those mentioned in this book to persons living or dead is purely coincidental and unintentional.

Tom Andrews

In 1900, President McKinley was reelected to his second term as president; however, President McKinley would not live to serve out his second term because of an assassin's bullet. The new president, Theodore Roosevelt, made America feel strong. He sent three warships to Panama to help secure the country's newly decreed independence from Colombia, in a revolution that the United States encouraged so it could build the Panama Canal.

By 1903, Americans were clearly industrialized. They knew about emerging technologies. Maybe 1903 was the year of promise. Henry Ford founded the Ford motor company in 1903. That same year marked the Wright brothers' first flight, as well as the establishment of Harley Davidson Motorcycle Company. I would later acquire a passion for two of those developments, but it was not until the age of 53 that I would buy my first Harley, and only after I had spent 35 years living the role I thought I was destined to live. Also, at that age, I would obtain my commercial pilot's license with multi-engine instrument and seaplane ratings.

Available land brought the settlers to Exeter, Nebraska, in 1870. For only a filing fee, setters could acquire 160 acres of land. The village of Exeter was named per the alphabetical system of naming towns every eight miles along the Burlington railroad.

Thus, the nearby towns were Crete, Dorchester, Exeter, Fairmont Grafton Hastings, Inland Juniata, Kenesaw and Lowell

By 1904, the technological and social changes had not yet arrived in Exeter, Nebraska. Tom Andrews was born into a subsistence farming family in 1904, the youngest of three brothers. Ironically, as in Colusa, California in 1964, the early 1900s Exeter, Nebraska did not offer many opportunities for young and uneducated men. A few years after Tom was born, his father died, and not long after that, his mother would marry Henry Brocker. Tom's half-brother, Marvin, was born shortly thereafter. Eventually his older brothers, Roy and Oscar, would leave Exeter and migrate to the west coast to look for work in the agricultural fields. Like many men of that time with no means of transportation or money, they would resort to hopping rides on freight trains and living in hobo camps as they travelled throughout the Western United States looking for work. In the fourth grade, Tom dropped out of school. He soon realized that opportunities for young a man with a fourth-grade education were few in Exeter, Nebraska. At age 16, Tom lied about his age and enlisted in the United States Navy, leaving the family farm for good. After six months in the Navy, his lie was discovered, and he was booted from the Navy in Treasure Island, California.

He had no job and no future. Like Roy and Oscar before him, Tom found himself riding the rails and living in hobo camps. In his younger years, Tom tended to fight with little provocation. Many times, in the hobo camps, Tom would find himself in conflict with others in the camps. Maybe the conflict was just over Tom wanting to borrow some Bull Durham tobacco so he could roll his own cigarette, or maybe he just wanted a swig of the other guy's hooch. Whatever the case, the fights were long and drawn out. No one in the camp would intervene. They would let the two men fight it out until one gave in. On more than one occasion, the two men would stop the fight so they could rest and then go at it again.

For the next 15 to 20 years, Tom would go from job to job, many times following the seasonal agricultural crops up and down the West Coast. During this time, Tom never married and never had any children that he spoke of. In his late 30s, Tom found himself in Tracy, California, where he landed a labor job with Granite Construction Company. In time, Tom would work his way into a foreman's position of a work crew. It was at this time that Tom finally settled into a common-law relationship with Sally Anderson. Tom and Sally never did marry; however, they did produce two children, a son named Tommy and a younger daughter named Sally. Tom's future looked a lot brighter now. He had a permanent job with some chance of advancement, a common-law wife, and two beautiful children.

Throughout this book, at times I will refer to Tom Andrews as Tom. Until I was 15 years old, I always referred to him as Dad. When I was 15 years old, my cousin Rusty suggested that Tom was not my father. As you read on, you will understand why I have my doubts. I would not know the truth until 2015, when I paid to have a DNA comparison with my three younger female siblings.

Naomi Homer

In 1921, Row, Oklahoma, and Colcord, Oklahoma, were nothing
more than wide spots in the road, just across the state line from
Siloam Springs, Arkansas. The two towns were little more than
a mile apart, so the Homer family used Colcord as their address.
Naomi Homer was the second of six children born to Will and
Ollie Homer. Will and Ollie would have a child every two years
like clockwork. The oldest sister, Nova, was rapidly followed by
Naomi, then brothers Freeman, Marvin, Onnie, and then a little
sister, Joy.

For the next seven to eight years, the Homers would continue
to try to scratch out a living for their family. Will had a very unusual quirk for a subsistence family back then. He raised cows for
milk, but milk was not allowed on the family table. Will had been
raised to believe that milk was bad for you. The family did milk
the cows but would separate the cream from the milk and sell the
cream, then feed the milk to the hogs. In those days, Will ruled the
roost, as the saying goes. Ollie's first four children were only fed
breast milk. Onnie and Joy were given canned milk. Toward the
end of the 1920s, Will and Ollie decided to leave Colcord to look
for work and find a climate better for Ollie's asthma. Like so many
families before them, they struck out for the West Coast.

The 1930 United States Federal Census shows Will and Ollie living in Asotin, Washington, where little Joy was born. For the next several years, Will and Ollie would remain in the Asotin, Washington, area supporting themselves by seasonal agricultural work. Around the time that Naomi was 14 or 15 years old, the family decided to move back to Colcord, Oklahoma. Once back in Colcord, Naomi nearly died from rheumatic fever. While Naomi was recovering from rheumatic fever, her mother showered her with attention to the point that Naomi was given "special handling." Naomi soon learned to use her illness to her advantage. When the other siblings were expected to get up in the mornings and do their chores before they went to school, Naomi would sleep in, claiming to not be feeling well.

This favoritism became a point of contention among the other children. Her mother developed a tendency to make excuses for Naomi as well. This tendency of making excuses would follow Naomi throughout her life. She learned to blame others for her misfortune. It was about this time that Naomi dropped out of high school, never to receive her high school diploma. In time, Naomi became the black sheep of the family as a result of choices she made. Naomi also learned to lie about her circumstances.

Naomi recovered enough to be able to go out dancing and partying with the local boys late into the night on a regular basis. However, when it came time to get up in the mornings, Naomi would often claim she was not feeling well. About this time, her older sister Nova would marry and move out of the house. This made Naomi the oldest of the siblings, a situation she readily took advantage of by ordering the younger siblings around. By age 19, Naomi would find herself pregnant by one of the local boys. Naomi would always claim that the father of the child was Homer Bossom Carine. Homer would deny to his death that he was the father of Naomi's little girl. His family as well would deny that their upstanding son was the girl's father.

At that time, Naomi had been dating Billy Smith for a long period of time and supposedly only went out with Homer Carine one time. Before Naomi's little girl Sadie was born in 1942, Homer Carine enlisted in the Army and was shipped out to fight in the war in Europe. The military was a good escape for young men who found themselves in such a situation. Billy Smith would end up marrying another local girl. Did Naomi find another plausible father to accept responsibility?

After Naomi's little daughter, Sadie, was born, she took pictures of Sadie and sent them to Homer in Europe. Homer sent the pictures back to Naomi, telling her that the child was not his. He was even willing to take a blood test to determine paternity when he returned from Europe. Like many young men who went off to war, Homer never returned. He was buried in Europe.

Shortly after she gave birth to her first child, Nova's husband died from complications from appendicitis. Nova, Naomi, and Ollie decided that they would leave Colcord again and head out to the West Coast to find work to support their children, but Will stayed in Colcord. Nova and Naomi would take their young daughters with them. Ollie later returned to Colcord, where she died at the young age of 46. Will lived on the family farm until the age of 88. Life was hard on subsistence families, especially child-bearing women. Nova would meet her second husband in California, and they would have two more children. Naomi remained in Sacramento, California, where she found a position working in a jewelry store. Naomi worked with a woman named Nellie, who would become my aunt.

Mystery Man

In late 1945, Naomi was living in Sacramento in a small upstairs apartment while working in the jewelry store downstairs. Her co-worker was Nellie Andrews, the wife of Tom's older brother, Oscar. At some point in time, Naomi was introduced to Oscar's younger brother, Tom. What will always remain a mystery is whether Tom was introduced to Naomi before or after she became pregnant. Naomi had originally told her mother that someone had broken into her upstairs apartment and raped her. Naomi's older sister, Nova, always believed that the father of Naomi's second child was some Army guy she was dating at the time. This raises some interesting questions. Was Tom the father of Naomi's child, or did he come to the rescue of unfortunate Naomi? Did Naomi dupe Tom into thinking he was the responsible party? Was she raped or was it the child of her boyfriend? The questions would be partially answered 69 years later. Originally, childless Oscar and his wife Nellie were planning to adopt Naomi's second child as their own. As it turned out, Tom became involved with Naomi and in March 1946, he married Naomi, leaving his common-law wife and two children behind in Tracy, California. Tom moved Naomi and Sadie to Modesto, where, three and a half months later, little Gil Andrews was brought into the world. Being born just a few months after his parents were wed, little Gil would be referred to as the "California sunshine baby." With all the sunshine in California, things just grow faster.

By now, Tom had two children of his own, maybe a third, and a four-year-old stepdaughter. With a steady job, he could make the ends meet, but as fate would have it, a few months after I was born, Tom was severely injured at work, permanently disabling him for life. Tom was supervising a job that required a portable cement mixer to be hoisted to the job location. The loaded mixer was secured to the hoist by a chain. The inexperienced laborer moved the hoist too fast, causing the mixer to slip loose. The loaded mixer fell on Tom, pinning him to the ground. The mixer cut into Tom's right bicep and broke his back. A piece of metal pipe attached to the mixer pierced Tom's neck into his left lung, collapsing it. Seeing of the pipe sticking out of Tom's neck, co-workers and onlookers were convinced that Tom was going to die. Tom asked for a cigarette, and one of his coworkers gave him a tailor-made cigarette (store bought). Tom, who smoked roll-your-own Bull Durham cigarettes all his life, most surely appreciated having a tailor-made cigarette before he died.

Tom was taken to the hospital, where he surprised everyone by surviving. The doctors reconnected Tom's right bicep muscles. However, Tom would never be able to completely use his right hand again, unable to fully extend the fingers on his right hand. He would have to teach himself to himself to be left-handed and live the rest of his life with one lung. He constantly suffered from back pain.

After spending weeks in the hospital recovering, the construction company gave Tom a $3000 check and told him his services were no longer needed. Tom had never seen $3000 at one time in his life. I am sure that in 1946, $3000 seemed like a lot of money. One of the first things Tom did was buy a new car, load Naomi, Sadie, and little Gil into the car and drive back to Colcord, Oklahoma for a visit. According to Aunt Nova, Tom was acting the big shot and "puttin' on the dog" with his newfound wealth.

After a brief visit to Colcord, Tom and family returned to Modesto, California. In no time at all, the $3000 was gone. Tom would find himself back doing the only thing he knew—looking for farm work to support his family. Tom moved the family to Turlock, California. By December, Naomi would find herself pregnant again, this time with twin daughters. Paula and Darla were born in August 1947 in Turlock, California.

The Fruit Tramps

By 1948, Tom, Naomi and the four children, including me, left Turlock, California, travelling up and down the West Coast, following the agricultural harvest. At times, we lived in migrant farm worker camps. Some were no more than tents with wooden sides and canvas tops. Many times, those of us that lived in these camps were referred to as "Fruit Tramps," people that followed the seasonal crops. We were society's underbelly, going from job to job, scraping out a living, just gettin' by, just "white trash," the invisible people. Most of the migrant camps did not have indoor plumbing, so we had to use community outhouses or washrooms when the need arose. We always had coffee cans under the bed to relieve ourselves during the night, which someone had to empty when morning came. Even the four children, as they became old enough, would find themselves in the fields and orchards picking apples, walnuts, peaches, prunes, and, on one occasion, hops. The workers were paid by the bag or box, so the more people that you had working, the more the family could earn. We moved from Sebastopol, California; to Petaluma, California; to Eureka, California; to Oregon and Washington State, and then back to the Sacramento Valley.

It was in Eureka, California, at about the age of four, that I began to accumulate memories of my childhood. One of my first memories is the time when an older neighbor friend, Ruben, and I were playing with matches, resulting in a forest fire. Ruben had gotten hold of the box of wooden matches, so we snuck off to a forested area not far from the migrant camp where we were staying. We decided that we would build a campfire in the fork of a tree trunk. Not realizing how fast dried pine needles would burn, we accumulated a small amount of pine needles to use as fuel to start the fire. Setting the lit match to the pile of dried pine needles was like setting it to gasoline. Within seconds, the flames shot up the trunk of the tree, burning out of control, spreading from tree to tree. We ran like hell back to the migrant camp to avoid being identified as the responsible parties. However, neighbors had seen us leaving the scene of the crime and reported us to the firemen when they arrived. Thanks to the efficiency of the fire crew, the fire was quickly extinguished. Ruben and I found ourselves standing tall in front of the firemen, our parents answering their questions. Fortunately for me, Ruben admitted that he was the one that had the matches. I don't think that my ass-whipping was as bad as Ruben's, but I know I never played with matches again. Needless to say, the incident was "burned" into my butt and memory. Pardon the pun. I was not allowed to play with Ruben anymore after that.

It was also in Eureka that I acquired my limited religious training. Our family regularly attended Sunday services at the local Pentecostal church. My older sister, Sadie, and I both were awarded complimentary Bibles for perfect attendance at Sunday school. For many years, I was very proud of that Bible and I kept it most of my life. The Bible would somehow disappear during one of my divorces.

It was also in Eureka, California, that I acquired the memory of Tom molesting my older half-sister, Sadie. At four years old, I did not realize what was going on when I walked into that bedroom, but I was perceptive enough to realize that something was not right. As I walked through the doorway, I saw Tom sitting in a chair with Sadie sheepishly standing directly in front of him. Tom immediately stood up, walked over to the dresser, and gathered up my slingshot and steel ball bearings, handing them to me and telling me to go outside and play. What stuck in my mind as unusual was that I had never been allowed to use the slingshot unless an adult was with me. I took the slingshot and did as I was told.

Sadie and I never spoke of that incident until she was 70 and I was 66. I had long since worked out what was going on in that bedroom on that day. When I asked Sadie about the incident, she was a little taken aback that I knew about it at all. Sadie told me that Tom had been molesting her for a while and when I walked in on them, she was finally prompted to tell our mother. Sadie wanted and expected our mother to leave Tom over the incident. She would resent our mother for not leaving Tom. But what Sadie did not know was our mother was pregnant with her fifth child. Our younger sister, Darlene, was born in August 1950. What could a single woman do with five children? But she would forever hold it over Tom's head, effectively emasculating him.

The only happy memory I have of my childhood was the time in Eureka when the Rodeo came to town. Tom bought me an all-black cowboy outfit: black cowboy hat, black cowboy shirt and pants, black cowboy boots, and two silver six-shooters with black holsters. I was the spitting image of Hop-A-Long Cassidy in miniature. On rodeo day, when we stepped into those grandstands and folks took notice, I was full of myself the entire day. I think Tom was somewhat proud to show me off.

After leaving Eureka, we migrated south to Petaluma, California, where Tom found a job on one of the many chicken ranches in the area. We lived in housing provided by the chicken ranch owner. Tom's job was to remove three to four inches of dried chicken manure from the floors of the chicken houses. Tom and Naomi worked side-by-side, using scoop shovels to remove the thick layer of dried chicken manure from the floor. The chicken manure was loaded into wheelbarrows, which then had to be wheeled outside and dumped. On many occasions, I accompanied them to work at the chicken ranch. As it turned out, this would become my first job. Almost five years old, I could barely balance the wheelbarrow when it was empty. I soon learned to balance the wheelbarrow with two partial shovelfuls of chicken manure in it. If I was on a flat surface, I could handle the wheelbarrow. Once I started down the ramp to go outside, many times it would get away from me, dumping my two shovelfuls. I then would have to start all over again. But I had entered the workforce.

As the only boy in the family with four sisters, I would often ask my mother if I could have a baby brother. Even though I was one of five children, many times, I felt a sense of loneliness and thought a baby brother would alleviate that. Three years later, my mother granted me my wish, but it would not be what I expected.

That chicken ranch job soon played out for Tom. So again, we migrated, this time east to Colusa California.

Colusa, California, is the county seat of Colusa County in the heart of the Sacramento Valley. The Sacramento Valley produces a large variety of agricultural crops, such as hay, olives, rice, wheat, barley almonds, prunes, peaches, and English and black walnuts, to mention a few. There was then, and still is, a need for seasonal agricultural workers. Today most of the work is done by Hispanic laborers.

Upon arriving in Colusa, we had no place to stay, and Tom had no job. Tom soon acquired a job driving a Caterpillar for a local farmer. Sitting on that jarring Caterpillar was murderous to Tom's back. One of the local churches in Colusa at the corner of Bridges and Fremont Street allowed us to stay in the church garage until Tom could get a paycheck and find a rental house for the family. The small garage had no privacy and no plumbing. Tom and Naomi strung a cotton clothes line down the center of the garage and hung bed sheets over the line to provide a measure of privacy for them. They slept on one side of the garage on a mattress on the floor and we slept on the other side on a mattress on the floor. Again, we had to use coffee cans to relieve ourselves during the night. In the daytime, we could use the restroom in the church.

As soon as Tom got a paycheck, we moved diagonally across the street to an old, dilapidated, wooden two-story house. The upstairs portion of the house had been condemned, so only the bottom floor of the house was inhabitable. But that was all that Tom could afford. That old house creaked and moaned at night and when the winds howled. At night, when I lay in bed, trying to go to sleep, I would hear every creak and moan. I hated when bedtime came. I would hear the rusty old hinges creak on the unlatched screen door as the wind blew it open and shut. I was convinced that ghosts lived upstairs and they were the ones that were making the noises. Since 1954, when Stewart Hamlbin released "This Old House," that song would forever bring back memories of that rickety old wooden house in Colusa. I was so glad when my dad's job played out again and we moved on, getting away from that rickety old house. I remembered the day that job ended. Tom always took a brown paper sack lunch to work and after lunch each day, he always neatly folded the bag to bring home to be reused. When he got home that last day, he waded up the paper bag and tossed it in the trash. It was time to move again.

That rickety old house was across the street from the Colusa County Fairgrounds at that time. That summer when the fair came to town, some of the carnival rides were set up directly across the street from our house. Having already entered the labor force back Petaluma, California, on the chicken ranch, I immediately saw an opportunity for another job. I could go across the street and be hired to help set up the rides. So, I borrowed a pair of my father's old leather gloves and boldly walked across the street, hoping to go to work. One of the carnival workers recognized what my purpose was when he saw me with those oversized leather gloves. He told me that he would pay me a quarter if I would move an iron pry bar from one location to another. Being the mountain of a man that I was at four-years-old, I was able to move the pry bar to its new location and I was immediately paid my quarter. Then the worker asked me if I wanted to read some of his comic books. Little did I know what he wanted in exchange for allowing me to read his comic books. He hoisted me into the driver side of his semi-tractor, went around to the passenger side, and climbed into the cab with me. He handed me several comic books and allowed me to look through them, all while he sat next to me fondling my little uncircumcised penis. Fortunately for me, I could go home, but I never spoke of that encounter until this day. Years later, I realized how lucky I was that I could leave.

Shortly after that incident, we left Colusa and moved to Seaside, California. We rented a house on the same street where Uncle Roy and Aunt Helen lived. Coincidentally, that rickety old house was torn down years later and the Colusa County jail would be built on the site. Just as ironic, twelve years later I'd return to live in Colusa, in a two-story brick house where the upstairs was condemned. Also, I would end up spending one night in that county jail for underage drinking.

Cannery Row

I think living in Seaside was the last time that I would have any fond memories of my childhood days. I entered kindergarten in Seaside, and soon came to love going to school. We lived on the same street as Uncle Roy and Aunt Helen and their two children, their son Charlie and youngest daughter Rusty. Their oldest daughter, Ginny, had already married and was living in Pacific Grove, California, with her husband. It was great to have older cousins to hang out with. I loved both my Aunt Helen and my cousin Rusty dearly. Charlie, who was 10 years older than me, became like a big brother. We would often take the bus to go to the beach and spend the day there. We thought nothing of taking the bus to go to the movies. Uncle Roy gave me my first dog, a Dalmatian mix I named after Ozzie of the Ozzie and Harriet TV show. Ozzie was mostly white with a few large black spots; not the typical looking Dalmatian. That dog and I were inseparable for the next five years. When I went to bed, Ozzie went to bed. When I got up, Ozzie got up. When Ozzie had grown to full size, he had to be restrained from entering the bedroom until I got in bed at bedtime. If he got to the bed before I did, he would stretch out full-length, making it difficult for me to fit in my single bed. I would bond with dogs for the rest of my life easier than I did with humans. I would always be a sucker for newborn puppies. I have always thought they were cuter than babies. I now have eight dogs.

In 1952, I would enter the first grade, but I would only complete half the year in Seaside. It would not be until years later that I figured why we abruptly left Seaside and moved to Arbuckle, California. The house we lived in in Seaside had indoor plumbing, unlike the house we moved to in Arbuckle. It seems that Tom was doing odd jobs to earn money to support the family. Uncle Roy was a house painter so whenever he could, Tom would help Roy on some of the jobs. Naomi decided that she could get a job and help support the family as well. One of our neighbors down at the end of the street worked at one of the fish canneries on Cannery Row, in Monterey. The "Negro" father, the politically-correct term used in 1952, who worked at one of the canneries offered to take my mother down to the fish canneries so she could apply for a job. None of us children were ever told what happened on that trip to Cannery Row, but years later, we would pick up bits and pieces of why we came to have a black brother. We do not know what Naomi told Tom about the incident, nor will we ever know what really happened. Sadie would later reveal that, during one of her visits to the family, the father had his hands all over her. Whenever the question of why we had a black brother was brought up, our mother would burst into tears, never answering. She could not even bring herself to tell our Eddie when he came of age and asked himself. We quickly learned to never broach that subject.

To our knowledge, the incident was never reported to police, nor was the neighbor ever charged with any crime. Maybe it was the shame of a white woman being raped by a black man in 1952, or maybe Naomi thought she would be held culpable due to her "flirtatious nature." We will never know, nor will little brother Eddie ever know who his father was. He did not learn how he became the only black child in a white family until he was 19, which was when I told him what I had learned.

Nor will we ever know how Tom handled the situation. Maybe he found himself forced to accept the situation after Sadie told Mom about Tom molesting her. We will never know if he ever confronted the neighbor. Tom did treat Eddie as well as he treated the rest of us. Maybe even he treated Eddie with "special handling" by being reluctant to discipline him, which would create developmental problems for Eddie in has adolescent years. Tom seemed to accept Eddie and even grew protective of him when racial issues were raised.

Even as the debate over abortion rages today, some believe that it should be allowed in cases of rape. In 1952 a white woman having a black child was not socially acceptable. I don't know if abortion was ever considered in my mother's case. But after reading the book Gosnell, The Untold Story of America's Most Prolific Serial Killer by Ann McElhinney and Phelim McAleer, I cringe at the thought of Eddie's life being ended that way. I firmly believe that abortion should not be used as after-the-fact contraception, and taxpayer's money should not be used to fund it.

I do know that having a black child in a white family creates issues for all. Even Eddie, to this day, will say he "has issues." There was a positive aspect of Eddie being in our family. Because of his presence in the family, we never learned racial bigotry or prejudices. We all accepted him as our brother. My biases are based on a person's values and character, not the color of their skin.

All things considered, Tom and Naomi decided that it would best to relocate again. I hated to leave my cousins and my beloved Aunt Helen. I would never see her again, as she would die shortly after we moved. I had no idea what living conditions we were about to encounter in the Arbuckle, California, POW camp.

POW Camp

When we left Seaside, California, we headed back to the Sacramento Valley. We initially found ourselves in Williams, California, ten miles west of Colusa. We first lived in the Smith Motel in Williams on the north end of town. At some point, Tom and Naomi decided that they would apply for welfare in the form of the Aid to Dependent Children program. Once they had money coming in, they learned of a place in Arbuckle, California, that was a converted German POW camp then renting to low-income families. The small agricultural towns of Arbuckle, Williams, Maxwell, and Colusa, just 10 miles apart, created a microcosm for those of us that were raised there.

The Arbuckle, California, POW Camp was originally built as a farm labor camp by the United States Department of Agriculture. The farm labor camp was built to house agricultural workers that were to produce guayule, a potential commercial source of natural rubber. The attempts to produce rubber failed to achieve favorable results.

The camp consisted of 30 barracks, a mess hall, and a community center. "In 1945, the War Department entered a memorandum of agreement with the US Department of Agriculture to establish a 250-man prisoner of war camp at the Arbuckle labor camp. The terms of the agreement stated that the Army would operate the camp for no more than one year."2

The Army took control of 18 of the barracks as well as the mess hall. The Army built two guard towers at the North and South ends of the camp. After the German prisoners were repatriated back to Germany in 1945/1946, the camp was transferred back to the US Department of Agriculture.

In 1948, Robert F. Alexander purchased the camp from the federal government and converted the barracks into low income apartments. The mess hall was converted into a bar and general store. By the late 1970s, the remaining buildings were removed, and a new apartment complex was built on the site.

Leaving Seaside and moving to the Alexander Camp was a step back in time. Most of the north end of the camp buildings had not been converted to the more modern apartment/duplex buildings as on the south end of the camp. On the north end of the camp, there still existed community showers and community latrines. The two guard towers remained. We did have indoor running water, but there were no restrooms inside the buildings. Again, we used coffee cans to relieve ourselves during the night, which I believe contributed to me becoming a bed wetter. The buildings were in the process of being converted to low rent duplexes. Naturally, the unconverted buildings were less expensive to rent. These buildings did have propane cooking stoves, but there was no central heating. A potbelly wood stove in the kitchen area provided the only heat.

Alexander Camp was a melting pot of races in 1953; however,

I do not remember any black families living in the camp. When our brother, Eddie, was born in October 1953, he stood out as the only black person in the camp, especially in an all-white family. We all were aware that our mother was expecting a child, so when she went to the Colusa County hospital 20 miles away to have the baby, we were somewhat excited, especially me, as I was still hoping for a little brother. When our mother returned home, we were surprised that he was a little, curly-haired black baby boy. Our parents told us that they had gotten the babies mixed up in the hospital to explain why he looked different. Sadie was somewhat suspicious, but the other four of us accepted this explanation blindly. We naively repeated that explanation until we got somewhat older and realized the story was not feasible. It would not be until I was a freshman in high school that I started telling those who asked that he was adopted. By then, I had pieced together some of what had happened on the trip to Cannery Row, but I could not bring myself to tell the curious that our mother had been raped by a black man. We had a mixed-race brother before Obama was cool. Many years later, when Eddie sought to obtain a copy of his birth certificate, he discovered that Mom was reported as the white mother and Tom was reported as the white father. The box reflecting the race of the child was left blank. Someone viewing the birth certificate would assume a white child was born to the couple.

On the north end of the camp where we lived, there were many Hispanic migrant workers or "wetbacks" as they were called at the time. At that time, the United States had the guest worker program, known as the Bracero Program, which was later ended

by President Johnson in 1964.³ Although there were some migrant workers that were here legally through the guest worker program working on the local farms, there were many that had entered the United States illegally. On more than one occasion, the
United States Border Patrol would raid Alexander Camp to round
up the illegal workers. My first encounter with the Border Patrol
raids happened when I was eight years old. It was like we were
being invaded by giant green men. From out of nowhere came a
swarm of Border Patrol cars occupied by giant green men. In 1954,
the United States Border Patrol had a minimum height require-
ment for Border Patrol agents. To an eight-year-old child, they all
looked more than 7 feet tall.

One of the families that also lived on the north end of the
camp was the Bagget family. The father, Bill (Sugar-foot, as he
was called), was of Native American heritage and his wife was of
Hispanic heritage. Their daughter Dorothy was Sadie's age, their
son Bill was my age, and the youngest son Frank was Darla and
Paula's age. Due to their dark skin, the family was always confronted during the Border Patrol raids. I do not believe that Sugar-
foot was full-blood Native American, but he had very distinctive
Native American features. Sugar-foot supplemented his farm laborer salary by playing in a country western band on the weekends. Country western music tended to be the only music preferred in the agricultural community.

As soon as the Border Patrol vehicles came to the screeching
stop in a cloud of dust, the agents piled out of the vehicles and
charged into the homes, whether they were occupied by Hispanics

are not. One agent spied my little brother's dark skin and rude-
ly asked who that kid belonged to. My mother boldly told the
agent that he was her kid. The agents went on about their business,
rounding up as many of the illegal workers as they could catch. In
the chaos of the raid, some of the workers were fortunate enough
to escape into the alfalfa field north of the camp, but some of their
family members were captured and taken into custody. As the fleeing illegals were running through the housing area, they shouted
warnings to the others, "Pinche migra, pinche migra!"

On picture day at school that year, my mother dressed me up a
nice shirt and the only pair of good slacks I had and sent me off to
school with instructions not to ruin my good clothes. These were
the clothes that I wore when we went to Sunday school. Everything
went well that day until the walk home from school. I was walking with my two younger sisters and one of their classmates when
I suddenly felt the urge for a bowel movement. Knowing that I
would not make it the next two miles back to the camp, I knew
I would have to find some place to relieve myself. We were about
halfway home when I spied an abandoned dump truck bed out in
a nearby field. I had planned to excuse myself from my sisters and
their friend and run off to relieve myself behind the abandoned
dump truck bed. But, as little sisters would do, they decided to
follow me, and in my desperation to convince them to not follow
me, I never did make it to the dump truck bed. Well, needless to
say, that was one long two-mile walk back to the camp in my best
navy-blue slacks. I cried all the way, knowing what I was facing
for messing my Sunday go-to-meetin' pants. As I expected, my

mother was not pleased with what had happened. I tried to explain, but to no avail. My mother decided that she would teach me a lesson. She placed a galvanized washed tub out in the front yard and filled it with hot water and soap. Then she forced me to stand out in the front yard washing out those navy-blue pants in that tub for all to see. That experience probably ranks as one of the more humiliating events in my life. Throughout most of my life, I regularly had dreams of being humiliated by appearing in public in just my underwear. I believe that this incident is what triggered those dreams.

I slept on a single bed in the kitchen near the wood stove, but at least I was near the only source of heat during the night. One night, I was awakened by someone pulling at my covers at the foot of the bed. Too scared to move, I pretended to be asleep, but the tugging on the blanket became stronger. I finally peeked and there stood a large white shape at the foot of my bed. I screamed and my parents rushed into the kitchen turning on the light. As I explained what had happed Tom asked, "What is that white thing over in the wood box, is that Ozzie?" As he walked toward the wood box to investigate, the white figure disappeared. Darla claimed that she saw the white figure in the wood box. As it turned out, it was the one-year anniversary of the death of my aunt Helen. For many years, I believed it was the ghost of my beloved Aunt Helen coming to visit me. I always had the sense that I was her favorite.

Sometime later, we could afford to move to the south end of Alexander Camp to one of the remodeled duplexes which had indoor plumbing. Looking back, I assumed the added welfare payment for Eddie is what allowed us to make the move. Our du-plex did not have bathing facilities, just toilet facilities. So now on Sunday nights, our mother placed that galvanized washed tub in the kitchen floor and filled it with hot water for us children to take a bath in. We still had to use a wood stove for heating, but at least we didn't have to go to the community bath houses and bath facilities anymore. We did not need the coffee cans under the bed anymore. In time, my bed-wetting stopped.

Many of my schoolmates lived in Alexander Camp, so there was always someone to hang out with. There was always some-place to explore, some mischief to get into, some adventure to be had. Boys at that age are prone to learn how to be stupid, and later, when you add girls to the mix we found age-old ways to be even more stupid. Even grown men tend to do some very stupid things when it comes to women. And, as I would also learn, women can do some real stupid things when members of the opposite sex are involved. We would spend the entire day outside without adult supervision. Today we would be considered "free range" children. We still did not have a television set, as some of the families did, so we spent the daylight hours outside playing. The evenings were spent listening to radio, The Lone Ranger, Boston Blackie, etc. If I truly have Attention Deficit Hyperactivity Disorder (ADHD), as I often am accused of, I believe it developed during this time. To this day, I must be on the move, physically doing something, or I get restless. When I get restless, I get into trouble, as I often did back then.

One of the families living in the camp was a Native American family, the Knights. They lived in a duplex next to the Holt family. The Knight family had four children: Philip, Rocky, Randall, and their little sister. Rocky was a classmate of mine, so I naturally hung out with him often. As boys our age would do, we spent a lot of time finding things to do, sometimes things that could get us in trouble. We became proficient at making our own toys and creating our own games. We played cowboys and Indians, we played army, all manly stuff. We had a rougher version of "kick the can," where we tended to tackle the others as they attempted to "kick the can" to avoid being caught. We were very proficient at making our own sling-shots out of old bicycle tubes and forked tree limbs. We became very accurate with those sling shots. Sometimes those glass windows in those abandoned buildings were too much to pass up. We also became very proficient at making our own bows and arrows out of tree limbs and got pretty accurate with those. We would make our own targets out of cardboard boxes and practice with those imperfect arrows.

The Holt family consisted of three brothers: Ronnie, Larry and Timmy. Their dad, Les, was married to one of Mr. Alexander's daughters, and he managed the camp store. Once, Les Holt mysteriously left town for an extended period. Several months later, we learned he had gone to a treatment center in Weimar, CA, to be treated for tuberculosis. Seems the family wanted to keep Les's tuberculosis a secret. The Holts had a collie dog named Pal that looked just like Lassie. Everyone knew better than to get down on all fours to play marbles with the Holts when Pal was around. The Holt boys took great delight in encouraging Pal to mount an unsuspecting friend. Pal could do not deterred once was he was locked on. That was the horniest dog I ever encountered. On a trash run to the local dump once, the Holt boys were in the back of their dad's pickup as Pal followed behind. Pal ran the several miles to the dump, following the boys, but when he got there, he dropped over dead.

Ronnie Holt had learned how babies were made, so he thought he would share that juicy tidbit of information with Rocky and me. When Rocky heard what was involved in making babies, he got very upset with Ronnie. He could not believe that his mother and father did that. After all, Rocky informed Ronnie, he had slept with his mother and father when their little sister was born, so they couldn't have done that. Rocky never forgave Ronnie for suggesting his parents would do such a disgusting thing.

In one of the duplexes behind ours lived the Reed family. Their son, Jerry, was in my class. Jerry's cousin, Lowell, also lived with them. As a young child, Jerry contracted polio and had lost the use of both of his arms. Jerry was a sickly individual, not much more than skin and bones. He reminded me of the photographs of the people who survived Auschwitz. When he was not sick, Jerry attended regular classes at the Arbuckle elementary school. He was in my class and sat across the aisle from me. Jerry had taught himself to print his school assignments using his toes. A special desk was made for Jerry and placed on the floor next to his seat. I had volunteered to retrieve Jerry's desk from the coat closet each day, place it by his seat, and then return it to the coat closet at the end of the school day. Jerry had a mean streak in him. If you made him mad, he would bust you with a rock when you least expected it. He had perfected the art of rock throwing with his toes. He always wore penny loafers with no socks. He could kick off those shoes, pick up a rock between his big toe and second toe, and throw that rock with surprising accuracy. Naturally, you could not retaliate against a "cripple." Even if you decided to return fire, Jerry would run back to his house, claiming you were the instigator. He took great delight in getting away with it and getting others in trouble. A couple years after leaving Arbuckle, I heard that Jerry had died of natural causes.

In the duplex directly behind ours lived in the Hart family. The Harts had four children, three daughters and a younger son. I came to dislike that imposing family immensely. By then, we were finally able to afford a black-and-white television. Once the Hart family found out, they became regular uninvited visitors almost every evening. They developed a routine, which became a constant irritant. Shortly after dinner, the parents would appear at our front door to visit. They would invite themselves to watch TV for the evening with our parents. Shortly thereafter, the four kids would appear at the front door. When you answered the door, they would always ask if their parents were there, knowing what the answer was. They would force their way in the door and invite themselves to watch TV for the evening. Now there were ten kids sitting in the living room floor and four parents sitting on the couch watching TV for the evening. They would not leave until the time for all to go to bed. One of my younger sisters told me that the second oldest Hart daughter had three breasts. I never did find out for sure if the story was true, but it was sure a curiosity. Many years later, just before leaving for the Air Force, the older sister, Ruby, and I would become intimate in the back seat of a car at the drive-in movies. I had the sense that Ruby was using that intimacy to catch herself a husband, but I was not falling into that honey trap.

Uncle Oscar and Aunt Nellie also became regular visitors to our house when we lived at the camp. I soon came to dislike their visits as well. Seems they had become "Bible thumpers." Each evening during their visits, we had to come in early from play to sit around listening to Uncle Oscar read from the Bible. I understand that Aunt Nellie had "gotten religion" some time before while she was serving a one-year prison term in a women's prison for embezzling money from a previous employer. I guess they thought we children needed saving. Oscar and Nellie never had any children and as the saying goes, "the best children are raised by those that never had any." They would eventually move from Eureka to Oroville, California, where Uncle Oscar got a job as caretaker at a state recreation area behind the Oroville dam. We visited them there one time, but Aunt Nellie was not comfortable having Eddie around, so we never went back. Sometime later, we learned that they were getting divorced. We soon learned that they had gone to visit a sick friend in the hospital. During the visit, the sick friend kept referring to Oscar and "Mable's" visits. Aunt Nellie became suspicious and started pressing Oscar about how he knew the friend and who Mable was. Under pressure, Oscar broke right there in the hospital room, admitting, "Damn it, I haven't had sex with you in ten years." Seems "Bible thumper" Uncle Oscar had a girlfriend on the side named Mable. Thereafter, the name Mable became a joke with me and my cousin Charlie. Anytime someone in the family would ask us where we were going, we would always respond, "Oh, we are just going to see Mable." Oscar and Nellie soon divorced and moved back to Eureka. Oscar went blind and died in an assisted living home. Nellie died of a heart attack. She weighed over 300 pounds most of her adult life.

One day, there was a knock at the front door. When Tom answered the door, there stood a deputy sheriff. The deputy sheriff told him, "Tom, I have a warrant for your arrest for welfare fraud." Tom casually asked the deputy if he could get his hat. The deputy told Tom to go ahead and get his hat. Mom and I stood there stunned. The deputy then looked at Mom and told her that he should be arresting her instead of Tom and that he would be back with a warrant for her arrest. It seems that Tom, and Uncle Oscar, had acquired some imperfect plywood, selling it to make some money on the side. At that time, Uncle Oscar worked in the lumber mill in Eureka and had acquired the plywood. Technically, Tom was not on welfare, so Mom was responsible for reporting the extra income to the welfare department. But who is going to arrest a woman with six children? Tom was only drawing a small government disability due to his accident back in 1946. Tom was hauled off to the Colusa County Jail in Colusa, 20 miles away. He pled guilty to welfare fraud and was sentenced to six months in the county jail. The culture back in the 1950s was that you took responsibility for your actions and you did your time. Colusa County Welfare Department back in that period was known for not having families of abled-bodied men on the welfare rolls, as is the mentality in today's society.

I believe that the deputy threatening my mother that day that he would be back with a warrant for her arrest created a trait in me I would carry throughout my life. On that day, I became a worrier, a fretter. For several days after Tom's arrest, I constantly worried that the deputy would return and arrest my mother. I could not shake that sense of impending doom. Throughout my life, I have found myself worrying and fretting about things that never happen. I always expect that dark cloud to show up in the sky, or, as they say, the other shoe to drop.

On a regular basis, we would all load up in the car and travel the 20 miles to Colusa in to visit Tom in jail. The visits were very informal. The deputies would bring Tom out to the lobby in the jail and allow us to visit unsupervised. On one occasion, Tom handed Mom a matchbox as a present. Curiously we watched as she opened the matchbox. Inside the matchbox was a small paper heart with the words I Love You across the front that Tom had cut out of a magazine. Mom coolly closed the matchbox without any reaction and continued with the conversation. Even as a 10-year-old, I thought her reaction was very cold. Looking back, I do not ever remember any show of affection between our mother and us children or Tom.

While Tom was serving his time in jail, a man and a woman from Arkansas moved into the adjoining duplex next to us. Shortly afterwards, the woman's brother showed up also and moved in with them. Sometime later, I overheard my mother asking my older sister Sadie, "What does it mean when a man flips you the finger?" As it would turn out, the brother of the lady next door had passed by the house while my mother was out in the front yard. As he passed, he flipped my mother the middle finger. Evidently, in his culture, flipping a woman the middle finger is a sexual proposition. Before we knew it, that guy, John Basil, was hanging out at our house spending the evenings watching TV. One evening, he spent the entire evening sitting on the couch with our mother watching TV. Our mother had placed a blanket over their laps, which we found hard to ignore. Throughout the evening, we all would regularly turn and check to see what they were doing. My mother became aware of our scrutiny and commented that we were "watching her like a hawk."

Until that evening, I had the potential to become a momma's boy, but after that evening, the bond between mother and son began to fracture. I had told her many times that when I grew up and got rich, I was going to buy her a Ford Thunderbird convertible, but as my resentment toward her grew, I soon forgot that promise.

On another evening, just as my mother was getting ready to leave to go pick up my sisters at the church, John Basil showed up drunk. He would not leave, so my mother left me there at the house with him. I was afraid of that drunken hillbilly. When my mother returned, she decided that she would drive John Basil over to College City, where he now lived and worked. College City was just a short drive from Arbuckle, but our mother never returned until the next morning. The next morning, when confronted by Sadie and our cousin Rusty, who was staying with us at the time, about being gone all night, I remember my mother saying, "Nothing happened. I had Eddie sitting on my lap all night." The bond between my mother and I was irreparably broken that morning, knowing that she had spent the entire night at John Basil's house. My trust and my faith in her no longer existed. I never mentioned the promise to buy her a Thunderbird again.

That incident created another lifelong trait in me that I would grow to dislike about myself. As I matured, I found that I could not bond with a female partner unless I had blind trust in her. The long-term relationships that I did developed in my life would start with blind trust. However, if the trust was ever fractured, I would step back and withdraw. I would build an emotional barrier around me to protect myself. I found that I could not superglue the trust back together. The barrier tended to make me callous and indifferent, so I could to protect myself from further disappointment. I would find solace in alcohol and tobacco to sedate myself. I would seek comfort in other women. If my partner did not have my trust, then she could not expect my loyalty. It would only be a matter of time before the relationship ended.

One of my mother's favorite sayings was, "If God loved a liar, he would hug you to death." I can only assume that when she died, that god hugged her to death. I could never believe her after that incident with John Basil.

One day, some time before Tom got out of jail, our mother called Sadie and me to the kitchen. There she told us that she was going to leave Tom to be with John Basil. I told her that if she did that, I would run away from home. Sadie seemed to agree, even though a few years earlier, she had wanted Mom to leave Tom. Maybe it was just the thought of that hillbilly John Basil becoming our father. Fortunately, that never happened. I never felt any fondness toward my mother after that.

A brief time later, Tom was released from jail and everything was back to normal, or so I thought. It was never explained to us why, but we were told that we were moving back to Williams, California, ten miles up Highway 99. I suspect it had to do with Mom's involvement with John Basil and his sister, who lived next door. Mom had not been discreet about her involvement with John Basil. I never did know if Tom found out about it. Again, as in Seaside, California, we found ourselves moving in the middle of the school year.

Highway 99

There are advantages to being the new kid in school. The girls think you are cute and the guys think you are cool. But once the newness wears off and others realize your economic situation, you find yourself back in that different social class than most of your classmates. You soon realize that the parents of the more affluent girls don't want them hanging out with you. As the saying goes, "I was from the wrong side of the tracks." So, you again only associate with kids in your own economic social class.

Initially, there was a positive aspect of moving to Williams. We moved into an apartment that adjoined the old abandoned movie theater right on main street, the old U.S. Highway 99 that ran up and down the west coast. Back in those days, Highway 99 ran through Main Street in most small towns, and at times, vehicle traffic was heavy. Attached to our apartment in the front was a large commercial store front. As Sadie would often say, Tom had another "hair-brained idea" about how to make some money. Seems Tom was planning on opening a used furniture store there. He did get the furniture store up and running but, as with most of his endeavors, it did not last long. For me, at least the appearance of a means of income relieved me of making up a story about what my father did for a living.

To my great disappointment, living on that busy highway would end my five-year bond with that great dog Ozzie, my best friend. According to Mom, Tom had chased him out of the house one day for being underfoot. Ozzie did not make it across that busy highway. It was a devastating thing to hear when Mom told me. It was as bad as when I learned about my Aunt Helen's death.

The furniture stored failed in a brief time and we moved again. This time, we moved south of town, near the drive-in movie. Economics determined what we could afford to rent, so rarely did we live in suitable housing for a family our size. Living next to us was the Capen family: Henry, Ruby, Gary, Virginia, and their little sister, Evelyn. The family was from Rogers, Arkansas. Like many men in the area, Henry supported his family by working at seasonal farm work. The oldest daughter, Virginia, was still living at home after having a child out of wedlock. Seems the guy who got her in a family way skipped town. The son, Gary, could have been who Fonzie from Happy Days was based on. He was cool, at least to a 10-year-old boy. Gary was a few years older than me. Gary had a good heart, but he was prone to getting into trouble, especially if he was drinking.

Seasonal farm work is what drew many migrant families to the agricultural areas up and down California's Central Valleys in the 1950-1960s. The seasonal agricultural jobs also provided summer jobs for the local youths until school began in September. Some high school youths could miss the first two weeks of school if they were employed in a seasonal job. The need for seasonal workers is still a draw to the area today, but most of the seasonal agricultural work is accomplished by Hispanic laborers, here either legally or illegally. Some are supposedly here through the Immigrant Worker Program, which allows them to stay from April to November, when the harvest is completed. However, many of these workers do not return to Mexico at the end of the harvest. Many have permanent residences here, some even apply for the benefits afforded to the "Immigrant Workers" from April to November, such as free child-care, so the parents can work in the harvest. Some do not even work in the harvest. Sadie's oldest daughter drives a bus daily to pick up children, infants, toddlers, and preschoolers to be taken to the child-care center. The family across the street from Sadie applies for the free child-care every year, even though they maintain a permanent residence in Williams, CA. One family that participates in Immigrant Worker Program drives two BMWs and a Cadillac and dresses their older children immaculately for school while maintaining a permanent residence, all at taxpayers' expense.

Across the irrigation ditch right beside the drive-in movie lived Chet, Vivian, Loretta, Dean, and little Chester Taylor. The Taylors were from Rogers, Arkansas, also. Dean was just one year older than me, so we regularly hung out.

Gary, Dean, and I soon started running together. Gary, being the oldest, was naturally the leader. Dean and I were the followers. Boys will be boys, especially country boys. As country boys, we spent a lot of time huntin' and fishin'. The Sacramento Valley is a spider web of irrigation canals fed by the Sacramento River. All country boys need to go fishin', swimmin', and froggin'. We never worried about all those chemicals or the dead sheep in those irrigation ditches. During the summer months, we thought nothing of riding our bikes for miles, checking out different fishing holes, fishin', and swimin' in the irrigation ditches. At night, we would wade the ditches with a flashlight and a frog gig, looking for bull frogs. On one of our fishing trips to Chaney's barn, Dean rushed ahead to beat me to the best fishing location. The irrigation pipe came out from under the road and emptied back into the irrigation ditch. The water draining out of the pipe had dug a deep hole there. Naturally, the larger fish would be found in the deeper hole. Dean dropped his bike as he arrived and ran to the drain end of the pipe to secure the best location. But, he forgot to stop and ran right off into the deep hole in the ditch. I heard a big splash and when I looked, there stood Dean, chest-high in the water with both hands raised over his head protecting his fishing pole. He forfeited the best fishing spot. Our parents never worried about us, even when we were gone all day. There were no cellphones back in those days. Once we left home in the mornings, our parents rarely knew where we were or where we would end up. A couple times, they did call the police on me when I did not show up for supper. We thought nothing of riding 10 miles to the next town to visit someone. When I got home, I was forced to call the police and tell them I was home. I had to be taught another lesson. On one occasion, they did coming looking for me, but to their surprise, I was already headed home. I had one of Dean's fishhooks stuck in my finger and I needed to be taken to the emergency room to have it taken out.

We regularly would sneak into the drive-in movie across the

street. We waited till after dark, and then we would grab our sleeping bags and head for the drive-in. There had been a hole cut in the fence just to the right of the movie screen. As soon as it was dark enough, we would sneak through the fence and head for the front row, where we laid out our sleeping bags next to a speaker pole. Most of the time, we were successful, but occasionally we were caught. Other times, we would get someone that had a car with enough money to pay for one or two admissions and the rest of us would hide in the trunk of the car till we got inside. On dollar night, a whole car load could get into the movies for just a dollar. I have been an avid movie-goer ever since, Western Movies being my favorite. They have always been great escapes for me from the reality of my life. I would forever be a visual person.

Ironically, the Capens, Taylors, and our family would move from south of town and end up renting houses on 9th street just a block apart. Ruby Capen was a regular uninvited visitor to our house to visit Mom. She spent most of her time complaining to Mom about her husband, Henry. Henry was unemployed at the time. I remember hearing her tell Mom, "All that old Henry wants to do is screw." Tom grew to hate Ruby's visits. Ole Ruby dipped snuff and during her visits, she would constantly have to go to the front door to spit. That irritated the hell out of Tom. I remember a saying he had about Ruby dipping snuff, "Anyone that would put that shit in their mouth would suck a dick." It goes without saying, that saying stuck in my mind, and I never tried snuff.

It was during my freshman year that I started telling people that Eddie was adopted. I realized how ridiculous the story about the babies being mixed up in the hospital was. Especially after little sister Darlene came home telling Mom what she had overheard her little friend's mother say. Darlene was at her friend's house and while the little friend and her mother were in the kitchen, she overheard her friend tell her mother that Darlene had a little black brother and that they had gotten the babies mixed up in the hospital. Darlene heard the mother say, "Honey, I don't think they got the babies mixed up, I think they got the daddies mixed up."

One day, I was riding my bike down Main Street headed home. As I passed Ziggy's Barber Shop, I heard a loud voice yell my name. I stopped and turned to look. Oh shit, it is a local cop, I thought. I went back and was confronted by the officer. I was shaking in my tennis shoes. He told me he had just come from my house and that he was investigating accusations that Gary, Dean, and I stole a microphone from the little league park behind the old high school. Damn, I knew what he was talking about but I could not proclaim my innocence fast enough. He told me I had better get on home because Tom was waiting for me. I peddled that bike as fast as I could the four miles back to the house. I knew what was waiting for me. Tom's way of disciplining me was raking the knuckles on his crippled right hand across my ears until I begged for mercy. I noticed that he did not do that to the girls or Eddie.

My usual worrying and fretting made it a very long ride home. After pulling up in front of the house, I just dropped my bike where I stopped outside the front gate. As I pushed the front gate open, Henry Capen and Tom came out the front door to meet me. At that moment, I lost control of my emotions. I stated bawling uncontrollably, all the while trying to proclaim my innocence the entire 20 yards from the front gate to the porch where Tom and Henry stood. I must have been a pathetic sight. I don't remember much of what was said during those initial moments, but I do remember Henry telling Tom, "Gary admitted to taking the microphone," and added, "that little son-of-bitch Gil had nothing to do with it." Oh, Jesus, there is honor among thieves after all.

After getting control of my emotions, I explained what I remembered happening that day. About three days before, the three of us had been out riding bikes. I had my own bike, but Gary was riding Dean's bike while pumping Dean on the handle bars. As we came upon the little league park, we stopped by the announcer's booth. Gary picked up the announcer's silver desk microphone and said, "Hey, look at this." I had a sense that I should get the hell out of there and took off on my bike. About a mile down the road, Gary and Dean caught up to me but I did not see the microphone or notice anything unusual. What I later learned was that Gary had taken the microphone and had Dean put it down the front of his pants. What they did not realize was that someone had seen us at the ball park. Gary returned the microphone and all was forgiven.

I learned two things from that incident. The first one is that life is about choices. You make some good ones, which you appreciate, but when you make some bad ones, they can haunt you for life. Hopefully you analyze the bad ones and learn from them, then move on. Some people never learn from their bad choices. But it is a bitch when other people's choices bite you in the ass. Ironically, death many times is also about choices, bad choices.

The other thing I learned was that I could never be a criminal, not with my fretting personality. If I ever committed a crime, I would worry myself sick about getting caught. Every time I would see a police car coming my way, I would be convinced they were coming for me. Once I was caught, I would probably confess almost immediately. As Clint Eastwood said, "A man has gotta know his limitations."

One aspect of being on welfare was particularly humiliating to me. Our welfare case worker had to make regular visits to our house. Arrangements were made to have all the children there during her visit so she could speak with us. Our case worker, Mrs. Lack, had an adopted daughter, Louise, who was a classmate of mine. Like in the movie "Claudine" with Diahann Carroll and James Earl Jones, if we had acquired anything that might be considered luxury items, we would have to hide them. During the period when our cousin, Charlie, was staying with us, he had to disappear.

Many years later, Mrs. Lack's son, John, would have the misfortune of crossing paths with Darla's adult daughter, Kim. John Lack was a Williams, California, police officer responding to a medical emergency at an apartment complex where Mom lived. Kim was visiting Mom as John parked his police car at the complex, blocking Kim's vehicle and preventing her from leaving. Kim blazingly confronted John, insisting he move his car. John foolishly handed Kim the keys to his police cruiser and told her to move it. She did, but 30 minutes later, John discovered that his cruiser was missing. In the 30-minute interval, Kim was driving around in the cruiser with the emergency lights flashing as she talked over the police radio. Approximately two hours later, a California Highway Patrol officer discovered the missing cruiser travelling down the highway and executed a felony stop on Kim, fearing that she may have gained access to the shotgun attached to the dash of the cruiser. No charges were pressed against Kim, but Officer Lack was terminated. Kim, however, has been in and out of jail most of her adult life on drug-related charges.

In the 60s, we got a welfare check at the first of the month. That money had to last the family the entire month. So, our mother was proficient at stretching a dollar. As soon as they got the check, she and Tom would go to Sacramento to the cannery sales. The store sold items in bulk, large burlap bags of potatoes and pinto beans as well as dented canned goods at a reduced price. They would load up all they could afford, hoping it would get them through the month. Tom was expected to kick in about half of his disability check, which was about $80. The other half he could keep for personal use for such things as Bull Durham tobacco and cigarette papers. Many dinners were nothing more than pinto beans and homemade bread, or pinto beans and cornbread. Mashed potatoes were a staple on the evening dinner table. By the time I joined the military, I had had my fill of mashed potatoes. If the monthly welfare check did not last till the end of the month, my parents might have to resort to getting U.S. Department of Agriculture commodities from the welfare office, such as powdered milk and cheese. Many times, toward the end of the month, we had "milk toast" or corn bread and milk for dinner. Just toast up a stack of bread, spread butter or jelly on it, then pour warm powdered milk over it. I learned to like milk toast and corn bread and milk, but once I left home, I never ate it again. Each summer before school started, Mom would break out the Spiegel's mail order catalog and order our school clothes for the upcoming year. It was understood that those clothes had to last you the entire year. It was a regular practice to come home after school and change into older clothes so you did not ruin the school clothes while out playing. My parents then spent the next year paying off the school clothes order on a monthly basis.

The practice of living from welfare-check-to-welfare-check greatly influenced my approach to making major purchases in my adult years. I never could convince myself to buy major items on credit. I would usually save the money until I could afford to pay cash for the item; cars and homes were the exception in my younger years. In my senior years, I regularly paid cash for my vehicles. I have even paid off the last two houses I have lived in. I learned to hate making monthly payments for purchases, mainly due to hearing Tom and Mom argue about how they could not afford another monthly payment.

Sadie turned eighteen in her senior year of high school, a few months before she was to graduate. That would be the first reduction in the welfare benefits during the next four years for Mom. Loretta Taylor had introduced Sadie to her uncle, Will. Will had recently arrived from Arkansas and was staying with his brother's family. Sadie and Will soon began dating, and before long, they were talking marriage. Will and Sadie were out on a date at the drive-in-movie one evening and during the movie, poor ole Will inadvertently brushed against Sadie's breasts, causing Sadie to faint. Will had no idea what to do, but fortunately for him, after a brief period, Sadie regained consciousness. Sadie and Will got married in the middle of her senior year. Maybe it was the loss of welfare benefits that induced Sadie to marry Will before she graduated, but to her credit, she did manage to graduate on the honor roll from high school. Will was a decent, hard-working guy but had little formal education. Will did farm work all his life, driving 35 miles to work every day. For the last few years of his life, the farmer he worked for kept Will working doing odd jobs even during the off seasons. Will epitomized the hardworking, American, blue-collar workers of the 1950s-1960s. He proudly went to work every day, at times holding down two jobs to support his family. He was proud of the work that he did and what he produced working on local farms. He proudly supported his wife and three daughters while pursuing the American Dream, buying his first and only home. I always thought that Will and Sadie were mismatched, but they remained married until Will died of a massive heart attack many years later. Sadie still lives in their first and only house. Will and Sadie had three daughters, one of whom died of asthma complicated by long-term meth use. She survived the asthma attack but was brain dead. She may have survived had her husband called emergency services sooner. Sadie had to make the decision to take her off life support.

Presumably because of the reduction in the monthly welfare payments, we were forced to move again. This would become the hardest move for me. We only moved 10 miles to the east to Colusa, but again, we ended up in a two-story building right across the street from the high school I would be attending when I began my sophomore year. Again, we moved in the middle of the school year. Just like that old rickety house at the other end of Fremont Street, the top floor of this brick house was condemned also. It actually had bats in in the attic that came out at night. That old house was right behind Rick's Frosty Freeze, a popular hangout for the high school students at lunch time and after school. I hated that house. The bricks were falling out of the walls, inside and out. I was so ashamed of living there that I would not invite friends to my house. I would sneak to and from school so no one would see me leaving or going to that house. My mother used to say, "Poor people have poor ways." Damn, I was tired of having poor ways. I could understand poor ways. I just couldn't understand trashy ways.

My mother had worked out a deal with my cousin, Charlie. She would do his laundry every week if he would drive Sadie and me back to Williams each day so we could complete that school year in Williams. Charlie started to live with us at that time, unbeknownst to the welfare dept. Charlie, Eddie, and I shared a bedroom for that year.

That old house and the adjoining property were owned by the town's Baptist preacher. The adjoining property had eight old bungalow-type motel rooms, which were rented out to low income workers. Sadie and Will rented one and lived there when they were first married. The preacher had a drop-dead-gorgeous daughter who was a year younger than me. She was out of my league. In her sophomore year, she would disappear from town for most of the year. She showed back up during my senior year. Seems the preacher's daughter had gotten herself in a family way and was shipped off to relatives to have the baby. The responsible boy disappeared about the same time and was not seen again in Colusa for years.

As my freshman school year ended, I found myself in a new town with no friends and at a loss for things to do that summer. I was not old enough to drive yet, so my mobility was limited. Several times during the summer, I hitchhiked back to Williams to visit friends there. I had inherited a Sacramento Bee paper route from a guy who had lived in Alexander Camp, Bill Baggett, when we lived there. When I tired of the paper route, I passed it on to Bill's younger brother Frank. I had my earnings from the paper route, so at least I had some money in my pocket. With money in my pocket and not much to do, I spent a lot of money at Rick's Frosty Freeze on ice cream and cokes. By the time I started my sophomore year, I had gained 70 lbs. I gained the weight so fast that my ankles would hurt if I just ran 10 steps. I also got man-boobs, of which I would be self-conscious of most of life. When you don't have much else, it is easy to find solace in food. I hated my life that summer and contemplated suicide several times. Now I was fat, poor white-trash who lived in a dump across the street from the high school for all to see. It all boiled down to my sell-image, my self-worth. I had no hope of breaking away from that overwhelming despair. My self-esteem would forever be directly proportional to my weight and financial situation. I was regularly teased about being fat, but years later, the "fat" comments would motivate me to get control of my weight. I would struggle with my weight most of my life. That year, I mentally started keeping score of all the reasons my life sucked. On that score card was some of the choices my mother had made during my life. I found myself blaming her for most of my misery. That was the year that I was first told that Tom was not my father. Evidently, it was common gossip within our family. It took me years to let go of that list and move on. I had to shake the victim mentality. I had to take control of my life. It was a huge weight off my shoulders. I had to stop blaming my mother and let go of the past. I had to stop listening to the sad songs. The sadness and misery I felt is captured in my eyes in my class photo that year.

One of my classmates, Monroe Cross, had the dubious distinction of being a polio survivor with no apparent side effects. However, Monroe did have hand tremors, which caused classmates to nickname him Shaky. Ironically, Monroe insisted on using a fountain pen to complete his school assignments. Watching Monroe refill his pen was amazing: the way his hands shock but never spilling a drop. Like me, Monroe was not accepted into the mainstream of high school. In my case, my economic situation and the fact that I entered Colusa High School in my sophomore year would bar me from acceptance by the clique of students that had grown up in Colusa, CA. When I attended by 40th year class

reunion, it became apparent I was not among friends. I left shortly after arriving. I did not attend my 50th reunion. Monroe never
had the opportunity to attend any reunions. One year after graduating from high school, he died from enemy machine gunfire in
Vietnam. I do not know if Monroe enlisted in the Army or was
drafted. Monroe was an only child. His mother and father must
have been devastated losing their only son in an unpopular war, especially after he survived polio as a child. Ironically, Frank Baggett
would also be killed in Vietnam after he graduated from high
school. Both are listed on the Vietnam Wall

Over the years, in talking to my siblings, we all have come
to a common realization. None of us can remember any words
of encouragement or praise from either of our parents. None of
us remember our parents ever nurturing our self-esteem, our self-
worth. None of us remember any words or showing of endearment
from our parents. It would take me decades of accomplishment to
validate myself. Having achieved the things I did, I was finally able
to convince myself that I have done more than just get by in life.
Some of my siblings have never accomplished that; they would be
content to just get by.

After the school year ended, things started to get better. My
weight dropped some and we moved from that house to a more
presentable one. I was no longer contemplating suicide. I had just
about lost all interest in school except for animal husbandry class.
The next two years, I was just gettin' by in school, just focusing on
what it took to graduate.

The summer before I started my senior year, I got a job "flagging" for a crop duster named Bob Dalton. In time, I was given the job of driving the loader truck for the airplane. That was the summer I got the bug to become a pilot. Bob was my hero. He made flying that plane look like child's play. He travelled up and down the California farming areas, crop dusting. He drove an all-white 1958 Chevrolet Impala with all-white leather interior. At the end of summer, Bob had me drive it all the way to Bakersfield for him while he flew his plane there. Bob had a girlfriend in Colusa, though I suspected maybe more in other places too. The one in Colusa was a divorcee he would visit in the evenings. To keep up appearances, he could not leave the car parked outside overnight.

My senior year is when I found myself spending the night in the Sheriff Mayfield Hotel, the Colusa County Jail. Dean Taylor and I were cruising around at two o'clock in the morning drinking beer. Cruisin' the square in Colusa was a favorite pastime for teenagers in those days. All you needed was a dollar and you could buy four gallons of gas. When we could not afford to buy the gas, we would resort to siphoning gas out of one of the many agricultural trucks around town. You could cruise all night on four gallons of gas. Well, dumbass Dean decided to toss an empty beer can out the window just as the local cop was passing by. Clunk, Clunk, Clunk. There was no escaping. Damn, it was the same officer who had confronted me out in front of Ziggy's Barber Shop. He must have changed jobs. Off to jail we went for underage drinking. When we got to the jail, the officer called our parents. Tom and Mom decided I needed to be taught another lesson. They told the officer that they would be down to get me in the morning. Well, morning arrived and no Tom or Mom. The officer arrived back at the jail and took me down to the old court house see the probation officer, Moses Dowell. He released me and let me go home. Tom and Mom were not there either. Apparently, they decided that they would go to the cannery sales in Sacramento to shop and they would pick me up at the jail on their way back later that afternoon. Spending all night in jail was another hard lesson. As Tom would say, "When you dance, you gotta pay the fiddler, boy." Like my mother used to say, "Gil, you have to learn things the hard way." I got off with six months' probation, which ended before I got caught cutting school. I didn't realize that growing up was going to be so hard.

That old court house still stands today. Out behind the court house there a plaque which reads:

THE LINCOLN ASSASINATION
INCARCERATION

On April 22, 1865, Capt Augustus Aashington Starr was sent to Colusa, called the Little South by some, by Brig. Gen. George Wright to find out what was happening. Upon arriving, he proceeded to arrest persons for making exulting expressions over the assassination of president lincoln. Among those arrested were editor of the Weekly Colusa Sun, William S. Green, District Attorney Dudly Shepardson, Deputy Assesser Charles Price, and Justice of the Peace Jasper Scoggins. They were identified as copperheads for cutting off the words, "United States of America" from Indian head cents and wearing the result as a badge.

In all 8 men were arrested and sent to Alcatraz.

On June 15, 1865, they were tried in the US district court in San Francisco for using disloyal language towards the federal government. After taking an oath of allegiance to the United States, they were released.

Three weeks before I was to graduate, Dean, Gary, myself, and a friend of mine named Billy decided we would cut school and go swimming up at Bear Creek, about 30 west of Williams. Only Billy and I were the only two cutting school because Dean and Gary had already dropped out. As fate would have it, the Vice Principal, Mr. Applegate, got suspicious when Billy and I came up absent on the same day. Mr. Applegate called my house and was informed by my cousin Charlie that I had left for school that morning. When I got home that evening, Charlie informed me of the phone call. Well, the next morning, Billy and I were called into Mr. Applegate's office and told that we were suspended for three days. Since we were suspended for those three days, he wanted us to irrigate his almond orchard. For the next three days, we showed up at his ranch and irrigated his orchard and killed gophers for pay. Not a bad deal, I thought.

During this period, our cousin Charlie lived with us, sharing a bedroom with me. He paid my mother rent and she did his laundry. Due to his generosity, I could experience things that I would have otherwise never experienced as a teenager. He had a job working at a truck stop south of Arbuckle and he made good money being a member of the Teamsters Union. He drove a 1963 gold Chevrolet Impala S/S, which he would eventually trade in on a Plymouth Barracuda Fastback when they first came out. Charlie provided opportunities for me that my parents could have never provided. He introduced me to rock-n-roll through his vast 45s collection. Our family had always listened to country music on KRAK, "KRAK Corral of Country Hits" radio station out of Sacramento. In the words of Barbara Mandrel's song, "I was country when country wasn't cool." The country songs were the sad songs I listened to. Charlie took me to the stock car races and wrestling matches in Sacramento, to bowling, the movies, and water skiing. These were all things that many teenagers took for granted. Sadly, we lost touch through the years. I feel I owe him so much and I would like to express my gratitude.

Charlie lived with us off and on from the late 50s and early 60s after Aunt Helen died. He was never married, though he did live with a woman for a brief time. Charlie had done a tour in the Army with the 101st Airborne in Germany. As a young boy, I found his military stories interesting. After moving to the Sacramento Valley area, he got a job at the Arbuckle truck stop, which he stayed with for many years. The Arbuckle truck stop sat on the southbound lane of Highway 99, which used to be referred to as "blood alley." There were so many fatalities on that two-lane highway that eventually Interstate 5 was built all the way up the west coast, bypassing towns like Arbuckle, Williams, and Maxwell. Truck stops along the way would suffer. Charlie would eventually move to the Watsonville, California, area where his sister Rusty had moved with her second husband.

Rusty, like Charlie, also lived with us off and on after Aunt Helen died. In Williams, she shared a bedroom with Sadie until Rusty got married. Rusty had been working as a waitress at the Arbuckle truck stop where Charlie worked. Like many waitresses at truck stops, she met a truck driver and eventually married him. They soon had a little daughter. After the baby was born, Rusty and her husband moved to Manteca, California. We visited them a couple times later while they lived there. On the first visit, her husband Ken was there, and their little daughter was approximately three years old. On the second visit, Rusty was living by herself. I overheard her tell Mom that Ken and the baby had been killed when a train had struck their car at a railroad crossing. This was the first anyone of us had heard of the accident. I recalled her telling Mom that the accident happened when the little girl was just two years old. After we left, I told Mom that Rusty's story did not ring true. The little girl had been older than that on our last visit. Mom disregarded my suspicions. As it would turn out, like many truck driver's wives, she was left alone a lot and grew lonely. Evidently, she got involved with a man and Ken found out about it. Ken divorced her and got custody of the daughter. The man she was involved with became her second husband. I always thought it ironic that it was through Rusty I heard that Tom was not my father. It seems another family rumor was that Uncle Roy was not her real father. I always thought it strange that she had red hair while Charlie and Virginia had coal black hair.

November 22, 1963: we all remembered where we were when the nation was shocked with the assignation of President Kennedy by Lee Harvey Oswald. I was in third period Ag. shop when we were told to report to the auditorium for an assembly. As we headed for the auditorium, across the school parking lot, some students were gleefully chanting, "We are going to get out of school early, we are going to get out of school early!" One of my classmates, Richard Zoller, literally was skipping across the parking lot . The student body president, Greg Boyer, had observed the chanters and was greatly offended by their insensitivity. As the student body assembled in the auditorium, Greg took the podium in front of the student body with tears in his eyes. He then proceeded to berate the entire student body for the actions of a few insensitive students. The Vice Principle, Mr. Applegate, had to step in to console all of us that had just been subjected to Greg's outrage. School was let out for the rest of the day. Naturally, we were all glued to our TVs for the next few days as the story unfolded, just as we did on September 11, 2001.

In 1963, when the twins were 16, Darla and Paula both started dating. Darla and Paula did not even look like sisters, much less twins. Like me, they had gained a lot of weight during the period that we lived behind Rick's Frosty Freeze. Paula was somewhat taller than Darla and much heavier. As I have learned over the years, being overweight limits your possibilities throughout your life, especially during your adolescent years, when those hormones start controlling your life. The old saying "water seeks its own level" applies. If you are fat and poor, your opportunities are very limited when it comes time to pairing off. Also, being raised in such economic conditions can be limiting to your social development. You are what you live, and living in a microcosm of a small town limits your social development. For me, being overweight during those adolescent years and being poor greatly affected my self-esteem. Many times, you find yourself withdrawing from social interaction because you do not feel you fit in.

Darla met a strikingly handsome high school dropout named Dennis Edmonds. Dennis and I got along well in the beginning, but when Darla announced she was pregnant that summer and Dennis stopped coming around, our relationship soured. Later that summer, I was driving back from Marysville, California, when I came up on Dennis hitchhiking back to Sutter, California, where he was living with his father. I picked him up and gave him a ride back to his house. During the ride, I made a point of pressing him about when he was going to visit Darla. He was evasive about his answers, but to my surprise, a few days later, he showed up and he and Darla soon married in 1964. They are still married to this day, despite Dennis being an alcoholic all his life. Darla was as "tender-hearted" as I was back then, but life's struggles over the years have hardened my heart. Mine has grown calloused over the years except toward animals. They have never disappointed me. Dennis has had multiple heart bypasses but never gave up drinking. Dennis and Darla are back living in Colusa where it all started. They have not spoken to me in years. Prior to that, the only time I would receive a call from Dennis was about two o'clock in the morning, when he was stone drunk. It would be the same each time. He would go on, "I love you, man, I am your brother," repeatedly.

Paula, on the other hand, met a fat, sloppy, arrogant, abrasive, worthless piece-of-crap named Bob Porten. By the same summer, she thought she was pregnant also. Fortunately for her, it was a false alarm. Paula and Bob got married anyway and soon started a family. She would admit later that she probably got married to get out of the house. The only good thing I can say about Bob is he was a hell of a body and fender man. He had a beautiful canary yellow 1952 Willy's sedan that he had customized. Bob could always find jobs doing body and fender work, but he could never hang onto them due to his abrasive personality. After I went into the Air Force, I learned that Bob had talked Paula into becoming a topless bartender to earn money. A couple years later, I learned that Bob and Paula were both arrested for rape. How in the hell does a woman get charged for rape, I thought. Well, as it turned out, Bob and Paula were invited to a party by a 21-year-old convicted felon. A 16-year-old girl accompanied them to the party. As the evening progressed and the drinking became heavier, the 21-year-old felon decided to rape the 16-year-old girl. Bob and the other guys then took turns raping the girl also. Everyone at the party was charged with the girl's rape. Bob got a year in the county jail and Paula got six months. Their three children would have been put in a foster care during that time, but Will and Sadie took them in for the six months that Paula was in jail. As you might imagine, their children had developmental issues going up. The oldest son went to prison for molesting young boys. Years later, Paula would confide to me that Bob had "pimped" her out during their marriage. Many years later, Paula wisely divorced Bob.

By now, Mom had lost three of her welfare recipients, Sadie, Darla and Paula, and would soon lose me. Eventually, she would also lose Darlene and Eddie, when he dropped out of high school at age 16. By then, Tom was almost completely marginalized. He had little to say about the day-to-day events around the house. It was almost like he was a boarder in the house. He had tried different endeavors over the years: TV repair, for which he had no formal training, car salesman, and the furniture store, among others. He even talked Will into buying a two-and-a-half-ton truck so they could collect scrap iron at the dumps and resell it at the Sacramento Scarp Metal. Tom's endeavors never lasted very long. My mother seemed to have turned into a desperate bitch, often talking to Tom in a condescending tone. By then, Tom was close to 60-years-old and just took the abuse. I remember a couple of loud exchanges between Tom and my mother. In one exchange, she told Tom, "If you don't like it, you old son of bitch, you can get out." In another exchange, she said, "I couldn't help what happened to me, but you could help what you did." Tom could not defend himself when she would bring up what he did to Sadie, and Tom could not support himself on his meager disability.

When Darlene was about 12-years-old, she started babysitting for a couple named Bradley and Francine, who had two young daughters. Bradley made a good income as a farm equipment mechanic at I.G. Summalt Caterpillar Company in Colusa. Bradley had some of the trappings of the middle-class family, such as nice cars and water ski boats, which seemed attractive to Darlene. Initially, Darlene would only babysit when Bradley and Francine needed her, but as time wore on, she started visiting them every weekend, leaving home on Friday after school and returning Sunday evening. She became almost like their third child, or so Mom thought. On one occasion, Darlene did asked Mom if she would allow Bradley and Francine to adopt her. Even at 17, I had the perception that something wasn't as it seemed with that arrangement, but my mother ignored my concerns. For the next five years, Bradley would always arrive by himself to pick up Darlene, even after our family moved 35 miles away. With Bradley and Francine, Darlene was introduced to experiences and a lifestyle that could not be provided for her at our house. Unfortunately for her, one of those experiences would haunt her the rest of her life. By the time I returned from my two-year Air Force assignment in Japan in 1967, Darlene revealed that she was pregnant. Initially, she told mother that her boyfriend, Tony, was the father. In time, she admitted that Bradley had been molesting her for several years and he was the father of her unborn child. Some would ask why she allowed it to continue so long, even after our family had moved 35 miles away from Colusa to Sutter, CA. Why was she still going to visit them on the weekends? I guess that question can only be answered by Darlene and professionals that are trained to deal with that situation. Darlene graduated from high school in May 1968. She turned eighteen in August that year. Thus, Mom would only be receiving aid to dependent children for Eddie. In 1968, Darlene briefly married a man, Louie, who was also Darla's uncle by marriage and would become her brother-in-law. Louie was also the brother of the man my mother married after Tom died. It is confusing, I know. Darlene would eventually marry an enlisted career Air Force SSgt, but it would be many years before she told him who the father of her daughter was. For many years, Darlene, would blame Mom for her situation, saying that Mom had never taught her about sex. Hell, sex was not even mentioned in the household. As it says in the Eagles song, Lyin Eyes, "every point of refuge has its price." She found a way out of just getting by at an early age. She would spend years in counseling because of the molestation.

While living in Sutter, Eddie continued to attend high school. However, he had no interest in doing so. He had to wait until he was at least 16 years old before he could legally drop out of school. One day when walking home from school, he was confronted by the high school principle for walking on the roadway. Eddie was wearing his new Sears mail order shoes and he did not want to walk on the rain soaked muddy shoulder for fear of getting his new shoes muddy. The principle told him to get off the road, but Eddie defied him and took off running home. In those days, the school was responsible for a student from the time they left home for school in the morning until they returned home after classes. The principle followed Eddie home and was met by Tom on the front porch. The principal told Tom that he intended to take Eddie back to the school, where he further intended punish Eddie by using a "wooden paddle with holes drilled in it" on his backside. Tom told the principle that no one was touching one of "his kids." When the principle insisted, Tom knocked the principal off the front porch. Even in his early 60s, Tom would not back away from a fight.

Once, Charlie, accompanied by Tom and Eddie, went out to at a Mexican restaurant for dinner. The owner of the restaurant informed Tom that he would not serve Eddie. Tom went in to a rage and began to destroy the furnishings in the restaurant. He even went in to the kitchen area and began knocking things onto the floor. The police were called and four uniformed officers arrived to subdue Tom. It seemed that the officers knew of Tom's violent reputation and thought there would be safety in numbers. Tom was hauled off to the county jail, where spent six months for destruction of private property.

On June 6th, 1968, Tom died of lung cancer in the one lung he had left. All those years of smoking Bull Durham cigarettes had caught up to him. He had been diagnosed earlier that year and was told with treatment he might survive eighteen months. Initially, he underwent the treatments, but they soon made him so sick he decided he did not want to fight it any longer and discontinued the treatment. He was buried in Sutter, California. Now Mom was without Tom's monthly disability check.

When Eddie turned 16 in October 1969, he dropped out of high school. As it was, he could barely read or write. He found himself a job shining shoes in a barber shop in Marysville, CA. The owner of the barber shop would regularly pay Eddie to leave for extended periods during the day so the owner and his girlfriend could have sex in the back room of the barber shop. Eddie later found a job driving a septic tank truck for the City of Colusa. The temporary job was a Man Power program to hire and train young people. After a few weeks, he was promoted to dump truck driver. The job could have become permanent had Eddie stuck with it, but he regularly would not show up for work. About this time, Eddie also started telling friends that he was adopted. He found it easier to explain why he had a white family. Mom's last meal ticket had flown the nest. Now she had to survive on what public assistance provided for her.

At age 16, Eddie experienced his first sexual affair with a 30-year-old married white cougar. According to Eddie, the woman "practically raped him" the first time they had sex. Eddie was visiting the woman and her husband, who lived in the apartment next door. After the woman's husband left for work, the woman started fondling him, then pushed him back on the bed. She then got him erect and climbed on top and had her way with him. The affair continued for several months, but from then on, Eddie was a very willing and enthusiastic participant.

A year after Tom died, Mom married Harold Edmonds, the father of Dennis Edmonds, Darla's husband. What a hillbilly, right out of the hills of Pea Ridge, Arkansas. I suspect that she felt that by marrying an able-bodied man, she could do more than just get by. Old Harold talked Mom into moving back to Pea Ridge, Arkansas, where he found a job working on a turkey ranch. The old house they lived in was provided by the owner of the ranch. In 1984, when I got transferred to New Orleans, I stopped at Pea Ridge to visit. Not knowing what to expect, I checked into a motel before I went to their house. I was glad I did. Talk about a step back in time. I didn't understand how Mom got herself talked into such a lifestyle with such a hillbilly. I only stayed briefly, claiming I was tired from the long drive, but before I left, I asked to use their restroom. That was a shock. It was a dingy dirty place worse than some porta potties. There were dark brown hard water stains in the bathtub, the sink, and commode. Evidently Harold had showered before I had arrived, and it was his habit to drop his dirty clothes where he stood and have Mom pick them up. He had dropped his dingy white jockey shorts right in front of the commode for me to step over. Those shorts had two-inch-long, caked-on, brown skid marks in them. I used to think that we were white trash—I never visited them again after that.

When Harold lost that job, he moved Mom to a single wide trailer that was located up on the side of a hill outside of Pea Ridge. It had no running water and only a wood stove for heating. About that time, Mom found out that she was to inherit approximately $30,000 from her brother, Onnie, who had been killed in an accident. Old Harold always called Mom "Granny," and when he heard Mom was inheriting the money, he would tell everyone that "he and Granny were going to take that money and move down to Mexico to live like kings." Thankfully, Mom had the good sense to leave him and move back to Sutter, California. Before she received the inheritance, she applied for SSI assistance and was surviving on that. When she received the inheritance, she did not notify social security immediately. However, vengeful hillbilly Harold did so for her. She was required to repay her monthly payments for that period. The remainder of the money was placed in an account controlled by Sadie for the next few years and then transferred to an account controlled by Darla and her husband. The remainder of the money was never accounted for. Mom lived out her final years in an assisted living community and died in March of 2000. As fate would have it, she could not be buried until fall arrived. That year, during the raining season in the Sacramento Valley, the ground water level was too high, so Mom had to be kept in storage until the water table dropped. Death was not any easier on her than life had been.

Breaking Away

In May 1964, one month before I turned eighteen, I graduated from high school, barely. I immediately started looking for a job, regularly visiting the unemployment office in Marysville, California, 35 miles from Colusa. I would hitchhike the 35 miles to Marysville, where I had signed up for a construction plumbers apprentice program. I had to regularly hitchhike to the unemployment office to go through the qualification process. One day, when I was hitchhiking back from Marysville, I was picked up by a Gridley Poultry delivery man who was making his delivery rounds. He suggested that I ride with him on his route and when he returned to Gridley, California, that evening, he would introduce me to his boss. The driver was hoping to go into fulltime sales for the company, which would leave a vacancy for his position. I made his rounds with him and we returned to Gridley, California, where I met the boss, James Brown. Then I rode with the driver back to Marysville. He dropped me off where he picked me up. I again began hitchhiking home.

When I turned eighteen, I received a notice to report for my pre-induction physical at Oakland, California. I mistakenly thought that I was just reporting for a physical, but fortunately, I failed the physical because the pupils in my eyes dilated at different rates. As we all stood there in our underwear, an Army Sargent stood in front of the assembled young men and point to two of the young men, stating, "You and you over there. You two are going in the Marine Corp, the rest of you are going in the Army." I thought, WOW, had I passed the physical, I would not be going home today. Again mistakenly, I thought failing the physical would make me safe from the draft. Not so. When Uncle Sam wants, you, he will get you, unless your family is wealthy or connected politically. I was not enrolled in college, so I would not be exempted by a college deferment. Even that would not protect those college students a couple years later when they started drafting students that had less than a "B" average. In 1970, the married paternity deferment from the draft was ended, and in 1973, the draft was ended.

The next week Mr. Brown called informing me that he would hire me for the delivery driver position. I started to work the next week and I rented a small cottage in Gridley, where I stayed during the week. The delivery route took me all over the Sacramento Valley. On Tuesdays, my route took me through Colusa where my parents lived. I would usually stop there and have lunch. On one Tuesday, I stopped at their house and it was vacant. You have heard the joke about parents moving and not telling their children? Well, it happened to me. I eventually located them in Sutter, California. Presumably the reduction in the monthly welfare payment forced them to move to cheaper housing.

That summer, when I was eighteen, I had my first sexual relationship with one of my sisters' friends. As fate, would have it, this 16-year-old girl had already had a child by, of all people, Gary

Capen. Seems Gary had gotten her pregnant then decided to move on. Well, when his older sister, Virginia, found out about it, she turned Gary in to the Sheriff's department. Having found herself in a family way a few years earlier, she would not allow Gary to get away with pulling the same stunt her boyfriend did. Gary pled guilty to statutory rape and was sentenced to one year in the county jail. I dated the girl briefly while Gary was in jail, but I had the sense she was trying trap anyone into marrying her. I was not falling for that honey trap. It was time to move on before I ended up in jail. As it would turn out, Gary would serve his time and when he got out of jail, he married the girl and they moved back to Rogers, Arkansas. Seems he also had to learn things the hard way.

The Gridley Poultry delivery job only lasted a few months. The company cut back on my position, forcing the salesman to return to his old position. Shortly after I was laid off at Gridley Poultry, I received a second notice to report for another pre-induction physical. I did not want to risk passing the physical exam and being drafted in the Army or the Marine Corp then being shipped off to Vietnam. I figured that I had better enlist in the Navy before I got drafted in the Army or Marines.

Like many patriotic young men of military age in 1964, when we heard about North Vietnamese torpedo boats attacking the USS Maddox in the Gulf of Tonkin in August that year, many of us were inspired to do our patriotic duty and "fight communism and the kill Viet Con." Years later, after reading H.R. McMasters's book, Dereliction of Duty, and learning what actually motivated President Johnson and Secretary of Defense Robert McNamara to persuade Congress to pass the Gulf of Tonkin Resolution, I was angered to learn that we Americans were deceived by our own President. I was angered that over 58,000 Americans lost their lives fighting a prolonged, unwinnable war that was based on falsehoods.

The guy I hung out with at that time, Ed Lund, suggested we enlist in the Air Force instead of the Navy. Ed's reasoning was that the Air Force had better electronics training. So, on November 4th, after President Johnson was reelected on Nov 3rd, we wisely enlisted in the Air Force. Ironically, Ed was trained in ordinance and shipped off to Vietnam. I had obtained a statement from my family doctor stating that my eyes would not prohibit me from military service. I took the bus from Marysville, California, to Oakland, California. There I would board a charter flight to San Antonio, TX. It was the first-time I was ever on an airplane. When Mom dropped me off at the Greyhound bus station in Marysville, there was no hug, no "I am going to miss you," no "Please write," just "Are you going to make out an allotment to me?" I didn't even know what the hell an allotment was. Looking back, I think she saw her male children as those who could help her out financially. I think it would have been perfectly fine with her if I had dropped out of high school at age 16, found a job, and contributed to the household.

At Oakland, California, airport, those of us from the Northern California area that had just enlisted in the United States Air Force assembled to be flown to San Antonio, Texas, to attend Basic Training at Lackland Air Force Base. Amongst those recruits were two African-American young men, Robbie Williams and Shellywood Rice. I sensed that both young men were not at ease amongst the mostly white group of young men. Robbie Williams was a very friendly, likeable person, but Shellywood Rice was more standoffish, keeping to himself. Waiting with Robbie was his white girlfriend, which did raise some eyebrows among those that were not from the more liberal San Francisco Bay Area. Having a black brother, I did not share the same sense of unease as some of the others. I got to know Robbie over time and learned that he had concerns about leaving his girlfriend. He feared that she would not be waiting for him whenever he returned home. He shared with me what his girlfriend's father had told her about dating an African American man. Her father told her that he "did not want any polka-dotted grandchildren." Obviously, Robbie's comment struck a nerve. I can't exactly explain it, but I felt his hurt. I did not share with him my brother's mixed race.

I originally had plans to make a career out of the Air Force. After I finished basic training, I was sent to Sheppard AFB in Wichita Falls, Texas, for telecommunications operator technical school. Much of the instructional material for the class was classified, so we were not allowed to take any study material back to the barracks. If you were caught doing so, you would lose your security clearance and be placed in another career field. Overall, the Air Force was a great learning experience for someone of my background who did not have much of a future. One of the first impressions I had of Air Force life was how difficult some of the young men in my squadron were having adjusting to being away from "momma." Their mother did not have the "mother bird" mentality and had not "prepared them to launch." Many had never experienced the regiment of being ordered around all their waking hours. Many found the "chow hall" food disgusting and could not bring themselves to eat the food because that is not the way "their mother fixed it." Many could not emotionally handle a drill sergeant standing nose-to-nose with them and screaming over some minor infraction. One of the young men approached the drill sergeant, telling him he did not like the Air Force and wanted to go home. He regretted that decision. The drill sergeant came unglued and went into a tirade, using all the curse words in his vocabulary. Sergeant Salazar, a short Filipino drill instructor, reminded the young man that he had enlisted for four years, which caused the young man to burst into tears. The individual bursting into tears enraged the drill sergeant even more, causing him to throw the young man out of his office. The entire exchange was heard throughout the two-story open bay barracks. No one ever entertained the idea of asking to go home again.

Instead of ending up in an electronics career field, Ed Lund ended up in ordinance and was sent to Vietnam after finishing technical school. Before deploying to Vietnam, Ed married his girlfriend, Connie. When he returned from Vietnam, Connie had gained 50 pounds, which Ed found displeasing. When he also discovered she had been unfaithful, he ended the marriage. After being discharged, he became a police officer for the Hayward California Police Department, where he was originally from. He married again, but that ended in divorce also when he discovered that she was having an affair with their African American neighbor. At the divorce hearing, his wife sought child support from Ed for the child that the neighbor had fathered. Fortunately for Ed, the presiding judge found in Ed's favor and he was not forced to pay child support for the child. Ed left the Hayward Police department, returned to Williams, and for a brief time, became a Williams City Police officer. He eventually left law enforcement and returned to the trade that his father had trained him for, becoming employed as a master brick layer. Ed died at a relatively young age.

Had I been placed in a different career field, I may have stayed in the Air Force. After finishing technical school, I was assigned to the 1956 Com Group at Fuchu Air Station in Japan. Being cooped up in a base communication center all day did not fit my short attention-span personality. Due to the classified materials in the com centers, there were no windows and access to the COMM center was restricted. To keep up the heavy workload in the COMM center in Japan, it was necessary to develop a capability for multitasking, but as I found out later, that can be a curse at times. Mentally, I would always be doing more than one task at a time. Even so, I enjoyed the two years I spent in Japan. I found the Japanese people to be very polite and warm.

On evening after returning to the barracks after a late night at one of the local bars, I found one of my three roommates, Fred Turner, lying face-down, spread-eagle on his top bunk. Fred had cut both of his wrists several times, causing substantial amounts of blood to pool on the barrack floor. I immediately contacted the First Sergeant, who had Fred taken to the hospital. The First Sergeant left me to clean up the mess, but as I used a towel, attempting to clean up the blood, the large pool of coagulated blood slid across the barrack's tile floor. Seeing that pool of blood slide across the floor in my inebriated state was more than I could handle. The First Sergeant had to had to get one of the Japanese National janitors to complete the job. Fred survived, but he was immediately sent home and discharged. I later learned that Fred had gotten a "Dear John" letter from his girlfriend back in the states.

I finished out my Air Force enlistment at Holloman AFB in New Mexico. While assigned to Holloman, I met my first wife, Elena. Like so many relationships, you get introduced, start dating, start a sexual relationship, and before you know it, you are engaged. When Tom died in June 1986, Elena and I drove to Sutter, California, to attend the funeral. That night after the funeral, Mom made Elena a place to sleep on the couch and a place for me on the living room floor. After everyone went to bed, Elena slipped down off the couch and joined me on the floor. I had no intentions of engaging in any hanky panky out of respect for the situation, but my son was conceived that night. It seems that back in the 50s and 60s, society had roles that males and females were expected to live out. You grow up, get married, have kids, and live happily ever after. And if you got a girl in a family way, you were expected to marry her. I know that conditioning influenced me. Over the many years, I would meet several people that would claim that they were never really in love with their spouses, or that their spouses were never really in love with them, they just got caught up in the currents of an ongoing relationship and married to give some sense of security to their lives at the time. As a Japanese woman once explained to me about a relationship she was caught up in, "Sometimes the tide is too strong to swim against it, it is just easier to swim with the tide." Or, as I have observed over the years, many weaker swimmers lash themselves to a stronger swimmer to navigate life's current. I always wondered if that is why Elena married me. Even Prince Charles eventually told Princess Diana that he had never loved her.

I was discharged from the Air Force on August 5, 1968 and married Elena on the same day. I did the right thing by society's rules. But did I do the right thing for Elena or for myself? Maybe it was the right thing to do at that time in our lives. After the wedding reception, we immediately headed out to Susanville, California, where I obtained a job as a seasonal firefighter. I had previously taken the civil service entrance exam and applied for any job I might qualify for. By January 1969, I was called to go for an interview at San Francisco International Flight Service station at San Francisco Airport. The job involved working for the Federal Aviation Administration, doing much the same work as I had in the Air Force. Jim Mason informed me that he would like to hire me but there was a freeze on federal hiring and he had no idea when the freeze would be lifted. Discouraged, I headed back to Sadie's house until I could figure out what I should do. The following Monday morning, I headed to the nearest unemployment office to look for work. While I was gone, Jim Mason called Sadie's house and said that the freeze had been lifted and I was hired. I began work in two weeks, starting what would become a 40-year federal career. My starting salary was $175.00 every two weeks, $5,732.00 per year. $175.00 was also what my monthly rent payment would be.

Two weeks later, my son Joseph was born at St Mary's Hospital in Daly City, California. My health insurance had not gone into effect yet, so I knew I would have to bear the financial burden of the hospital charges. But I had not figured on complications. I took Elena to the hospital on Saturday evening and she was in labor until Sunday evening. Like many women enduring labor pains, Elena said that she did not want to have to go through that again. I had to be at work at midnight Sunday, so I left and went to work. Shortly after I got to work, the hospital called and said that the baby was delivered via c- section. The bills started mounting. But at least mother and baby were doing fine. Elena was supposed to be released in three days. However, when I arrived at her room on the third floor on the third day, she was no longer there. I was informed that she was in intensive care because she had developed a staph infection in her incision. The bills were really mounting now. The business manager for the hospital called me into her office to discuss how I was going to pay. I explained my financial situation to her, but she insisted that I obtain a loan to pay off the hospital. I told her that was not possible and asked her not to mention our conversation to Elena. However, the bitch ignored my request and visited Elena, pressuring her over the hospital bill. Elena would be required to stay at least a week longer in the hospital, but they would release my son. Initially, I did not know what I was going to do with a newborn with no way to stay home to care for him. I decided to call Sadie to see if she could take care of the baby until Elena was released. She was a lifesaver. She kept my son at her house for a week until Elena was released. I believe that this week-long separation hindered the normal mother-child bonding. Elena never exhibited affectionate mothering characteristics toward our son and was not comfortable breastfeeding him.

After Elena was released, I secured a second part-time job working for Wackenhut Security Services. They were very accommodating regarding scheduling my assignments around my full-time job. Many days, I would work two 8-hour shifts, back to back. One of my regular assignments was working the San Francisco Giants baseball games. I also worked rock shows at the Cow Palace and baggage checks at the airport. I soon had the bills caught up, but I did not have much money left over. Money was tight, so on the occasions when I got an unexpected call to go to a second 8-hour assignment, I did not always have money in my pocket to buy lunch during the second shift. I lost a lot of weight and was always tired. There were days when I was literally falling asleep standing up. One day, when I was working baggage checks at the airport after my F.A.A job, I started getting very sick, experiencing headaches, fever, and vomiting green slime. I asked the shift supervisor if I could go home, but he insisted I stay till the end of the shift in about two hours. I stuck it out and made it home. When I tried to eat dinner that evening, the food kept trying to come back up. Evidently, I had gone so long with any substantial food that my body was rejecting it. In time, I would quit the second job.

In August of that same year, Elena took our son back to New Mexico to visit her family. She forgot to take her birth control pills with her, so by the time she returned home, she had disrupted her menstrual cycle. For about a three-month period, we thought she was pregnant again. I was depressed for the three months until she found out she was not pregnant. I just got everything paid off and now I thought I was starting over. True, I did have health insurance this time. But I decided I needed to do something about the situation myself. In January of 1970, at 24 years old, I had a vasectomy. The whole experience of the pregnancy, the hospital bills, working two jobs, and then the possibility of having a second child within a year and a half was too much stress for me. It was a feeling of overwhelming despair that I had experienced back in high school. Not to mention the commuting in the bumper-to-bumper traffic on the four-lane Bay Shore freeway to and from work every day. Some days it would take an hour and a half just to drive the 34 miles to San Francisco Airport. Being from farming country, moving to the San Francisco Bay area was somewhat of a culture shock. I was not prepared for the high-cost of living, high rents, and the congestion. Just to get out of the bay area on weekends could take up to three hours, and returning on Sunday evening, you could encounter the same commute. Feeling overwhelmed at times also put a strain on my relationship with Elena. Even then, the Bay Area was a very liberal environment. I was shocked when we attended a Jefferson Airplane concert at Santa Clara County

Fairgrounds and many of the attendees were passing around lit marijuana joints while police ignored their activity. I was so naive about the cultural revolution that was just beginning in the liberal San Francisco Bay Area and other parts of the U.S.

I think it was during this emotionally stressful period that I subconsciously became estranged from my family. I was having enough problems dealing with my own issues and I could not handle additional issues created by others. One of life's lessons I have learned is that some people are addicted to chaos in their lives and they constantly bring chaos in to the lives of others. Emotionally, I distanced myself from family members' chaos. Rarely would I visit them, and when I did, it seemed all we talked about was the chaos in different family members' lives. On one of the rare visits to Sadie's home, my mother was there. When I got out of the car, she ran out to me and hugged me. I was caught completely off-guard. That was the first and only time I remember her hugging me. I soon realized it was all for show. Her two sisters were in Sadie's house, and she was doing it for their benefit.

During this time, I came to the realization that I was not good at riding life's roller coaster. Because of my reserved personality, I could not feel the exhilaration of the peaks of the ride, but I could feel the depression of the depths. I always hid my depression, always hid my fears by keeping them bottled up inside, not even sharing them with my spouse. That can drive a wedge into a relationship. I would drive myself deeper into depression by keeping things bottled up, looking at the issues with blinders on. It is easier to see the darker side of things. I would carry that trait through most of my life. What is needed is another perspective from someone else, but it would take me a long time to realize that. It seems for me, the negative life experiences cut deeper and the scars lasted longer. I would develop a self-deprecating sense of humor to mask what I was feeling inside. I think that sense of humor saved me from myself.

After a year with the F.A.A., I received a pay increase. However, that was the top of the pay-grade for my position. I would have to apply for other positions if I hoped to keep climbing the career ladder. So I took the test for Air Traffic Controller, obtaining a relatively high score. My name was placed on the roster of eligible applicants.

In late 1970, I received a letter from the United States Customs Service office in Los Angeles, California, stating that they were contacting applicants off the Air Traffic Control roster to determine if they were interested in applying for the new position of Sky Marshal. The position title was Customs Security Officer (CSO), however, I had no idea what the position entailed. I would learn it was created to attempt to put a stop to the rash of airline hijackings that occurred in the early 1970s by putting armed officers on high-risk airline flights. I had never aspired to a law enforcement career, nor did I know if I had what it took to perform in a law enforcement position. The human resources lady in Los Angeles told me if I was interested, I should contact the HR specialist in San Francisco, because they were hiring also. When I contacted the HR specialist there, I was advised that they were hiring, but only for Anchorage, Alaska, and New York City. I thought Anchorage,

Alaska, and New York City? Hell, I was having a hard-enough time surviving in the bay area. When asked if I was still interested, I said yes for fear of being eliminated from consideration. The HR specialist then scheduled me for a psychological test for that November. Somehow, I passed that test. I figured by staying "middle of the road" on my answers, not going too far to the right or left with my answers, I could get through the test. After receiving the results of the test, I never heard from the HR specialist. I soon forgot about the position.

In April 1971, the San Francisco HR specialist called me at work, asking if I was still interested in the position. I hesitated to answer, thinking I would end up in Anchorage, Alaska, or, even worse, NEW YORK CITY. Without thinking, I asked, "Where is the position?" To my surprise, she answered, "Right here in San Francisco. You will be working out of the San Francisco airport." WOW, talk about luck, I thought. As the saying goes, "Luck is opportunity meeting preparedness." It was a fantastic opportunity. I would have to get prepared. She further informed me that I would have to be in Ft. Belvoir, Virginia in two weeks. I would have to successfully complete a month-long intensive law enforcement training with an emphasis on firearms training. I accepted the position with reservations. I had a wife and child that I would have to leave alone for a month while I trained. I would have to resign from my current secure position and gamble on successfully completing the training program. What if I wash out? I thought.

Fortunately for me, when I discussed the opportunity with my supervisor, he encouraged me to accept the position, telling he would hold my job open until I successfully completed the training. He would hire me back if I did not successfully complete the training. After discussing with my wife, I decided I could not pass up the opportunity—the pay grade was three levels above my FAA position. Now I would have to prepare myself. I bought a book on law enforcement defensive tactics and practiced them on my wife. I bought an old H&R nine-shot 22-caliber revolver at a pawn shop and a book on how to shoot a handgun. I would spend hours at the Coyote Point pistol range practicing at the 25-yard line. I practiced one-handed single shots, shooting at a bull's-eye target, concentrating on my breathing and the trigger press. I became somewhat proficient. Now I felt somewhat prepared.

I reported to Ft. Belvoir for my training on April 16, 1971. I was glad I had gotten familiar with firing a handgun. It made the rest of the training less stressful. Throughout the training, classmates disappeared with no explanation. Each day, we dreaded someone opening the classroom door and calling out our name. The background-check process was still being completed as we attended class. If your name was called out, that usually meant the "hook" got you. You were summarily removed from the program, usually because of something they had discovered in your background. You would be escorted back to the barracks, where you packed your belongings. Then you were escorted off the base. The "hook" never got me, and I made it through the training.

One of my classmates, Charlie Bokinski, was also being assigned to San Francisco. Charlie was originally from Utah. After serving a tour in the U.S. Army as a military policeman, he was hired by U.S. Customs Service as a Sky Marshal. When Charlie reported to San Francisco, I assisted him in getting settled into the area. Charlie could have been a double for a young Glen Campbell. The Pan American female flight attendants and the female employees at San Francisco International Airport competed for his attention. Charlie was a chick magnet. Charlie had a bright future with the U.S. Customs Service, or so it would seem.

Flying High

After completing the training, on the flight back to San Francisco, I kept thinking to myself, Wow I have been issued two service revolvers, a gold badge, and a government check for $1200 to be used as a revolving expense account. I found it all hard to believe. The Sky Marshal position began my conversion from small-town country boy to a more sophisticated man of the world. It would introduce me to temptations I probably never would have encountered otherwise. In 1971, the Sky Marshals at the San Francisco office were being assigned 8 and 14-day trips on Pan American Airways 747s to the Far East and 21-day trips around the world. I never imagined I would be visiting such places. I never did get assigned an around-the-world trip, but I was regularly assigned to the Far East trips. I went to Tokyo, Hong Kong, Bangkok, Singapore, Manila, Guam, Hawaii, and Saigon. We were also assigned Air West Airlines flights up and down the west coast. I also did a 30-day detail to Minneapolis, where we were assigned flights all over the northwest and northeast U.S. on Northwest Airlines. We were scheduled to flights for two months, and on the third month, we were assigned security at the airport boarding areas. Ironically, 30 years later, my son would be hired as an Air Marshal, a newly recreated position after the 9/11 attack.

When assigned to the two months of flight status, you were required to arrive at the departure boarding area two hours before your departure. It was our responsibility to spend those two hours mentally screening the passengers waiting in the boarding area for the flight. We were "profiling" the awaiting passengers during those two hours. Profiling is not a politically-correct term in today's political environment. Law enforcement today is not allowed to profile in the performance of their duties. However, it is human nature to assess the characteristics of those we meet throughout our life. Many times, we form unfounded first impressions of individuals we encounter in our day-to-day life. After many years in law enforcement, certain characteristics are triggers that heighten our alertness to certain individuals. A term now used by some in law enforcement is "evaluating the human terrain," or "collecting human intelligence."

On the Pan American 747 flights, there were three marshals assigned to each flight. One was assigned to economy class and the other two were assigned to first class. While the plane was airborne, one marshal had to be in the upstairs lounge, which had access to the flight deck. To avoid singling us out from the other passengers, the flight attendants treated us as first-class passengers. I was treated to foods I had never heard of before. There were usually 17 female flight attendants assigned to each Tokyo flight. The temptations were there but, fortunately, we usually stayed with a flight crew for only one leg of the trip and we always had different hotels accommodations when we arrived at our destinations. It was quite the experience for a 25-year-old young man from farming country who was raised on welfare to find himself a world traveler. You can take the boy out of the country and you can take the country out of the boy, if he wants you to.

I never had any incidents on any of my flights. I was thankful for that. My only ripple on a flight was in Tokyo, when a Pam American Captain announced during the crew briefing that he did not want any armed officers on his flight. We would have to check our weapons and "dead head," not in a work status, just in transit back to San Francisco, which meant we would traveling as passengers only. Ironically, his attitude in 1971 was, "I can fly that plane any place in the world." Maybe after 9/11/2001, thirty years later, he would realize that the plane could also be flown into a tall building.

A highlight of one of those flights was riding in first class with Angelo Dundee and Muhammad Ali when Ali was going to the Philippines to fight Smokin' Joe Frazier in the "Thrilla in Manila." Probably the hardest part of the job was staying awake on those long 14-hour flights. Also, trying to maintain a relationship with my family became difficult at times. The stress of living in the bay area, commuting, going to night school, and Elena and I both working jobs at different ends of the peninsula was taking a toll. My absence was forcing Elena to assume many of the responsibilities I normally would have shouldered. She soon would shed her small-town personality.

During one of my 14-day trips to the Far East, another Sky Marshal, Jimmy Smith, revealed to me a bizarre incident he had created at San Francisco International Airport just a day before our trip. Jimmy was detailed to San Francisco to work from New York City for 30 days. He was staying in temporary lodging in downtown San Francisco. Jimmy had been out drinking heavily in downtown San Francisco even though he was scheduled to work the "desk watch" at 12 midnight that night. Jimmy was scheduled to work at our Burlingame, California, office just three miles south of the airport. Jimmy rode the city bus from downtown to San Francisco International Airport, where he was dropped off. He then realized that he had no way of getting to the Burlingame office unless he walked the three miles. Jimmy, in his intoxicated state, decided that he would "borrow" a Pan American Airways 747 stair van and drive it across the airport to the south perimeter. Without any thought for airport regulations or arriving and departing aircraft, Jimmy drove the van across the airport to the south perimeter. There he abandoned the van, then hopped the perimeter fence, and began walking the remaining half mile to the Burlingame office. A passerby stopped Jimmy and confronted him about what he had just done. As it turned out, the passerby was an off-duty California Highway Patrolman. Jimmy presented his gold Customs Badge and convinced the passerby he was just going to work. The passerby then gave Jimmy a ride the rest of the way to the Burlingame office. After Jimmy relieved the person that had been working the "desk watch" that evening, he passed out for the rest of the night.

After I arrived back in San Francisco, I was confronted by my supervisor about the incident. He wanted to know if Jimmy had discussed the incident with me. I could only confirm what he already knew. I also learned that after Jimmy was dropped off at the Burlingame office, the passerby then drove back to the airport perimeter where he encountered the airport police looking into the incident. He informed the airport police of where he had dropped off Jimmy. They returned to the Burlingame office to confront Jimmy. They banged loudly on the door of the office but got no response from Jimmy. By the time that Jimmy had returned from the Far East, the police had completed their investigation into the incident. I never saw Jimmy again. He was sent back to New York City and terminated. I never learned if he was ever charged with a crime.

Over the next few years, I worked with several Customs Officers that were originally hired in New York State. It seemed that some had a "New York State" of mind when it came to having a "gold shield." They seem to think it gave them special privileges. Some thought nothing of using their assigned government vehicle to take their wives shopping or their children to school. Some thought it was ok to use their government credit card to fuel their personal vehicles. They thought nothing of using their badge to gain access to movies or get free coffee and donuts. Several of these officers lost their jobs when the abuse of their "badges" was revealed. Their mentality seemed so foreign to me.

After about a year, the flights were phased out and we were assigned full time to the pre-departure screening of passengers. Originally, we set up the screening process, but in time, that was contracted out to a private security company. We were then responsible for providing the arrest authority for any violations of air piracy laws. We also found ourselves arresting people for drug violations when narcotics were found in their carry-on baggage. I also learned that airport terminals are little communities within themselves and they tend to be Payton Places. It was an eye-opener for a country boy to see all that went on in the airport terminals.

In 1972, my brother Eddie visited me for the first of only three times in his life. He was returning from a tour of duty with the Navy in the Philippines. I picked him up at the airport and he spent the night at my house. The next day, he headed up north to Mom's place. It was during this visit that I told him how he came to be in the family, about our mother being raped by a black man. He did not seem affected by what I told him. He told me that he had asked our mother a couple times, but she always would break down and cry, so he dropped the whole issue. One thing he told me on that visit I had never given much thought to until he said it. He told me that shortly after joining the Navy, he was faced with an identity crisis. He didn't know if he was supposed to be white or black. He said he was raised as poor white trash, but his skin color was that of a black person. The blacks in the Navy resented him for hanging out with the whites, and even had kicked his ass for doing so. Ironically, the only discrimination he felt was from the other black sailors. I would later learn that he had gone AWOL and the FBI was looking for him. I am glad I did not know where he was: as a law enforcement officer, I would have had to turn him in. I would also learn that while he was in the Philippines, he was mainlining and selling heroin. That was not something I could bring into my life. According to Eddie, during one heroin party, a girlfriend of one of the sailors laced her boyfriend's heroin with some chemical, presumably poison. The girlfriend had discovered that he had "butterflied,"—cheated on her—and she was getting her revenge. The sailor immediately started foaming at the mouth and his eyes rolled back in his head. Everyone fled the party, leaving the sailor to die.

Over the years, Eddie and I have talked about our childhood. The conversation often led to how Tom treated him. He would often say that as far as he was concerned, Tom was his father, and that Tom is the one that raised him. Tom treated him as well as he did me, maybe sometimes less harshly, and at times, it seemed that he treated him with kid gloves. Maybe that was Tom's way of showing that he did not harbor any resentment towards Eddie. Maybe that speaks to Tom's character, or lack thereof, but that is for Eddie himself to decide. Eddie will tell you himself that he has a lot of "issues," as might be expected, but Tom's treatment of him does not appear to be one of them.

By late 1973, the Sky Marshal program was being phased out and the remaining personnel were being transferred to different positions within the U.S. Customs Service. I saw it as an opportunity to get out of the bay area, so I applied for a new position of Customs Patrol Officer in Arizona. Ironically, Charlie Bokinski also saw an opportunity to get out of the area. He was transferred to Nogales, Arizona. Before my transfer came through, I found myself in the hospital for 10 days with a ruptured appendix. While still in the hospital, a lab technician came to my room and asked if I had experienced similar symptoms before. I told him that almost a year before, I'd had the same symptoms, but I just ignored them and continued to go to work. He told me, "You must have one hell of immune system. You have scar tissue on your appendix from a previous attack." Shortly after I was released from the hospital, I was notified that I had been selected for a position as Customs Patrol Officer in Nogales, Arizona.

Bound for Yuma

Some people thought I was crazy for accepting a position in Arizona. However, I felt relieved to be leaving the Bay Area. Nogales was and still is a major drug corridor into the U.S. The illegal alien issue was then, as now, a concern we also would be dealing with, but not intentionally. I would only spend two weeks in Nogales. Then I was reassigned to San Luis, Arizona, where our new office was located, at the port of entry, 25 miles south of Yuma, AZ. The acting Patrol Director, Oran Neck, handpicked those that he wanted to retain in the Nogales Office. He reassigned those not selected to outlying offices. Fourteen of us were reassigned to Yuma/San Luis, AZ.

Oran subscribed to what he referred to the "Big Oak Tree" philosophy. If you found yourself huddled under the shade of Oran's Big Oak Tree, he would see that you received favor when it came to promotions and assignments. In the beginning, his protégés were the ones that were rapidly promoted. At times, the promotional opportunities were in the outlying offices, so the protégés were promoted to these positions with the assurance that they could return to the Nogales Office after approximately one year. Several times, Oran's protégés did not qualify for the positions, so the position description was rewritten to qualify the person that Oran wanted in the position. Horace Cavitt was transferred into Nogales to assume the District Patrol Director's position. The Assistant Patrol Director's position was then announced, with the position description rewritten so Oran could qualify. He later told me that he was called in the Horace's office and told to find his application amongst all the applications for the position—he effectively selected himself for the position. Oran expected loyalty from those huddled under the shade of the Big Oak Tree.

Of the 14 or so officers originally assigned to the newly-created San Luis office, all came from large metropolitan areas. Two were from New York City, five were from Los Angeles, four were from Baltimore, one was from Portland, one was from Hawaii, and one was from Texas. We were jokingly referred to as the "menagerie of misfits." Most had never driven a four-wheel drive vehicle in the soft desert sand. One guy from Baltimore did not even have a driver's license. In the beginning, it was like a keystone cop movie. Every shift, someone called for assistance to have their vehicle pulled out of the deep sand. On one occasion, four other vehicles got stuck trying to pull out the first vehicle. These city boys did not adjust well to the Yuma desert.

Several of these new employees were transfers from other agencies. Many of them found small town Yuma unpleasant to live and work in. Their wives and families were less pleased. In time, we were tasked with manning a remote, soon-to-open new office in Lukeville, AZ, 127 miles to the east. Initially, our office detailed several officers to Lukeville on two-week assignments. Soon, several single officers volunteered to transfer to staff the new officers.

Jack, Sly, Steve, and Dennis found they liked the unsupervised environment of the remote office. Sly would be the only one to make Lukeville a permanent move. He soon brought his young Asian American girlfriend from Texas to live with him. He was soon promoted to first line supervisor.

Elena and I bought our first house in a foothills subdivision 12 miles east of Yuma. Things seemed to be going well. I liked living outside of town, where we had privacy. The subdivision had a recreation area for the families, which included a huge swimming pool. One of the frequent visitors to the pool was a retired ATF agent who weighed close to 320 pounds. As he floated around the pool like a walrus, he would often say, "I wonder what the poor people are doing." I thought things were going great. A year and a half later, Elena found that she disliked being so far from town. We sold that house in the foothills and bought another in a subdivision on the west end of Yuma. It was in a nice neighborhood not far from one of the better schools, and the house had a swimming pool. I would have never imagined 10 years before that I would ever own a house with a swimming pool. Only rich folks had pools. Now I found myself floating around the pool, drinking margaritas, saying, "I wonder what the poor people are doing." I knew only too well what they were doing: just gettin' by.

In the initial years of the deployment of the Customs Patrol Division to the southern border, there were many conflicts with our sister agency, the U.S. Border Patrol. We had different missions but in the same geographical areas. Border Patrol's primary mission was the apprehension of illegal aliens crossing into the

U.S. The Customs Patrol Division's primary mission was the interdiction of narcotics and merchandise being smuggled into the U.S. Many of the conflicts arose out of both agencies being in the same areas trying to accomplish different goals. At times, the uncoordinated activities in the same areas would interfere with the others operational goals. Usually the agents could work things out, but management created intentional conflicts at times.

Ironically, several of those hired to fill vacant positions within the San Luis Office were Border Patrol Agents that had jumped ship from Border Patrol to U.S. Customs. Initially, we encountered many illegal aliens that were attempting to enter the U.S. to obtain work. Many times, we found ourselves apprehending these aliens and then turning them over to Border Patrol. But after they purposely took hours to respond to relieve us of those we had apprehended, we stopped detaining the aliens. We then would just place a call to the Border Patrol Office and advise them of the alien's location.

One night, I was patrolling the river area when I noticed an unmarked Ford LTD traveling on the levee southbound parallel to the river. I watched it as it traveled along, stopping, then moving forward for several minutes. I pulled up on the levee to investigate. I pulled in behind the vehicle and stopped it with the use of my red emergency lights. The driver identified himself as Jerry Jackson, an Anti-Smuggling Agent with Border Patrol. He demanded that I give him my name and badge number because he was going to press charges against me for stopping him without any probable cause. I informed him that I was only required to provide him with my badge number and that, as a Customs Officer, I did not need probable cause in a border area. I could stop and search without probable cause. I provided him with my badge number, #157, and went about my business. As my luck would have, it sometime during the rest of my shift, I lost that badge. I know it sounds suspicious, but I spent most of my next shift retracing my travel from the night before trying to locate the badge with no luck. I heard later that he tried to pursue the matter, but he did not get very far with the charges. Evidently someone enlightened him regarding a Customs Officer's authority in a border area.

In the mid-1970s, with the implementation of EEO (Equal Employment Opportunities) hiring policies, the law enforcement ranks were being staffed with a few female officers and others considered minorities. Border Patrol in Yuma initially hired three women. Two were younger women and the third was an older Immigration Inspector. One woman was assigned a Senior Border Patrol Agent as her training officer. It was not long before the rumors started circulating that he and the young lady were having an affair. Someone informed the agent's wife, an Asian lady, who did not take kindly to his infidelity. His wife went to the young lady's home and confronted her in her front yard, in broad daylight. The agent's wife pulled out a gun and shot the young lady. The young lady survived, but she learned, as others have learned, not to mess with an Asian woman's husband. Sharing a patrol vehicle with a male training officer for eight hours on the midnight shift could lead to temptations. During the period that I served in uniformed patrol, Customs did not hire any female officers in Arizona.

During periods of budget constraints, we had to keep our patrol cars parked for lack of fuel. Management decided that one vehicle per shirt would be used by a supervisor. We would load up in one of the four wheel drive vehicles, then be taken out to known crossing points along the border and dropped off in two-man teams. We were provided with a handy talkie so we could communicate with the shift supervisor if we observed any smugglers crossing with contraband. On one occasion, we observed four individuals carrying contraband crossing through a hole in the fence just east of the port of entry. As we notified the supervisor, the four individuals met up with a vehicle, loaded the bags in the truck and headed toward Yuma. As the supervisor entered the area, the load vehicle sped off. When the supervisor attempted to give chase, his vehicle stalled and was unable to apprehend the vehicle. Those were long nights lying out in the desert during the chilly weather.

Often when we seized a vehicle with narcotics, we would put the vehicle in government service. We had seized a Volkswagen Van, which was placed in service as an unmarked undercover vehicle. Bob and I were utilizing the van as our assigned vehicle. As the summer temperatures became hotter in Yuma, we decided to take the van to the shop to have the ventilation duct work checked out because would could not get any ventilation through the forward vents. At the shop, the mechanic discovered several kilo bricks of marijuana stuffed up into the vents blocking the air flow. Later, we took the van to the shop again for routine maintenance, and again the shop discovered several more bricks of marijuana in the undercarriage of the vehicle. We had been utilizing that vehicle for

months with a substantial amount of marijuana still concealed in
it.

I found myself really enjoying my new job. I felt uneasy taking days off for fear of missing out on something exciting happening at work. As uniformed patrol officers, we worked rotating
shifts patrolling the border area looking for drug and merchandise
smugglers. I liked the mobility and variety of being out in the undeveloped areas trying to catch the smugglers. Much of the time, I
was working by myself. I liked the independence. I had no fear of
making vehicle stops out in remote areas late at night by myself.
One aspect of responding to calls or situations that quickly became apparent to me was that there is always "a gun involved"—
yours. Even if the suspect did not have a gun, there was always the
possibility of the suspect taking yours, especially if there was more
than one suspect. I became very protective of my weapon in enforcement situations. I particularly liked "profiling" vehicles that
were preferred as load vehicles: full size Ford/Mercury, Chevrolet,
and Chrysler/Dodge sedans. The larger trunk areas of these vehicles could accommodate approximately 600 pounds of narcotics. When loaded with 600 pounds, these vehicles would ride low
in the back, at times bottoming out on bumps in the road unless
they were equipped with air shocks. Even with air shocks, having
all that weight in the rear caused the vehicle's steering to become
very unstable. If the air shocks were fully inflated, it would cause
the vehicle to be noticeably higher in the rear. In most cases, it was
not possible to profile the occupants due to window tinting or low
light. Once you could articulate "founded suspicion" and had the

vehicle stopped, you could develop "probable cause" to search the vehicle. Many times after stopping the vehicle, the smell of marijuana was detectable. One afternoon, I was leaving my residence, which was the second house from the stop sign on first street in Yuma. As I pulled up to the stop sign, a very dusty, older model Chrysler Imperial passed in front of me. I noticed as the vehicle passed that it rode very low in the rear. On a hunch, I stopped the vehicle and questioned the driver. When I asked to inspect the trunk area, he consented. The trunk contained approximately 400 pounds of marijuana wrapped in kilo bricks. In just five minutes of work, I had seized 400 pounds of marijuana and a Chrysler Imperial and arrested a smuggler. Narcotics seizures and arrests were the way that to get noticed by management and get promoted. In the first year of its existence, the Arizona-based patrol division seized over 100,000 pounds of narcotics, accelerating the careers of many. I did well in that regard, but working rotating shifts and long hours continued to take a toll on my relationship with my family. I would often work my days off. I never really felt like I was going to work. Elena was not pleased that I was spending so much time working.

In late 1974, the U.S. Customs Service was rocked by the violent deaths of two of its unformed patrol officers in Nogales, Arizona, Charlie Bokinski and Bud Dixon. Early that morning, two teenage children on their way to school came upon their bodies lying outside their government vehicle. The teenagers lived on a ranch several miles northeast of Nogales, Arizona, and routinely drove the isolated road into Nogales to attend classes. Initially, law enforcement had few clues as to how the two died. It would take months of investigation to discover what had happened to the two during that 12 midnight to 8 a.m. shift on that remote road.

The investigation into the deaths, along with the coroner's autopsy, revealed how violently the two officers had died. Officers were routinely assigned to monitor the activity on the remote road, which was regularly used by drug smugglers to smuggle large shipments of drugs into the United States. Charlie and Bud were assigned the duties that night. Due to the remoteness of the area, law enforcement radio communications were not reliable, leaving the officers at times with no available backup from other officers. Sometime during the night, the two officers observed a pickup truck driven by a lone male traveling out of the area. The officers intercepted the vehicle and attempted to affect a stop. The driver, realizing law enforcement was blocking his path, turned the vehicle around, attempting to flee back toward Mexico. Charlie and Bud gave pursuit. Bud was driving while Charlie literally rode "shotgun" in the passenger seat. During the high-speed pursuit, Charlie leaned out the open passenger window and fired a shot from his shotgun at the fleeing vehicle. One of the pellets from the "00 buck" round penetrated the cab of the fleeing vehicle and entered the driver's back. The fleeing vehicle came to an abrupt, unexpected stop. Bud was unable to stop the Custom's vehicle in time to prevent it from coming up alongside of the stopped pickup. As the vehicles came to a stop, the driver of the pickup extended his arm out the open window and fired a shot at Charlie with a 32 caliber semi-automatic pistol. The bullet struck Charlie in the upper body, causing him to drop the shotgun on the ground outside their vehicle. In the excitement of the moment, Bud hurriedly drew his 357-caliber service revolver and accidentally discharged the weapon into Charlie left side.

The driver of pickup then exited his vehicle and retrieved the shotgun lying on the ground. He then deliberately walked around the front of the government vehicle and shot Bud with shotgun as he was exiting the driver's side door. As Bud fell to the ground, the driver of the pickup walked over to Bud and bashed him in the head with the butt of the shotgun. Leaving both officers for dead, the driver then got back in his pickup and fled the scene.

Several hours after assistance arrived that morning, an alert officer noticed tire tracks leaving the roadway and disappearing over an embankment into a ravine. The pickup, approximately 400 pounds of marijuana, and the dead driver were discovered at the bottom of the ravine. The investigation indicated that while fleeing the scene, the driver had passed out from bloodloss and drove the vehicle into the ravine. I have heard other accounts of what happened on the remote road that night, but the only three people that know for sure are no longer with us.

Several days later, a massive funeral service was held in the little border town of Nogales, Arizona. Dignitaries from Washington D.C. and law enforcement officers from throughout the southern United States attended the ceremony to show their respect. It was an impressive turnout.

In 1975, two DEA agents, Roy Stevens and Don Ware were kidnapped, shot with automatic weapons, and left for dead while conducting surveillance in San Luis Mexico, The only thing that would save their lives was a stroke of luck and outstanding immediate medical care. During the surveillance in Mexico, the "dopers" had "made" blond-haired, blue-eyed Roy and Don as "narcs." At first, Roy and Don thought that they were being approached by Mexican Federal Judicial Police, but they would find out in a very brutal way that they were mistaken. They were jumped by the men, badly beaten, and their guns were taken. Don was barely conscious, but Roy was still aware of his surroundings. They were thrown in the back of an open pickup truck headed out of town, followed by another vehicle occupied by men with automatic weapons. They knew they were being taken to be murdered.

On the way out of San Luis, Mexico, a municipal bus came between the pickup and the vehicle with the armed men, temporarily separating the two vehicles at a stop light. It was now or never, and Roy knew it. By a stroke of luck, the dopers had missed Don's back-up gun in his waistband, a snub nose five shot 38 Smith & Wesson. Don was in no condition to defend himself, so Roy grabbed Don's gun at the stop light, jumped out of the back of the pickup and put the gun to the driver's head. The gun went off, killing the driver instantly. Now Roy only had four shots left, and they were no match for automatic weapons. Seeing what had transpired in front of them, the men in the follow vehicle opened fire on Roy and Don with automatic weapons. Both agents were shot multiple times. Don was in bad shape. The agents were left for dead. Both Roy and Don did play dead. They were rescued by other agents working in Mexico that day. Not waiting for an ambulance, they loaded Roy and Don into an agent's car and hauled ass for the hospital in Yuma. It was code three, balls to the wall, get the hell out of the way, the entire 30 miles to Yuma Regional Medical center. By the time the agents arrived at the hospital with Roy and Don, they had almost burnt out the brakes on the car. They were not able to get the car stopped in time and crashed into the side of the hospital, causing minor damage. Roy and Don were saved. After Don was stabilized, he was medevaced to a hospital in San Diego, where he spent six months in critical condition.

Twenty years later, Don and I would be partnered up on a task force case and develop an uncommon personal and professional relationship. Don had become a hero, almost an icon, to younger agents. Don worked the streets in Las Vegas his whole career, turning down multiple offers to take a medical retirement or to become a "suit" in Washington D.C. He would not die from the bullets of an assassin, but rather the nick of a surgeon's scalpel.

It was also during this time that I worked up the nerve to write my mother a letter to ask her if Tom was my father. On that midnight shift, I was the only one working. I had been assigned to desk duty monitoring "sensors," electronic sensing devices activated by motion. There had been many sensing devices planted along known smuggling routes in our area. When activated, each sensing device sent out a numerical code indicating where the device was located. They were also equipped with microphones so that when they were activated, you could tell if a vehicle or person had set them off. I anticipated some possible activity that night, so I backed a patrol car into a space behind the office and left the keys in the ignition. I then contacted the shift supervisor in the other division and asked him to back me up if the devices were activated. When I got two activations in sequence, I would notify him, and he would assume my watch at the desk. I would run like hell to the car and race off to the location that was activated. Just as I was halfway through my letter to my mother, I got 10 & 11 sequence activation, so I put my plan in motion. I raced three miles up the road, where the route entered the highway. Just about the time I got to the location, the supervisor advised over the radio that number 12 had activated as well. The car was trapped, and by the time I turned down the dirt road, I found a sedan with its engine still running stopped on the dirt road with the driver's side door wide open. The driver had skipped, but I got his car and 600 pounds of marijuana. I had to get assistance from the sheriff's deputy to get the car back to the port. I had to finish the letter to my mother another night. I eventually sent the letter. She answered, saying that Tom was my father, but for years after, even after her death, I would hear information to the contrary from other family members.

On another evening shift, I was assigned to the west side of San Luis, Arizona, patrolling the river area in an open, military-style jeep. It was hot and I was tired and dirty as I headed back to San Luis at the end of my shift. Just as I was about three miles from the office, I noticed a vehicle turn its lights on as it was coming out of one of the agricultural field roads approaching the highway toward me. Oh, I thought, it is probably just an irrigator leaving work, but I will check it anyway. I did not even have a red light in the jeep, so I just used the bright spot light I had rigged up and signaled to the driver of the vehicle to stop. The vehicle stopped just short of the highway, so I left my vehicle running and walked over to the car. I asked the young male driver for identification, which he presented. I then asked him the basic questions: what was he doing, where was he coming from. He told me he was an irrigator, but he seemed too young, about eighteen years old. Since he was coming from the direction of the river area and the international border, I asked to search his vehicle. When he responded that he did not have the keys to the trunk, I had him step out of the car as I reached in and retrieved the keys from the ignition. His response was a red flag and should have heightened my alertness, but I was hot and tired and just wanted to end my shift. I was inattentive. With the vehicle keys in hand, I walked the young man to the trunk area of the vehicle to try the keys in the trunk lock. A key fit and the trunk opened. Holy shit, the trunk area was loaded completely full of marijuana bundles.

I turned to place the young man under arrest, but he was gone. What a dumbass! I had let the young man get behind me, out of my sight. He had taken off running back down the dirt road, back toward the border. I was only 28 at the time and still in decent shape, so I took off after him. He was about 10 steps out in front of me, but I could not gain any ground on him in the chase, so I thought I would fire a warning shot with my Smith & Wesson Model 66 357 revolver as I ran. Bah-whom! The shot had the opposite effect of what I had hoped for. The young man kicked his skinny little ass into high gear and now I was losing ground on him. About 100 yards into the chase, it dawned on me, damn, I left my vehicle running alongside the highway, and his vehicle is sitting there with the keys still in the trunk lock with the trunk open. I had better go back. But just as I broke my stride, the young man stumbled about 20 yards out in front of me and rolled over on his back, scrambling backwards on all fours, trying to get to his feet. Before I could regain my stride and resume the chase, he was back up on his feet, disappearing into the darkness. When I got back to my vehicle, I called for assistance, requesting a driver for the loaded vehicle. I was lucky that time. I made a rookie mistake. I got complacent, which could have had dire consequences had the young man had ill intentions. I was shaken, knowing I had screwed up.

Our office received information from the DEA office that smugglers were using a river crossing to smuggle loads of marijuana at around 12:30 a.m., when the Border Patrol was changing shifts and the area was not patrolled. So, a young Puerto Rican officer from New York named Ramon and I were assigned to watch the area during that time period. We watched the area for two nights with no activity. On the third night, late into the shift, we observed a faint flashing red light in the area. As we watched, we soon realized that the flashing red light was a Border Patrol vehicle chasing another vehicle. The two vehicles traveled about three-fourths of a mile to the south and then turned off the paved road onto a gravel road, heading in our direction. We decided to assist in the chase, knowing we had a faster vehicle, a 1978 Plymouth Fury police pursuit vehicle. As we approached the intersecting gravel road, I realized we were traveling too fast to stop before the intersection. We slid through the intersection. I regained control and joined in the pursuit, but the dust was so thick from the other vehicles it was hard to see anything in front of us. As we approached the next intersection, we encountered two other Border Patrol vehicles joining the pursuit. The area was soon swarming with other Border Patrol vehicles, so we decided to leave the area and head back to the office.

The next morning, Ramon and I were called into the office to explain our actions in the pursuit. I explained that we were only involved in the pursuit for two miles before we discontinued the chase. The Border Patrol agents claimed that we interfered in the pursuit, causing one of their vehicles to roll over on the gravel road. It turned out that the vehicle that rolled over had two illegals in the back. They were injured so they were looking for a scapegoat. I made a point of telling my supervisor that they were not going to hang the accident on me. Ramon and I drove back to the accident site and discovered that the accident happened at least 200 yards before the intersection where we joined the pursuit. I believed that the Border Patrol agent did not want to admit that he had just lost control of the high profile four-wheel drive vehicle traveling at a high rate of speed on the gravel road. We reported back to our supervisor, but I got the impression that he did not want me to be so vocal about defending myself.

The next morning, Ramon and I were again called into the office, but this time we were told that we were being assigned to a two-week desert detail 80 miles to the east of Yuma. The detail would be a campout detail. We would be living out of a camper for the next two weeks, watching an isolated smuggling route. It seems that we were to be isolated, so we could not have any input in the inquiry into the accident. By the time we could return to Yuma, the incident was forgotten.

I was regularly assigned to work with an officer who would become another longtime friend. Ole Levi and I spent many long hours together. He was from Norwegian farming stock out of North Dakota and, like many of Norwegian stock, he did not talk much, unless it was a subject he was interested in, which was usually mechanical. He would usually prefer to zone-out, having a conversation with himself. You could not get him into any idle conversations to pass the time during those long midnight shifts. He seemed irritated when I spoke, interrupting the conversation he was having with himself. Years later, on one of our many motorcycle trips together, he rigged up a portable citizen band (CB) radio on the handlebars of his motorcycle. I asked him if he wanted to monitor the CB so we could communicate with each other while riding. His response was, "You have anything worthwhile to say?" I had no response.

I had been married to two women that tended to zone-out, deep in thought. One could sit for hours manicuring the split ends from her long hair while deep in thought. After many years, I discovered that she was ruminating about a love that might have been. The second wife was addicted to social media. She could spend hours on her cell phone, Kindle, or laptop, surfing the internet, playing games, or reading. One of her former colleagues had used the term "Bob," referring to her battery-operated boyfriend, her vibrator. So I referred to my wife's devices as Bobs, her battery-operated boyfriends. She could lose herself in her games or on Facebook for hours. As Libbie Custer explained in the book "Custer" by Jay Monaghan, when George was writing magazine articles, reading, or studying, he focused so hard that she felt like she was the only person in the room. She would leave the room and withdraw to another. I have often experienced the same feeling. I find it very unsettling to be in a room with someone who is not even aware that you are there. I tend to withdraw to the outdoors.

One morning, we found the tracks of a group of five people who had crossed the river during the night. We were leap frogging, taking turns checking the next farm road in their direction of travel, following their tracks across the highway into agricultural fields. Levi found where the individuals had stashed 400 pounds of marijuana in a dry drainage ditch. We left the marijuana there, planning to set up surveillance on it and wait till someone came to pick it up. We spent all day watching the stash of marijuana, but no one showed up. When night fell, we left our vehicles and snuck into the field, so we could be closer to the stash and watch it. Levi and I were lying down on our stomachs in a newly planted cotton field, but the plants were not tall enough to conceal us. We positioned ourselves to the south of the stash, thinking that whoever came to pick up the marijuana would then proceed to the north or the east, surely not the south. Well, no sooner had darkness fallen than we noticed five individuals walking along the drainage ditch.

It was like watching a black and white video unfold before your eyes. Levi and I could not talk to each other, even though we were just a couple feet apart. We did not dare talk on our portable police radio. We just lay there silently, not daring to move, watching, as four of the individuals loaded the homemade backpacks on their backs. And then it happened. They turned back south and headed right for us. I did not know what Levi was thinking, nor did he know what I was thinking. We waited till two of the "mules" were in arm's reach of us. We jumped up with flashlights and hand-guns. It sounded like a herd stampeding. Three of the individuals immediately dropped the backpacks and ran into the night. I was trying to get the guy I caught to sit down, but he was staring off into the dark, as though thinking of running. Finally, I gave him a "love tap" to the back of the head with my flashlight, just to get his attention. Back in the politically incorrect days, "undocumented aliens" were called "illegal aliens," "wets," "wetbacks," "mojados," "Julios," and "Tonks." "Tonks" referred to the sound made when they were hit upside the head with a flashlight. We only ended up with two out of the five original individuals. The individual that Levi apprehended was carrying pieces of shag carpet. The group would place the carpet down on the dirt farm roads, allowing them to cross without leaving any footprints, but the carpet pattern was noticeable in the soft dirt. We had arranged for a backup team to be on standby, but as luck would have it, they were three miles up the road, all out of the vehicles, in the middle of a discussion. We finally got through to them, but it was too late. Then one of the officers decided that he would ignite a pop flare to illuminate the area. The only problem was that it landed in Bermuda grass field and set it on fire. Great, we had three people loose out in the dark and a grass fire we had to put out. I will need a beer when this is over, I thought to myself.

A few months later, the two individuals went to trial. They both took the witness stand denying that were involved in smuggling that night, insisting that they were just poor "wetbacks" who had the misfortune of running into the smugglers while they were crossing the river. The one I arrested said that he was not doing anything wrong, and the next thing he knew, that guy over there—pointing to Levi—pistol whipped him. Levi, of all people! He is one of the most even-tempered people you will ever meet. I had a tough time containing my laughter. For a long time, I would not let Levi live that down.

In 1976, a former Sky Marshal from Honolulu, Joe Badyl, transferred to the Yuma Patrol Division. Why would anyone in their right mind transfer from Honolulu to Yuma? As it turned out, Joe was going through a divorce from his older Japanese wife and thought the distance between the two places would help him handle the breakup. I had met Joe on one of our flights to Manila, back in 1971. I had even visited his home in Honolulu, where I met his wife and two beautiful Amerasian children. Joe was a very likeable young man, but he had issues with his parents. Since I knew Joe, I was regularly assigned to work with him and show him around. Most of the time, he was pleasant to be around, but I soon learned he had been diagnosed with bipolar disorder and was taking lithium medication. He was having a tough time dealing with the pending divorce. If he was on his medication and not drinking, I did not mind working with him. I was very uneasy around him otherwise.

Joe could turn from pleasant to volatile in a New York minute. On more than one occasion, he erupted into a hostile outburst. You could not predict what he would do in an enforcement situation. It made me uneasy knowing he had that 357-service revolver strapped to his hip. One night, he and I were assigned to patrol duties north of San Luis, Arizona. We were travelling down a paved road on a rainy night. The visibility was very low. Joe and I were talking as I was driving the new, marked patrol sedan. Looking into the darkness, I noticed a blurry white patch in the road ahead. I strained to make out what the object was. Just then, the black and white paint horse running down the middle of the road turned its head. I braked, but it was too late. I slid on the rain-slicked road into the horse's back side, knocking him forward about 10 feet. The horse fell over on the side of the road. Damn, what a mess that was. The new patrol vehicle had damage to the grill and hood. While I was attempting make radio contact with a supervisor, Joe was shouting, "We gotta shoot the horse, we gotta shoot the horse!" I was shouting back at him, "Do not to shoot the horse!" The horse was laboring to breathe, but I did not want Joe to shoot it. The horse died shortly thereafter. Evidently, the impact of the vehicle broke his back. I took a lot of harassing over killing the horse and wrecking a new patrol vehicle.

I never reported Joe's erratic behavior, but he soon left me no choice. Several times, Joe reported late for his shift because he had over-slept. It was usually because of his heavy drinking. During one of our shifts together, Joe recounted to me an incident the weekend before at Los Angeles International Airport. Joe had convinced his wife to travel to Los Angeles, where he would meet her so they might talk about a possible reconciliation. By the time the flight arrived, Joe was very intoxicated. Things were about to go from bad to worse. When Joe and his wife left the terminal for the parking area where Joe had parked his vehicle, Joe realized that he was disoriented. He could not remember where he had parked his car. Joe anxiously began looking for his car but had no idea where it was. As time wore on, Joe became very excitable and loud, climbing onto the tops of parked vehicles, trying to spot his car. A passerby called airport security, reporting Joe's erratic behavior. Airport Police arrived and confronted Joe. They got him calmed down and helped him locate his vehicle. Joe identified himself as a Federal Officer, so the Airport Police let him off with just a warning. Fortunately, Joe had left his service revolver at home. Not surprisingly, Joe's wife decided that reconciliation was not possible.

All things considered, I felt it was time to report my concerns about Joe's erratic behavior. I contacted my supervisor, Guierllmo Juevo, and related my concerns about Joe's mental health. I soon learned that two supervisors went to Joe's home and relieved him of his service revolver and badge, placing him on administrative leave with pay. A brief time later, Joe did the right thing and resigned. Initially, Joe found himself living in a tent in the backyard of his girlfriend's house. He eventually married her and found a job working at her place of employment, Arizona Public Service, in Yuma. I never had any contact with Joe again.

One evening, I was assigned to work the San Luis, Arizona, area in an unmarked sedan. I was sitting just one block north of the port of entry in the parking area of an auto parts store, just watching the evening traffic. Suddenly, an older model Cadillac sedan hurriedly pulled into gas station across the street. The driver of the vehicle stopped at the water hose and air pump facility, but no one exited the vehicle. A couple minutes later, a red Chevrolet II sedan pulled up alongside the Cadillac. The drivers of both vehicles then got out of their vehicles and opened the hood of their vehicles. The two spoke for a moment and got back in their respective vehicles. The red Chevrolet then proceeded back to Mexico. The blue Cadillac then took off at a high rate of speed north toward Yuma. I began to follow the Cadillac as it proceeded north. I was having a tough time keeping up with it, and when we arrived in Yuma, the vehicle continued at a high rate of speed. I was able to catch up with him when he stopped at a red light. On reaching the Yuma Cabana Hotel in Yuma, the vehicle turned into the parking lot and proceeded around to the back of the hotel. The driver quickly exited the vehicle and entered the hotel.

I had contacted other officers working that night for assistance in watching the hotel. One of the officers, Monwell, partnered up with me in my vehicle. As the night wore on, Monwell started talking about a device called an "auto suck" that he had read about in a magazine. He described how it plugged into the cigarette lighter and could bring a man to an orgasm once placed over the penis. Monwell's wife coincidently had been visiting her mother for the past two weeks, so he quickly talked himself into a sexual frenzy, proclaiming loudly, "Man, I need blow job!"

Just then, the Sector Communications Operator announced over the police radio, "Someone has a stuck microphone." Then a second voice announced, "Ya and I have it all on tape." I checked my microphone switch, and it was stuck open. All that time, we had been sitting exchanging "sexual scores" with an open mic for all the west coast to listen in on.

After several hours, it looked as though there would be no further activity for the rest of the night. We discontinued the surveillance, planning on returning the next morning.

Bright and early the next morning, I again established surveillance on the hotel. I was soon joined by other officers. Within a brief time, we observed the Cadillac leave the motel and drive a short distance to a Taco Bell. The driver entered the Taco Bell briefly, then returned to his vehicle. The Cadillac then proceeded westbound out of Yuma toward the California border. As the vehicle was crossing over the bridge into California, I affected a stop of the vehicle, assisted by the other surveillance officers. I had the driver step out of the car, then step to the rear of his vehicle, where I questioned him briefly. I learned that the 57-year-old male driver was from San Jose, California. His story was not consistent with what I had observed the night before. While looking into the vehicle, I observed a wrinkled brown paper bag lying on the front seat. The bag contained six condoms, each filled with an ounce of Mexican brown heroin. We placed the driver under arrest, but physically we were in California judicial district, so we had to turn the old man over to our sister office in Calexico, California.

A few months later, we were required to appear in San Diego Federal Court for the old man's trial. He had pled not guilty, but after a brief trial, he was found guilty and sentenced to five years in prison, plus ten years' probation. A couple years later, he was released from prison. He hired an attorney to petition the court to set aside his ten years' probation. I was subpoenaed to testify at the hearing. While waiting for court to convene, the old gentleman approached me outside the courtroom and struck up a conversation. He informed me that due to the mandatory drug testing associated with the probation, he was trying to get his probation "trial" set aside. Then he made the mistake of telling me, that if he did not get this "trial" off him, he was going to skip. He said he could not do the 10 years' probation. I needed to inform the judge and the Assistant U.S. Attorney of the old man's statement. The judge denied the old man's petition. I never did hear if the old boy skipped and went on the run or if he did his probation.

I had received information from a local female citizen that some individuals were in the San Luis area to purchase some narcotics from individuals living just short distance from her house. She pointed out the residence and the vehicle that was to be used to transport the narcotic. I obtained the license number of the vehicle, and after running a registration check, I learned it was a rental vehicle out of Phoenix, AZ. A criminal history check on the person that rented the car revealed that the individual had a prior record for narcotics violations. I was assigned to uniformed patrol on that day, so I relayed the information to Levi and Wally, who were assigned to plain clothes. They then established a surveillance on the residence and vehicle. The next morning, as the vehicle left the Yuma area, Levi and Wally stopped it as it travelled eastbound on Interstate 10 toward Phoenix. I arrived at the scene as they were getting the three occupants out of the vehicle. As I approached the passenger side of the vehicle, one of the occupants was standing outside talking to another of our officers, Bill. I noticed as the individual turned, he consciously pivoted on the ball of his right foot, without lifting the foot off the ground. I asked him to lift his foot and when he did, I observed a condom containing an ounce of Mexican brown heroin. We placed all occupants under arrest and transported them back to our office for processing. Two additional ounces of heroin were later discovered. Wally was designated case agent of the case with the other officers as witnesses.

The following day, I received a call from Don, who was assisting Wally in the preparation of the criminal case report. Don informed me that Bill claimed that he also saw "something" under the passenger's foot but had failed pursue the matter. Don stated that Bill seeing the object also would "give more credence" to my observation. I just told him I did not care what they put in the report. The report minimized the information that I had passed to Wally from the local citizen. I later overheard Wally bragging to others that he had "made the office's first heroin case."

Sometime later, George, the station chief, called me in to his office to discuss a matter. After closing the office door, George informed me it had been reported that I was having sexual relationship with a female informant. I pointed out to him that I had never documented a female informant, nor had I ever paid a female informant. I further informed him that the female citizen who provided the information about the heroin case had even refused to be paid. The explanation seemed to satisfy George. Ironically, I had met the local lady through Monwell. He had an interest in the lady due to her more-than-abundant breasts. She was known locally as "Chichona" (the big breasted one). The lady was not interested in Monwell, supposedly because he was African-American. Monwell tried to convince the lady that he was "Cubano," not African-American. The lady worked the agricultural fields daily with the migrant workers. I regularly encountered the lady in the area, but we were never an item. However, she did tell me later that she was interested in me. She soon married, but as she said, she did so to get out of the fields. Twenty years later, I would encounter the lady again in New Mexico, and she was still married to her husband.

Monwell and his wife were going through a rough patch in their marriage. His wife had been told by her sister-in-law, her brother's wife, that Monwell had cheated on her while they had visited her family in Denver. Her brother and Monwell had been out bar-hopping and encountered a couple of young ladies. Her brother had confessed to his wife that he and Monwell had gotten blow-jobs from the young ladies. Her brother did not consider blow-jobs to be cheating. Monwell"s wife was not so liberal-minded, and routinely berated Monwell on his infidelity. After Monwell and wife transferred back to Oxnard, California, they soon divorced when Monwell was accused of sexual harassment for groping a female coworker in the building elevator. He eventually remarried, but on the flight back from their honeymoon in Europe, he became very ill. He was subsequently diagnosed with terminal cancer. The Special Agent in Charge promoted Monwell before his death, so his new wife would get a larger insurance payout.

In early 1978, a supervisor position opened in our sister station 127 miles east in Lukeville, Arizona. I had been assigned to a two-week detail in Lukeville before it had opened as a permanent office. Lukeville was small port of entry 80 miles south of Gila Bend, Arizona. The closest town was Ajo, a Phelps Dodge copper mining town 40 miles north of Lukeville. They also had the closest hospital. During the summer months, the population of Lukeville was approximately 57 people, mostly government workers at the port of entry. I found that I was one of five officers on the list of the best qualified for the position. I figured that the number one guy on the list, Bill, was a shoe-in for the position. He had just received an award for a project he had been assigned to. What I did not know was that after he got the award, he informed management that he did not want the project anymore. I could have told him not to piss off the selecting official. As it would turn out, I was selected as the least of the five evils on the best qualified list. Seems the others also had made some missteps along the way, while I had not made any yet. I was told by the selecting official that my selection was probably the fairest selection that had happened in four years. According to the Station Supervisor, Jerry, Oran's number one protégé, it was the first time in the Nogales patrol district that the position was not pre-selected. Oh yeah, I forgot there is no such thing as pre-selection in the federal government.

The Bird Man of Lukeville

In April of 1978, I reported to Lukeville, Arizona, as a new first line supervisor. Elena and my son would follow when my son finished the school year in Yuma. My counterpart in Lukeville was a guy about my age named Sly "Snake Eye" Lovelace. When Sly got mad, he would slightly squint his left eye and stare at you. He looked like a rattlesnake getting ready to strike. He was usually thinking about what he was about to say, which was usually, "You're an asshole." We were responsible for supervising fourteen uniformed patrol officers.

The town of Lukeville consisted of the government port of entry on the east side of town and a mini strip mall and gas station on the west side. The strip mall consisted of the duty-free store, the post office, a grocery store, a small café, and the Lukeville bar. Just north of the port of entry was a small motel and RV park. At the time, the whole town, other than the port of entry, was owned by a guy named Al Gay, who lived in Alaska. Just before I arrived, the government built a modern port of entry to accommodate the U.S. Customs Inspection Division, the U.S. Customs Patrol division, and the U.S. Immigration Service personnel. The town and port of entry were surrounded by the Organ Pipe Cactus National Monument.

After getting settled in, Sly decided that I should be initiated to my new job. The initiation consisted of a three-day horseback trip out 20 miles to the east, then overnight camping. The next day, we would ride another 20 miles back to the northern part of our area and camp out overnight again. We had a third officer meet us at the prearranged stops with our sleeping bags, army cots, food, and of course, beer. On the third day, we would return to the office. Sly expected me to not be able to endure the twenty-mile ride. He said that I surprised him when I did not commandeer the support vehicle to return to the office and have the young officer ride my horse back.

On the second day, we arrived at the prearranged camp site and met the other officer with the supplies. After unsaddling the horses and securing them in the corral, Sly and the young officer decide to take a quick nap. The young officer rolled up his jacket to make a pillow for his head and found a shady spot under a tree. Sly found some old bed springs and made himself comfortable. I was standing, leaning against the corral, when I heard the young officer yell, "Good god damn!" As I turned to look, the young officer jumped up and ran about 10 yards, then stopped. All the commotion startled Sly, causing him to jump to his feet and try to run also. However, as he tried to escape the unknown danger, his spurs got caught in the bed springs, dragging the springs a few feet while he stumbled to get away. Once he got clear of the springs and danger, he turned to the young officer, yelling, "You crazy son-of-a-bitch, what are you doing?" The young officer explained that while he was lying in the shade, he heard a rustling, and as he looked out of the corner of his eye, his saw a large snake slithering under his neck. Fortunately, the snake was a harmless one. Sly was easy to startle, and easy to anger.

On another occasion, Sly and I were returning from a trip to Nogales, AZ. I was driving west on two lane highway 86 from Tucson to Why, AZ. Sly was napping. He liked to drive in the mornings and have me drive in the afternoon. I was the junior supervisor, so that was fine with me. As I proceeded along the two-lane highway, I came up on a semi travelling westbound also. The semi was going slower than I was but I could not pass because of oncoming traffic. Anticipating an opportunity to pass, I pulled up close to the rear of the semi. I edged out enough to the left to see past the semi, but traffic still prevented me from passing. As I pulled back in behind the semi, I braked slightly, causing Sly to wake up. As he opened his eyes, all he could see was the back of the semi-trailer. Instinctively, he panicked, grabbing the dash board with both hands and jamming both of his feet into the passenger side floorboard, attempting to stop our vehicle from rear-ending the semi. In his startled, angered state, he yelled, "You crazy son-of-a-bitch, are you trying to kill us?" I could not help but laugh. He was not so eager to nap when I was driving after that.

Sly decided to share with me some desert survival wisdom he had somehow acquired over the years. According to Sly, whenever you become lost out in the desert, and you have run out of food and water, when you have lost all hope of being rescued, just climb up on the highest rock and start "beating your meat" (masturbating), and surely someone will walk up on you. I never did ask how he had acquired that bit of wisdom.

Some years later, when I was assigned to El Paso, an El Paso County Narcotics Officer and I were traveling to a training session in Alpine, TX. The officer had been nicknamed "WUP" (World's Ugliest Policeman) by one of our officers that worked with him on a regular basis. On the way to Alpine, our vehicle broke down, so we pulled off an I-10 exit to be rescued. We discovered that our battery did not have enough charge to utilize the law enforcement radio to call for help. We knew that other officers were traveling the same route behind us, so we decide to wait for their help. After a substantial amount of time, we were still stranded along the desert highway. So, I shared with WUP the desert survival wisdom I had learned from Sly. I told WUP to climb up on the overpass guard railing and start "beating his meat." As I told WUP, surely a passing motorist would call the police and we would be rescued. WUP game me the dirtiest look but said nothing. In time, we were rescued and continued our trip. After returning to El Paso, word got back to me that WUP had told others about the incident and had decided I was a pervert. Word even got back to my wife, who did not find the humor in Sly's wisdom.

Within the first few months after my arrival, I was sent to two different two-week supervisory training sessions in Los Angeles, where "by-the-book" supervisory policies and procedures were taught. During those two-week training sessions, all the attendees had lodging accommodations on the Queen Mary. By-the-book policies and procedures had little application in remote Lukeville.

Due to the remoteness of the area and lack of amenities, things were more relaxed. The only available TV reception was with a very tall TV antenna with a booster on it. During the summer months, due to the heavy draw on the electrical lines, we often had brown outs. The only recreation outside of the Lukeville bar was 40 miles north in Ajo, and even that was limited. Sly and I spent a lot of time in the bar. Drinking soon became a favorite pastime of ours. Until then, I was not much of a drinker. I was jokingly referred to as a "six-packer" because that was about all I could handle in one session. However, after two years in Lukeville and the Birdman Caper, drinking became the usual way I would attempt to alleviate my stress. I think drinking was a way to step outside the reserved me. Fortunately, I did not tend to fight when drinking. The only time I did get in a fight, I only agreed to step outside because I could not think of a reason not to. The fight only lasted a couple of blows, then it was over with. We went back in the bar and continued drinking.

Shortly after I arrived in Lukeville, Jerry, the Station Chief, was promoted to a position in Los Angeles, CA. Jerry was replaced with the consummate protégé, Storming Norman. According to Sly, Norm was married to the niece of then Arizona Senator, Dennis DeConcini. Norm had entered Customs at the Nogales Station at a higher pay grade than most due to his relationship with DeConcini. He immediately worked his way into a staff position as District Intelligence Officer. Within a brief time, he was then promoted to a newly created position of Customs Air Officer at the Phoenix Aviation Branch. When he arrived in Phoenix, his supervisor, Bill Gately, told him, "I did not want you, but you were forced down my throat." Norm had a very exalted opinion of himself due to his relationship with DeConcini. Customs management soon learned to use Norm's political clout to their advantage. They found that they could get assets for the Customs Service through Norm.

Norm only lasted about a year in Lukeville, after which he was promoted to the position in Los Angeles that Jerry was vacating due to him being transferred back to Nogales as Assistant Patrol Director under Oran Neck. Oran pulled off a thought-to-be-impossible transfer of Jerry back to Nogales. I won a ten-dollar bet with the Lukeville Port Director because of the transfer. The Port Director bet me that Jerry would never get the position because he believed that District Director Lee Volee's disliked Jerry immensely. However, Oran seized the opportunity to transfer Jerry back to Nogales when Volee made the mistake of taking two weeks annual leave and leaving Oran in charge as Acting District Director with full authority to sign off on promotions and transfers. By the time Volee returned to work, Jerry was already back in Nogales. Jerry would subsequently become District Patrol Director himself when Oran was promoted to Regional Patrol Director in New Orleans, LA.

Approximately one year after being promoted to the position in Los Angeles, Norm was then promoted to Aviation Branch Chief in Belle Chasse, LA. He was there a brief time, then was promoted to a position in Washington D.C., then subsequently became Director of the National Aviation Center in Oklahoma

City, OK. Norm retired from there and became Chief of Staff for DeConcini in Washington. In December 2000, I ran into him at a service station in Yuma, AZ. He was standing in line, waiting to use the restroom. During our brief encounter, he made a point of telling me that he was Under Sheriff in Cochise County, AZ and that the Customs Service was "calling him back to service" in Washington.

One of the ways I dealt with the remoteness of Lukeville was to regularly go fishing either with my son or my regular fishing partner, Guillermo "Fish Bait" Juevo. He called me "Catfish" because I once caught a catfish during a bass fishing tournament. I called him "Fish Bait" because when we fished, he had to have every conceivable kind of bait that might attract the fish, as well as every kind of artificial lure known to man. I don't think there was ever a trip where we did not have some type of problem. One time, I almost got my boat seized in Mexico for not having the proper paperwork for the boat trailer. Another time, the cable came off the steering spool, preventing me from being able to steer the boat in a narrow channel. The current wedged the boat sideways in the channel while the current prevented us from breaking the boat loose. I had to crawl up into the bow of the boat in 100-degree heat on my back to re-wrap the entire cable back around the spool so we could get back to the dock. What miserable day that was.

One year, "Fish Bait" got the idea he wanted to fish some "pot holes" off the main channel of the Colorado River during an upcoming tournament. So we rented a plane and flew over the area to scout out the inaccessible pot holes. On the first day of the tournament, we were up at zero-dark-thirty out on the river. We had to run the river with a spotlight. We took a channel off the river to a jumping-off point, where we would have to leave my boat then walk in a couple miles to the pot holes. As we walked, we carried buckets of waterdogs (salamanders), minnows, worms, and all our fishing tackle. We had both our hands full. We also were backpacking our inflated truck tube waders on our backs. We were loaded down like pack mules. As soon as we get all loaded up, we were swarmed by mosquitoes. Being unable to swat the mosquitoes made it a miserable two-mile walk to the pot holes. I cussed all the way to the pot holes. We never caught a single fish. Fish Bait claimed he got a "good hit," but you can't believe any fisherman. Then Fish Bait got the idea that we would walk out to some open water surrounded by cattails. The only problem was getting to the open water. We had to wade through a mud bog. Every time I took a step, I would sink down into the mud past my calf. I lost my shoe more than once, and I had to retrieve it from the mud. Every step was a chore with my long legs. Again, I cussed all the way back to dry land while Fish Bait laughed his ass off. We didn't catch a fish the whole day.

Our most disastrous adventure was at a Law Enforcement fishing tournament on Roosevelt Lake near Globe, Arizona. Fish Bait had rented a small aluminum flat-bottom boat to use during the tournament. Roosevelt Lake is seven miles long end to end, a big lake. Well, Fish Bait decided he wanted to fish the shallows at the south end of the lake, seven miles from our camp. We fished the shallows with no luck most of the first morning. Then a storm started moving in from the north, where our camp was located. The winds picked up, so we pulled the boat into a small cove and warmed up by a camp fire. Sheltered in the cove, we could not gauge how bad the winds were out on the main body of the lake. I suggested to Fish Bait that I hitchhike back to camp and get the truck and trailer so we could load up the boat and trailer it back to camp. He insisted that the winds would die down in a while and we could just wait them out. Or so he thought.

We were joined in the cove by some other fishermen in a nice $7000 top-of-the-line fiberglass bass fishing boat. At dark, the men in the large boat suggested that we follow them in our boat back to the north end of the lake. They had a spotlight and would lead the way. It sounded great. But, as we were leaving the cover of the cove and rounded the point out into the main body of the lake, all hell broke loose. The winds were blowing gale force and the lake literally had white caps. We had water coming over the side of our boat. I was in the bow of the boat, getting hit with the direct force of the wind and the mist coming off the lake. We were taking on water fast as the larger boat continued on up the lake. I told Fish Bait to get that damn boat to shore before we sank. He angled diagonally into the shoreline since he could not turn cross-ways to the wind without capsizing. I jumped out of the boat in a couple feet of water, grabbed the tow line, pulled the sinking boat back around to the leeward side of the point, and tied it to a tree to stop it from sinking.

Then Fish Bait decided he wanted to stay overnight with the rented boat. I told him, "Bullshit! I am wet, I am cold, and I am miserable. I am walking out of here tonight if it takes me all night. At least walking, I will be warm." Fish Bait decided to go with me. It was pitch black when we started out. We barely could make out the rocky shoreline, but I was going to walk out. I was leading, feeling my way along the rocky shoreline, when I came upon couple trees blocking our way. I forced my way through the branches of the trees. I didn't realize that when I let one go, the branch caught Fish Bait across the bridge of the nose, almost knocking him unconscious. I have to admit, I did not feel too sorry for him. He saw stars for a while, but we continued on. After several hours, we made it to a camp, where we begged a ride back to our camp. When we got back to camp, the other concerned campers approached us. They told us that they were starting to get very worried and planned to call out an air search first thing in the morning. One said they thought both of us were "fish bait" at the bottom of the lake. Had we continued as we were, we probably would have been just that.

During our drinking sessions at the Lukeville Bar, I learned that Sly had been tagged with another nickname: The Lemon Drop Kid. Sly tells a very good story, especially when he is drinking. He tends to exaggerate a bit, but it makes his stories funny. As the story goes, when Sly was a young K-9 officer at the San Luis port of entry, he almost got himself fired. Seems Sly and young kid from Mexico had found themselves trying to outsmart one another. The young kid would try to sneak northbound in the southbound pedestrian lane at the port of entry to the U.S. Sly would always try to catch him, but the young kid would run back to Mexico. One day, Sly saw the kid sneaking up the northbound pedestrian lane and figured he would let him get halfway up the lane before he made his move. Sly picked up a large lemon that had been confiscated from a traveler coming into the U.S. At what he thought to be the right moment, Sly hurled the lemon with all his might at the kid. But at the last moment, another young kid, an innocent bystander, stepped in front of that lemon. The kid went down with "blood and snot" everywhere. Sly also accused the kid and his mother of overacting in hopes of getting immigration papers. There was an immediate cry to fire Sly, but luckily for him, he had a supervisor that preempted any efforts to do so. The supervisor realized that he had to discipline Sly before upper management got involved. So Sly got off with a stern verbal reprimand.

Other than when Gary Tison and Randy Greenwalt broke out of an Arizona state prison, aided by Tison's three brainwashed sons and were on the run for weeks,[4] things went smoothly that first year. During the period that the gang was on the loose, we were on constant high alert, always subject to being called out. Some officials thought the gang might try and flee the U.S. into Mexico through the Lukeville Port of Entry.

However, on New Year's Eve 1979, things went from bad to worse. A couple people in the community were hosting New Year's parties. By the time I made it to the second party, I was very intoxicated from drinking Scotch and water. Sometime after midnight, I left the party and went home. As I was walking down the hall toward the bedroom, I was literally bouncing off the walls. Before making it to the bedroom, I stopped at the restroom. As I entered the bathroom, I turned toward the vanity and fell face-first onto the water pick reservoir, which had the water pick's beveled end sticking straight up. That beveled end went into my face just below the right eye, then up in the eyeball, just missing the pupil, and then up into my eyelid.

As I stood up, blood went everywhere, but I felt no pain. I just wiped the blood off with my hand and went to bed, not realizing how bad the damage was. Well, the next morning, I quickly realized the extent of the damage. My eye was completely swollen shut and caked over with a large amount of dried blood. Not only I could not see out of the eye, I could not even get it open. I had to soak it for an hour before the caked blood finally came off and I could pry the eye open. At least I was not blind. I woke up Elena and had her drive me to the hospital. The doctor said that due to the swelling, there was nothing he could do. I was a sorry sight for weeks. While we visited the hospital, we left our son at the house in Lukeville. While we were away, our son ran into Sly and told him that Elena had taken me to the hospital. When I got home, Sly was waiting to see the damage. As Sly's wife used to say, the three fastest ways of communication around here are, "telephone, telegraph, and telling Sly." Within a few hours, it was all over Lukeville. I never drank Scotch and water again.

Two other officers and myself decided one day that we would do a three-day horseback detail out to the west side of our area. We had a fourth officer meet us at prearranged locations with the supplies. After securing the horses on our first day, we settled in around a campfire for a few beers. The spot we chose had corrals but was located on Darby Well Road, a main thoroughfare through the Organ Cactus Nation Monument. Later that evening, we got a radio call from Sly, who was at the office. Sly asked if we were at the corrals on Darby Well Road. We confirmed that we were. Sly informed us that he had just received a call from Monument Headquarters inquiring if we were at the corrals. It seemed that an irate tourist had stopped at the Headquarters to complain about his solitude being disturbed as he visited the Monument. He was not pleased that the Air Force A-10 Warthogs had bussed him as he drove along the remote Darby Well Road. He also was not pleased that there were a bunch of men camped out with a big bonfire drinking beer out on the remote road. Sly informed us that the Headquarters was dispatching a Park Ranger to investigate. We immediately dosed the fire, digging a big hole to bury all the evidence before the Ranger could arrive. Fires were not permitted on the Monument. By the time the Ranger arrived, we had buried all the embers, covering all traces of the once campfire. When the Ranger arrived, we denied having a fire. I was sitting in my lawn chair over the buried fire pit. The young probationary Ranger was very aggressive in chastising us for the selection of our campsite, but he took no action.

Sometime months later, Sly and I were out driving on the north perimeter of the monument when we discovered the young Ranger's personal pickup parked off road near a sheer mountain cliff. The Ranger and a friend were scaling the cliff, which was prohibited. We reported the suspicious vehicle being parked off the access road to Monument Headquarters, never identifying it as belonging to one of their employees. Evidently, the violation led to the probationary Ranger's dismissal.

The isolation of that remote border station tended to have an ill effect on the wives of some officers. They never anticipated the conditions their husband's job had brought them to. There was not much for them to do. In the summer months, the heat was unbearable outside. In the evenings, we had to be on the lookout for rattlesnakes and scorpions. There were even occasional sightings of Gila Monsters. At times, we would even find scorpions in our houses. Housing was provided by the government. Some lived in the housing compound behind the port of entry, where I lived. Others lived in single wide trailers just north of the gas station. Some lived in the housing provided by the national monument.

Not long after I recovered from my New Year's accident, another officer and I were out riding horses we had borrowed from our sister station to the east, the Pappago Indians. Our horses were in quarantine due to a dead rabid fox being found in the corral. Because our patrol area was mostly within the bounds of the national monument, we were not authorized to use our vehicles to patrol off the established roads. So, we used horses to patrol the off-road areas. The two of us were heading south from the corral at the monument headquarters. We decided that we would race our horses down the power line road toward the border, so we spurred them to a full gallop. In no time, his horse took the lead. His horse was running on one side of the power line poles while mine was running on the other. My horse decided that he wanted to run on the same side of the poles as the other horse, so he started pulling to the left. I instinctively pulled back to the right to keep the horse to the right side of the pole. In the struggle between the horse and me, the horse headed straight for the power line pole. I could not pull him back to the right. So, to avoid a head on collision with the pole, I jerked his head to the left. The horse side-stepped around the pole. As he went by, he slammed his shoulder into the pole, along with my shoulder. I twisted my body to the left so my head would not hit the pole, but the pole caught me in the right rib cage and the right thigh. I went flying off the horse, landing in a grease wood bush about ten feet away. I bounced right back to my feet, only to glimpse the horse disappear out of sight over the horizon, still racing the other horse. The other rider never noticed. All the breath was knocked out of me, so I could not yell or even talk on my portable radio. In time, I caught my breath but did not want to communicate on the radio and advertise that I had been separated from my horse. Just about that time, the other officer could be heard on the radio asking, "Where are you?" advertising to the whole area that I had been separated from my horse anyway. We rounded up the wayward horse and rode back to the corral, but when I stepped off the horse, my right leg gave out. It had swollen to one and a half times its normal size. I was taken to the hospital again, and I was told that nothing could be done for the cracked ribs, and there was nothing they could do for the leg. I would have to stay off it for six weeks. I had broken some blood vessels in my leg and the swelling was caused by the blood draining into my leg. In time, I mended again. But things would only get worse for me.

When the new port of entry was built in Lukeville in 1977,

the east and west sides of the building had large plate glass windows running almost the entire length of the building. Due to the extreme temperatures in the summer, the windows were covered with a reflective film to keep out some of the heat. In late May of 1979, a small black bird regularly landed on the window ledge and would spend hours pecking at his reflection in the window. Almost every evening, when the east side of the building was shaded from the grueling sun, the bird would begin the same routine. Sometimes it pecked its way from one window to the next. The peck, peck, peck became very annoying to some employees, prompting them to chase the bird away. The bird would always come back. The annoyance prompted some of us to devise ways to rid ourselves of the little "son-of-a-bird."

On July 29th, I got my chance. I had prepared myself. I loaded my old H&R nine shot, 22 caliber revolver with bird shot and brought it to work, placing it in my locker in my office. The bird shot was also effective for killing rattlesnakes. That afternoon, I had just received a radio call from one of the officers out on patrol, requesting assistance in extricating his vehicle from a sandy wash west of town. Just as I was about to leave, the little son-of-a bird arrived. Ah-ha! This is my chance, I thought. I had to wait for the bird to proceed along the window ledge before I could get a shot at it. I slid the window pane open about two inches and waited for the bird. As I did, the bird hopped down off the ledge to the flower bed below, allowing me a shot. I placed the muzzle against the nylon screen and fired. BANG! I got it. Little did I know that the shot would become known as the shot that was heard around the U.S. Custom service, even though no one had heard it locally. Little did I know what a shit storm I had just created. When I met up with the officer needing assistance, I mistakenly told him that I got that little son-of-a-bird. Seems he repeated it to others.

The first indication I had of the gathering storm came when I learned that an internal affairs agent was in Lukeville and had been to the "post" office looking for a bird in the refrigerator. When he visited the post office, he was told that they did not have a refrigerator. The agent then proceeded to leave town but was told that the "port" office did have a refrigerator. It seems that the anonymous letter the agent had received had a 'typo" in it. The agent then proceeded to the refrigerator and retrieved an ice cream bag that had a little black bird in it.

A few days later, I received a call from the internal affairs agent in Tucson, Arizona, wanting to come interview me. I told him I would save him the trip and give him a statement over the phone. I admitted that I had shot the little-son-of-a-bird. I was informed that he had to do the interview in person. A couple days later, the agent showed up in Lukeville and interviewed me. The agent read me my rights per the Miranda warning. I waived my rights. Considering his own safety, he also had me unload my service revolver and place the ammunition in my pocket. I gave him a statement in which I admitted shooting the bird. He then informed me that the bird was taken to the University of Arizona in Tucson, where it was identified as a bronze headed cowbird, a protected wild fowl in the state of Arizona. He also informed me that U.S.

Fish and Wildlife had received a copy of the anonymous letter and they would be conducting a separate investigation.

A few days later, a U.S. Fish and Wildlife agent showed up to the interview me. Fortunately for me, I knew the agent from the days when we worked together in Yuma. He too read me my rights and had me unload my service revolver. He proceeded to tell me that there are only two birds in the State of Arizona that are not protected, sparrows and starlings.

Now, this is where it gets complicated. The bird that was retrieved from the port office refrigerator did not have what is known as an "evidence chain of custody" with it. Theoretically, the bird in the refrigerator could have been planted in an attempt to frame me. Without a chain of custody, it could not be proven that the bird in the refrigerator was the bird I shot. That being said, the agent then would have to determine through the interview if the bird I shot could possibly be the bird found in the refrigerator. He explained to me that a bronze headed cowbird and an immature male starling look very much alike. He then proceeded to determine through the interview which species of bird I shot. Now this is where ignorance is bliss. When asked to describe the color of the bird's head when the sun shined on it, I responded "purple." Ah ha. Good answer. Then I was shown a "photo lineup" of birds and asked to pick the one that most resembled the bird I shot. I picked the one with the shorter beak. Ah ha, another good answer. The agent informed me that based on my answers, he would have to conclude that the bird I shot was an immature starling, one of only two birds not protected in the State of Arizona. He also informed me that a bronze headed cowbird has a longer beak and when the sun shines on their head, it looks bronze. I would be exonerated by U.S. Fish and Wildlife.

Not so with U.S. Customs Service, however. When the Regional Commissioner heard that I shot "a non-seneschal creature" his reaction was "fire that son-of-a gun." Damn, you would think I shot a bald eagle. At the direction of the regional commissioner, I was approached by my immediate supervisor to "take a voluntary demotion and transfer to Phoenix and make it easy on everyone." I respectfully declined the offer. Sometime later, I received a letter proposing a five-day suspension without pay for acting recklessly and setting a poor example as a supervisor. I was notified that I had the right to appeal through the agency grievance procedures.

I appealed the proposed action to a national grievance examiner in San Francisco. I had to conduct my own investigation, emphasizing the minimal damage done to the screen, the non-lethal ballistics of the birdshot, stressing the remoteness of the Lukeville area and the less than traditional lifestyles in the area. Also, about that time, President Carter was attacked by a vicious jackrabbit while out in a lake in a row boat. An article in the paper was accompanied with a picture of Carter "whacking" that poor non-seneschal creature with a boat oar. I thought the article and picture would make good fodder in my grievance. I was successful in the appeal process. The examiner agreed with me that the proposed disciplinary action was too harsh and I should only receive a strongly-worded letter of reprimand.

Shortly thereafter, I received a call from the Human Relations specialist in Los Angeles, Cleo Moses, informing me that the regional commissioner stated that he would not consider reinstating me for the entire five days of the suspension and he wanted to know what I would consider. Having already incurred the loss of pay and feeling overly confident regarding the examiner's finding in my favor, I maintained my position that any suspension was too harsh. Wrong answer! Since I was unwilling to compromise, the commissioner decided that he would let the five-day suspension stand. I had no further grievance remedy. Live and learn. The whole thing was an exercise in futility.

For years after leaving Lukeville, I would be known as the Birdman of Lukeville. Over the years, when I would introduce myself, people would say, "Aren't you the Birdman of Lukeville?" Seems the version of the story many had heard was that, due to the stress of living in the remote area, I had "cracked up" and drawing my 357-service revolver, shooting out the window and endangering the families who lived behind the port of entry.

One morning, I was notified by Inspection personnel that a male driving a pickup truck pulling a horse trailer had just entered the port of entry from Mexico. The vehicle was waiting to enter the U.S at 6 a.m. when the U.S. port of entry opened. After being released by inspection personnel, the vehicle then proceeded about one-fourth of a mile north of port of entry and stopped on the side of the road. Suspecting the driver may intend to meet up with persons who had crossed the border during the night with narcotics, several of us positioned ourselves so we could watch the vehicle. Another officer and I walked into the desert west of the vehicle's position, so we could establish a better vantage point to watch. After several hours, we were notified by an officer who was monitoring the sensing devices that a "sensor" west of the port of entry had been activated. We were sure that smugglers were heading in our direction to meet up with the vehicle. Shortly after, we were surprised to see three individuals on horseback appear out of the desert and met up with the driver of the pickup. As they approached the vehicle, we left our hiding places and confronted all four individuals.

After a lengthy interrogation of the male driver and his 53-year-old American wife, who was riding one of the horses, we learned that they were smuggling the horses, not narcotics. Initially, we were not convinced of the couple's story. But after a lengthy search of the desert nearby for narcotics, their story proved to be true. According to the couple, they lived in San Jose, California, and they had visited Mexico to participate in a charity rodeo. The couple decided that if they returned to the U.S. with their horses through the port of entry, the horses would have to be quarantined. Not wanting to have their horses quarantined, they decided they would sneak the horses across the border during the night. The husband hired two Mexican cowboys to ride two of the horses while his wife rode her horse. The husband dropped the three horses and riders off along the border fence 8 miles west of the port of entry the night before. The three riders rode most of the night to get to the arranged meeting place. I was amazed that the husband would even consider having his wife ride most of the night out in the isolated desert with two men they barely knew.

We seized the horses and stabled them with our three government horses, Clyde, Spic and Buck. Our horses had been seized years before when they were being used to smuggle narcotics. The two Mexican cowboys were turned over to Border Patrol. The couple and their vehicle were allowed to leave. We boarded the three horses for close to a year while the couple petitioned to have them returned. I rode the husband's quarter horse often when patrolling the desert area. That horse knew one speed: full out. He would run until he was exhausted. More than once, I broke bridle reins trying to rein him in. The couple was finally successful at having their horses returned, but they were shocked when they learned that they had to pay the government substantially for boarding the horses for almost a year.

Later that year, 1979, Fish Bait and I were detailed to New Orleans, Louisiana, for a 30-day operation throughout Louisiana. I ended up being detailed to the Lafayette area while Fish Bait was assigned to New Orleans. I was assigned to a boat operation trying to interdict shrimp boats being used to smuggle marijuana into the area from South America. The first day of the operation was spent posing as fishermen while watching the intercostal waterways. Posing as local fishermen was not a stretch for me and the others assigned to the boat. Tackle in hand, all we needed was a cold beer, but we had to settle for sodas. The second day, we decided to venture out into Vermillion Bay to check shrimp boats as they came into the bay. The boat belonged to DEA and was operated by their captain, a bona fide Ragin' Cajun native "coonass," a term used to refer to native Louisianans. Just as we entered the bay, we encountered a shrimp boat approaching us as it entered from the Gulf of Mexico. One of the local Customs officers recognized the "Cindy Ann" as a boat that was suspected of being used for smuggling. We allowed the boat to continue into the bay, noting that it did not have its shrimp nets hanging out to dry after an alleged day of shrimping. The boat continued until, just before entering the intercoastal waterway, and they laid anchor. After dark, we laid anchor nearby, allowing us to watch the boat till the next morning. The DEA boat was equipped with radar so we could monitor any activity at the boat during the night. Throughout the night, we observed on the radar monitor some smaller boats approaching the shrimp boat and then departing.

The next morning, we decided to board the Cindy Ann and search it. The DEA boat captain pulled alongside the Cindy Ann at first light and four of us boarded the boat. It was a little risky trying to board the large boat from the smaller boat because our boat was moving around in the water. As we boarded the boat, we thankfully discovered that there was only one crew member on board, but as we searched, we discovered what was later determined to be 19 tons of marijuana in the hold. We handcuffed the Colombian crew member to the wheel in the wheel house and continued searching the boat. We were on the boat for less than an hour when we heard a smaller boat approach and the occupants of the boat yelling to the crew member in custody. Oh shit! It was the off-load crew, and they were here for another load. We thought we would unhandcuff the crew member so he could catch and secure the smaller boat's tow line, then apprehend the two men in the smaller boat. I asked, "Who has a handcuff key?"

Jimmy said, "Leo does, but he is down in the hold counting the marijuana bundles."

I yelled to Leo, "Hey, Leo, we need the handcuff key." There was no answer from Leo, so Jimmy grabbed his shotgun and leaned over the railing of the shrimp boat, pointing the shotgun down at the two men in the smaller boat. The operator of the boat looked at the shotgun, then looked at his partner, and then decided to get the hell out of there by applying full throttle to the boat. We were able to radio to the DEA boat. They then apprehend the smaller boat after a high-speed chase and some shots fired as they fled in the intercoastal waterway. I later learned that the ground units were able to identify the stash house where some of the loads had been taken, recovering that marijuana and a large amount of U.S. currency. I never did hear what happened to that currency.

We took the shrimp boat back to the dock and secured it under guard until the next morning, when we planned to offload it. We had to wait till the Parish Sheriff showed up so he could do a press release and get his picture taken with the shrimp boat. So that night, I drove over to New Orleans to hook up with Fish Bait and check out the night life in New Orleans. After a night on the town, I ended up sleeping on the floor in Fish Bait's motel room. I was not about to sleep with him. I got up the next morning to head back to Lafayette.

Once I got on Interstate 10 westbound, I cranked that newly

leased Camaro up to 85 mph. As I was crossing one of the long causeways, I noticed another vehicle up ahead in the same lane travelling as fast as I was. Gradually, I closed the distance between our two vehicles. Just as I recognized the rear deck amber lights, they lit up, and I saw an officer waving me to the right side of the road. Damn, it was as if the state police officer could read my mind.

As the officer approached my vehicle, he asked for my license and registration. As I handed him my license, he glanced at my license, then said, "Mr. Andrews, where are you going today at 85 mph besides to jail?"

"Uh, ah, well, I am going over to state police headquarters in Lafayette to help off load a shrimp boat we seized yesterday." The nice officer told me to wait while he checked. In a short time, he came back, handed me my license and told me to hold it down. He was letting me go. Wow! That was close. He took off up the road in front of me as I fell in behind him at 65 mph. Just then he turned his rear deck amber lights back on and waved me over again. Damn, I was sure he changed his mind and I was in trouble. As he approached my vehicle, he told me to fall in behind him and he would give me a police escort the rest of the way into Lafayette. With red lights flashing, he escorted me the rest of the way to Lafayette. I never did have to show him my badge, always something I avoided doing when being stopped on a traffic stop by state and local police. I always waited till they asked for it, because some state and local police take offense when "badged by the feds."

Living and working in the isolated area of Lukeville lent itself to a less-than-favorable living conditions. As usual, I was keeping all the stress bottled up inside me. Living behind the port of entry only magnified the stress. I could not get away from the job. I was drinking a lot to release the stress. As you would expect, it took a toll on my relationship with Elena. We decided that we would buy an undeveloped piece of property 30 miles north of Lukeville and move to the property. We bought 1.5 acres of land, developed it, bought a double-wide manufactured home, and moved it to the property. We moved to Why, Arizona, right across the highway from the XYZ Bar. Why, Arizona, is named so because it is at a "Y" intersection in two highways. At least on my days off I was not finding myself hanging out at the office. Our marriage soon had gotten to the point where she asked for a divorce. We mutually agreed to go our own way and filed divorce papers. Elena wanted to go back to where he parents lived in New Mexico. She was only gone a brief time when she called and said she wanted to come back, but she wanted to stay at her parents' a while longer.

Not long after Elena returned, I was offered an opportunity to transfer back to Yuma, Arizona. At that time, Levi was a first line supervisor in Yuma. Due to some personal issues, he decided he wanted to take a reduction in grade back to patrol officer. That left a supervisor vacancy in Yuma. Guillermo Juevo, who was now a first line supervisor in Sierra Vista, Arizona, wanted to transfer back to Yuma to fill the position. However, it turned out that he had recently had some issues with the District Patrol Director. So, the director was not in favor of giving him the position. I soon received a telephone call from the Assistant Patrol Director posing the question to me about taking Guillermo's position in Sierra

Vista, if he was transferred back to Yuma. My response was that I still had my house in Yuma and now I had the home in Why, Arizona. Evidently, he liked that answer.

The next day, I was notified that I was being transferred back to Yuma. We sold the place in Why and moved back to Yuma. I thought maybe Elena and I could work things out. But within a year or so, she moved back to her parents again. She stayed there about a year, then moved back to Yuma, where she moved in with a girlfriend. In time, we would start seeing each other again, but it did not last. Initially, she purchased a mobile home for her and my son to live in not far from my house. She did move back in with me for about a year, but it was obvious we had become different people. By February of 1984, it was over for good, after 16 years together. The final straw was served up at lunch one day.

Several of us from the office were having lunch at a local restaurant. During lunch, Levi accusatorily said, "Who are seeing you over at your wife's mobile home during lunch?"

I asked Levi what he was talking about. He replied that a friend of his lived in the same mobile home park as Elena and he had, on several occasions, around noon, seen my little brown Toyota vehicle and another vehicle parked at her house.

I challenged Levi, stating, "Think about it Levi. During the day, I drive my assigned government vehicle, which is gray. And Elena uses my Toyota to go to work."

Levi immediately realized his error, stating, "Oops, I guess I shouldn't have said anything." My initial thought was to try and catch Elena in the act of getting a "nooner," but the more I thought about it, the more I realized what a waste of time that would be. After about three days, I confronted Elena, telling her that someone has seen my vehicle at her mobile home during noon hour. Her immediate response was, "Who do you have spying on me?" It was obvious that it was time to move on. I just told her I wanted her out of my house by this weekend. One thing you learn about divorce is that, in most cases, each partner owns 50 percent of the responsibility for the break-up. If you do not accept your share of responsibility, you can't put things behind you and move on. You cannot put all the blame on the other person. When I married Elena, like most people, I believed it would be for "life." But, as many have discovered, it is only for the "life" of the marriage.

In time, George was notified that he was being transferred to New Orleans, LA, leaving his position vacant. Kenny had just been transferred to Tucson, so I was temporarily promoted to Station Chief for 120 days while the vacancy was advertised under the Merit Promotion System. The rumors circulated that one of Jerry's protégés would be selected for the position, so I had resolved myself to that fact. It was soon announced that Brian Player from Tucson, Jerry's number one protégé, was selected for the position. On the day that Brian was to report in at the Yuma Office, I had scheduled an all-hands meeting at 9:00 a.m. at the office to welcome him. By 10:00 a.m. Brian had not arrived, nor did I receive information pertaining to his arrival, so I released everyone to resume their normal duties. I left the office myself but returned around 11:00 and noticed Brain was in his office having a conversation with Steve, one of the officers. Not wanting to interrupt the exchange between the two, I did not immediately present myself to Brian. Shortly thereafter, Brian and Steve left the office for lunch. Through the rumor mill, I soon learned that Brain had originally planned to return to Tucson that same day. However, Steve had convinced him to stay until Tuesday evening to attend the monthly Yuma Area Law Enforcement Meeting. Brian did stay to attend the meeting but departed for his home in Tucson Wednesday morning.

I soon learned that Brian had only reported in to the Yuma Office only to occupy the position and receive the increase in grade, but then detailed back to the Tucson Office indefinitely. The plan was to promote Brian to the higher grade in Yuma, but he would continue to work in Tucson until he was alternate staffed to a position in El Paso, TX. I was never informed of who was to serve as Station Chief while Brian was away. My management never did communicate to me what they had orchestrated. I then contacted the H.R. Specialist in Nogales, inquiring about the turn of events. When I explained to the Specialist, Sue Whales, what had transpired, she commented, "I think someone is pulling a sneaky." When my management learned that I had called, they were very unhappy with me. I was then informed that I was to remain in the Station Chief position but without the increase in pay. I would serve out the remainder of my time in Yuma in that status.

Leaving Las Vegas

One week to the day after Elena left for the last time, I walked into the Chilton Inn in Yuma, looking to hook up with a friend of mine. The night before, I had been out bar-hopping and I was suffering from a hangover. I was not in the mood to drink that evening. My friend was the manager of the hotel, but she was not there that evening. However, two of her employees, Joy and Coleen, were there, along with two of their friends. Joy saw me as I entered the lounge and waved at me to join them at their table. Joy and Coleen introduced me to their two friends, Flo Gutierrez and her younger sister, June Lansing. I noticed that June was overdressed for a night out in Yuma. I remember thinking as I sat down that June looked high maintenance. Flo was long divorced and June was recently widowed. Considering the condition I was in, I was not in the mood for anything other than hanging out. Since I was interested in the manager of the hotel, I thought it wise that I not be making any moves on her employees or the other two ladies.

June kept offering to buy me a drink, but I kept declining. June and Coleen both tried to get me to dance, but I was not in the mood for that either. I learned that Coleen had recently found out that her boyfriend was married, and he just happened to be sitting at the bar. Coleen was fairly well intoxicated, trying to medicate the hurt she was feeling. Attempting to make her boyfriend jealous, she pleaded with me to dance with her one dance. I agreed. While dancing, she suggested that I take her home and "screw her." I told her she did not mean that, she was just feeling hurt. Then she wanted me to walk her out to the car, so her boyfriend could see us. I agreed to that but returned to the lounge immediately.

That must have triggered an affront to June. June was a flashy, voluptuous, long-haired honey blond that was used to being hit on by men. She was not used to a simple small-town boy playing hard to get. She went to the bar and got me a coke, then began pressing me to dance with her. I agreed to one dance. The next thing I knew, her sister, Flo, left and June asked for a ride home. I gave her a ride home, dropping her off at her dad's house with no intentions of furthering the relationship.

The next day, as I was just leaving the house, June called, asking me to accompany her to the rodeo in Yuma. Since I had been planning on going to the rodeo anyway, I agreed. During the day, I learned that she was executive administrative assistant to Wayne Newton's business attorney, Mark Moreno. One aspect of June's physical attributes that did not melt my butter was her large posterior spread. Even squeezed into those tight Levis, it was more potatoes than this country boy cared for on his plate. She suggested that I visit her in Las Vegas and see Wayne's show. February 25 was my son's birthday, so I agreed to visit her with my son. I never thought a long-distance relation would last and, based on the way she dressed, I did not think I was in her league. It would turn out that she was originally from Yuma and regularly returned to Yuma to visit family and friends. Occasionally, we would take turns visiting. I never saw the relationship going anywhere. She was a beautiful woman, but she was high maintenance, and I could take or leave all those potatoes.

On a Thursday in late April 1984, I got a telephone call from Sly who was now assigned to the U.S. Customs Aviation Branch in New Orleans, Louisiana. Sly informed me that Customs had just created a new position within the aviation branch and wanted to know if I was interested in it, and transferring to New Orleans. The job sounded interesting. I agreed to accept the position. Sly said he had no idea when the position could be filled due to budget constraints. It could be months. The next day, I planned to go to Vegas to visit June. I thought it was the right thing to do to tell her of my pending plans during my visit. I had not anticipated her reaction to my plans.

Bright and early the following Monday morning, Sly called again, telling me I had been selected for the job. He said that he had hand carried my application to the regional HR specialist and she had signed off on the selection the previous Friday afternoon. He wanted to know when I could be in New Orleans. I agreed to a reporting date in 30 days. I called June and told her, not realizing what she was planning. I discussed it with my son, who was then 14 and could choose who he wanted to live with. He was staying with me most of the time in Yuma anyway, so he decided to go with me to New Orleans. It turned out that June decided to go, too.

Before I realized it, June decided to quit her job, sell her house, and move to New Orleans with me. I had never discussed such arrangements with her, but since I was not saying "no," I was passively saying "yes." How did I get myself into this position? What was I thinking?

When I arrived in New Orleans, the Aviation Branch there was known as the "Seagull Squadron" because all they did was squawk and shit, and you had to throw rocks at them to get them to fly. When they did fly, it was to get something to eat somewhere in the neighboring states. After finding a place to live, I returned to Yuma to move my furniture and my son. June was also packed and ready to go. I was very unsure of the arrangement, but it had taken on a life of its own, with someone else in control. New Orleans was a new experience, but I did not like living in an apartment. I was back dealing with heavy traffic again. Fortunately, the new job was a great adventure that would require me to attend flight training for fixed wing aircraft. The job duties required me to serve as an inflight radar operator on Customs aircraft. When I was not assigned to flights, I was assigned air smuggling cases, which would take me all over the southeast. I did a lot of traveling in Customs aircraft and found myself often flying the aircraft, logging the hours. While focusing on the new job, I did not give much thought to my relationship with June. I realized my childhood dream of becoming a pilot, like Bob Dalton. I got to fly as co-pilot in Customs helicopters, though I never did get a rating in helicopters.

Soon after arriving in New Orleans, I received information

that an individual in Tuscaloosa, Alabama, by the name of Julius Caesar Pate was involved in smuggling marijuana into the U.S. from South America utilizing his Cessna 210 aircraft. I contacted the original source of the information, Investigator Earl Walden of the Alabama Bureau of investigation. Earl's brother, Trash, was also an investigator with ABI. Earl informed me that J.C. was still involved in the smuggling operation and that he had located some property outside of Tuscaloosa belonging to J.C. where he had built a dirt airstrip and an aircraft hangar.

I travelled to Tuscaloosa and met with Earl, documenting all the information pertaining to J.C. and his operation. I learned that J.C. and members of his organization were old bootleggers who had gotten into the marijuana business. I prepared an affidavit supporting an application for a court order to have a law enforcement tracking transponder installed in the aircraft. The court order was signed by a local magistrate. At zero-dark-thirty one morning, Earl, a certified technician, and I forced entry into the hangar and installed the transponder. It was very important that we leave the hangar in the same condition in which we found it to avoid alerting the organization of our visit.

Several weeks went by before any activity was reported on the aircraft's movement. Then I received information from the Federal Aviation Administration that they were tracking a Cessna 210 aircraft as it was leaving the southern coast of Louisiana heading toward South America. I immediately contacted Earl to have him check J.C.'s hangar to determine if his aircraft was gone. But Earl would have to wait till night fell before he could sneak into the hangar. As fate would have it, a Customs Agent in Mobile, Alabama, also had installed a transponder in a Cessna 210 aircraft that he was working a case on. That agent would eventually advise me the next day that his suspect aircraft was still in Alabama. Earl would soon advise me that J.C.'s aircraft was missing. Now it was a waiting game. I did not have to wait long. Later that afternoon, FAA advised that they were tracking a Cessna 210 as it entered the coast line just south of Mobile, Alabama. Evidently the aircraft had been flying at a very low altitude across the Gulf of Mexico to avoid radar detection. A Customs Cessna Citation II aircraft was launched to intercept the suspect aircraft. A Customs pilot and I launched in twin engine Piper Navajo aircraft, but it would not be fast enough to intercept the suspect aircraft, which had a head start on us. But the Citation could.

The Citation aircraft intercepted the Cessna 210 aircraft south of Tuscaloosa, but the Citation would not be able to land behind the aircraft on the remote dirt airstrip. We could not affect an arrest on the ground crew and pilot. The aircraft was tracked to a dirt airstrip away from J.C.'s hangar, where it landed and offloaded its cargo. The pilot then got the aircraft airborne again, heading to J.C.'s hangar. The ground crew observed the Customs aircraft overhead and fled the area with their cargo. The pilot, Thomas Pianzo, landed the aircraft at J.C.'s hangar, then fled the area himself. The shipment of marijuana was never recovered, but all of the organization was eventually rounded up and charged. After J.C.'s very young wife was indicted in the case, J.C. agreed to cooperate in exchange for the charges being dropped against her. J.C. owned many luxury assets such as a new home, vehicles, a caterpillar, an airplane, and land, all which IRS found very interesting for someone that only reported $14,000 income that year.

Sometime later, Earl contacted me again with information regarding a Cessna 404 aircraft that was being readied for a smuggling organization. Earl informed me that an aircraft mechanic for Hughes Aircraft Company had been hired to install wing locker fuel tanks in the newly purchased aircraft at a small airport north of Birmingham, Alabama. The installation was being done during night time hours. I immediately drove to Tuscaloosa to meet with Earl, again documenting all the information pertaining to the purchase of the aircraft to support a court order requesting the authorization for the installation of a law enforcement transponder in the aircraft. Late that evening, we located a federal magistrate in his motel room, where he was staying while attending a conference, and the order was signed. We planned to go to the small airport later that night and do the installation. We got to the airport about 1:30 a.m. the next morning but discovered that the mechanic was still working on the installation of the fuel tanks. We waited, hidden at the airport, while the installation of the fuel tanks was completed. Evidently, someone had noticed our presence and reported it to the local police.

When the police cruiser pulled into the airport area, we all hid, since we did not know if the local police could be trusted. I ducked into an open hangar, attempting to conceal myself as the officer scanned the darkened hangar with his spotlight. I flattened myself against the hangar wall, but I was soon spotted. With the light shining in my eyes, the nice officer said, "Come out with your hands up." For the second time in my career, I found myself on the wrong end of a gun. Fortunately, both times it was good guys on the other end. But it still was a very uncomfortable feeling.

After we all identified ourselves, we noticed that the aircraft was taking off from the airport, presumably to test the fuel modification. I called FAA immediately and learned that the aircraft had landed at Birmingham International Airport. Damn, that was where we had just come from that night. We rushed back to Birmingham and located the aircraft at the executive terminal. But it was broad daylight, so we would have to wait until that night again to try and do the installation of the transponders. Damn, later that day the aircraft took off and headed for New Orleans Lakefront Airport. Now the aircraft was in a different judicial district, and I would have to find another federal magistrate to sign a new court order. Utilizing a Customs-owned aircraft, we headed back to New Orleans where we had started out two days before. I located a federal magistrate, but we had to go to his house to get the court order signed. Finally, later that night, we got the transponder installed. But bright and early the next day, the aircraft took off for Naples, Florida. The Customs pilot and I jumped in the Customs aircraft and gave chase. I had more work to do, as I had not identified the pilot of the suspect aircraft yet.

En-route to Naples, the pilot told me that he was giving me a new nickname: "OT" for overtime. He said he had not seen his wife in three days. I told him I hadn't seen mine either, but that was not necessarily a terrible thing. I figured maybe when we did get home, they would appreciate seeing us and show due gratitude. He said that in his case, that was not likely. Arriving in Naples, I finally got lucky and identified the pilot, Robert Dugas of Fort Lauderdale, Florida. Dugas used his passport as identification to rent a car at the Naples airport.

I then called the Customs Patrol Supervisor in Fort Lauderdale, Charlie Jordon, asking for his assistance in obtaining background information on Dugas. I also provided him with all the information I had on Dugas and the aircraft. It would be another waiting game to catch the aircraft coming back into the U.S. transporting narcotics. I could not anticipate how long a wait it would be. The next morning, the aircraft departed Naples and flew to Marco Island, Florida, the southernmost airport on the west coast of Florida. I asked an officer from that office to go check the airport for the aircraft He reported back that the aircraft was gone.

I then contacted Charlie Jordon, again seeking information, and told him that the aircraft had disappeared. Charlie said, "That might have been the aircraft that crashed into the ocean off the coast of Florida when it was being chased by Customs aircraft." When I ask him how long ago that was, he said it had only been a couple days. I then contacted a supervisor for the U.S. Customs Aviation Branch in Homestead, Florida, following up on the information I had received from Charlie. The supervisor had no idea what I was talking about. Naturally, I called Charlie again, telling him that the aviation branch had no idea what he was talking about. Charlie said, "Let me get back to my "source" and I will call you." I never heard from him again. It would be two years before I learned what had happened to the aircraft.

In 1987, after I had transferred to Las Vegas, I got a call from an Internal Affairs agent in Florida asking me if I remembered the investigation into Robert Dugas. I never liked those calls from internal affairs. I sure as hell did remember. I related all the information I had stored in my little brain to the agent regarding the investigation. He informed me that they had arrested Dugas for smuggling 500 pounds of cocaine in the aircraft.

"Great," I said.

He said, "Not so great." Charlie Jordon had informed the pilot of the installation of the transponder and the pilot removed it when it was at Marco Island airport. The agent said that the organization had been using that aircraft for two years to smuggle narcotics from South America. The agent then informed me that Charlie Jordon and his District Patrol Director, Frank Kinney, were arrested for providing information to the organization and directing law enforcement assets away from the organization's operation. All I could say was, "What a no-good son-of-a-bitch."

Charlie fled before his sentencing and was on the run with his wife and new baby for many months. But he eventually screwed up. When agents did a search warrant on his mother-in-law's house, they discovered a video of the child that Charlie and his wife had sent to the mother-in-law. Charlie did not realize that he had also videoed the vehicle he was driving, as well the travel trailer that they were living in as they traveled around the country staying in recreational areas. That video was featured on a law enforcement show, which resulted in Charlie's capture. Charlie and Frank spent several years in federal prison in Florida.

After just a little over a year in New Orleans, I learned that the U.S. Customs Office of Investigation was expanding their office in Memphis, Tennessee, and I was being considered for a position as Special Agent in Memphis. At that time, Memphis was a one-man office staffed by a good ole boy from Louisiana. Ole Scooter was a laid-back guy with a terrific sense of humor. He also had a way with the ladies even though he was married. Memphis would be another adventure. I was selected for the position and was to report in September of 1985. June and I got married in New Orleans. But I wondered if it was the right thing to do. I think I felt obligated to go along with it since she had quit her job in Las Vegas and sold her house.

Shortly after I was selected for Memphis, Sly was also selected for a position in Memphis. This would become our fourth assignment together. The Memphis office was considered a "bird's nest on the ground" at that time, but nothing lasts forever. Scooter hired a sweetheart of a lady to be the office secretary. So now we were a three-man office with Scooter as the agent-in-charge. We were a sub-office of the New Orleans Office. One could not ask for better working conditions. Our area of responsibility was Western Tennessee and Arkansas. Little did we know the misfortune that was about to follow us.

Shortly after arriving in Memphis, I was scheduled to attend a four-month criminal investigator course at the Federal Law Enforcement Training Center in Glynco, Georgia. My son and

June would remain in Memphis while I attended the academy. June had been hired as executive secretary to the City Attorney in Memphis. During those four months at the academy, I returned home for the Christmas holidays and June visited me once at the academy. It was during this time that I realized I did not miss June when I was away and that I might have made a mistake.

I returned to Memphis in February. For the next few months, things were great. Our whole office regularly went to lunch together at places around Memphis with Scooter serving as our local guide. That spring, we regularly attended happy hour at the Sunset Serenade atop the Peabody Hotel, where the ducks rode the elevator each morning and evening. But there was a storm a brewing. We had no idea what terrible thing was about to happen in New Orleans, something that would send shock waves all the way to Memphis.

We would soon learn that the Special Agent in Charge in New Orleans was being demoted and reassigned. Originally, he was to be reassigned to the New York Office, but he had cut a deal and got his reassignment changed to Memphis. What did we do to deserve such a fate? He would displace Scooter as agent in charge. As a consolation prize, Scooter would be offered a position as agent in charge in a new office in his home town of Shreveport, Louisiana.

The rumors we heard did not paint a pretty picture of what we were about to encounter. We would learn that the Special Agent in Charge, Barry Grisham, had fostered a hostile work environment in New Orleans due to his management style. Washington had supposedly tried reassigning Barry to neighboring Mobile,

Alabama, for one year to resolve the issues. The agent in charge of Mobile was reassigned to New Orleans for one year hoping to smooth things over. After a year, he asked to return to Mobile, and Barry returned to New Orleans. Within another year, Barry had things back as before. Washington felt that they had to remove Barry from his position. Normally, Washington would force transfer someone like Barry to Washington and bury him in some staff position where he did not have oversight of other employees. But instead, Barry was going to New York City. But that was not to be in Barry's case. Barry had a "hook," a rabbi, who intervened, so Barry negotiated a transfer to Memphis.

Before Barry arrived, Scooter and Janet, the office secretary, were scheduled for an imprest fund training class in the New Orleans Regional Office. They travelled together in Scooter's government assigned vehicle to attend the three-day training. When the two returned, there was a subtle, but noticeable electricity between the two. As time wore on, tension between the two replaced the electricity. Janet would later confide in me just before I transferred to Las Vegas that she and Scooter had started an inter-office affair while in New Orleans. The tension arose out of Scooter's ongoing relationship with another married female, Linda, that worked for another federal agency on the first floor of our federal building. Janet, a married mother of two young daughters, was not pleased that Scooter, a married father of two young daughters, would disappear from our office to visit Linda. Apparently, Janet was willing to be "the other women," but not one of two other women. Scooter found himself in a very precarious situation, being pressured by his secretary to end the relationship with Linda. Scooter now was under a cloud of Sexual Harassment. Jane knew she could not file on Scooter for fear of being exposed herself. But the tension between the two soon caused Scooter to seek medical treatment for a bleeding ulcer. To alleviate the tension, he arranged to be sent to the Training Academy in Brunswick, Georgia, for four months.

Presumably because I was leaving the office in a couple months, Janet confided to me about the affair, which she herself was having difficulty dealing with emotionally. To me, it was obvious that she was crazy about Scooter, who had told her "he was in love with a woman he couldn't stand." Scooter was not used to a woman making demands on him. Janet further confided in me that Scooter was not her first affair. When she lived in Seattle, she had an affair with her daughter's piano teacher. She said something that I found unusual coming from a woman that attended family services at their church of choice every Sunday. She said that "once you have an affair, it is easier to cross the line the second time." She equated it to murdering someone: once you have done it, it is easier the second time. When Scooter returned from the Academy, he then transferred to a new office in Shreveport, LA. I never did hear what happened to the relationship.

When Barry arrived, the whole atmosphere of the office changed. Now it was coat and tie with Barry micro-managing all cases. Barry was very short and had a receding hair line and a beer belly. He reminded me of Napoleon Bonaparte. Sly had nick-named him "Low Rider." He and I did not hit it off. Seemed he did not think that I should leave the office at quitting time. I regularly came in an hour early to get a head start on writing reports, but that did not seem to pacify Barry. It was downhill from there. I would regularly leave the office at five to go to the gym or jog to maintain a level of physical fitness, which was encouraged. I also completed my flight training at Memphis Naval Air Station Fight School, obtaining my private pilot's license.

Fate would intervene on my behalf. Fate intervened for everyone working for Barry. In the fall, June got a call from her old boss in Las Vegas, wanting her to come back to work for him, and asked what it would take. Seems he had gone through eight secretaries since June left. June told him she would have to receive a substantial raise and he would have to get me transferred to Las Vegas. The raise would be no problem, but he did not know how to get me transferred. It seems a couple of well-placed letters, one to Senator Harry Reid and one to Frank Fahrenkopf, head of the Republican National Committee from Wayne Newton's office, did the trick. June left that fall and by December, I was in Las Vegas. Within a few months after I left, Scooter left for his hometown in Louisiana, Sly left for Arizona, and the secretary transferred to the FBI office in Memphis.

Now Barry was supervising himself. He tried to recruit fresh staff from inside the ranks of Customs, but his reputation had proceeded him, so he could not get anyone to take the positions. He then tried recruiting from outside the Customs Service and eventually staffed the office again. A few years later, his micro-management style would create an intolerable environment for his staff again. After some time, Barry arranged a transfer to his home town of Norfolk, Virginia. Supposedly, one of the conditions of the paid transfer was that Barry had to agree to retire one year after arriving in Norfolk.

I do not think the Barry situation is unique to the federal government. I understand that similar situations also occur in state and local governments and work environments of all types, for that matter. Some employees in the federal government accept positions with no intention of performing the duties of that position. In the law enforcement ranks, the protégés, "fast trackers," the "bootlickers," and the "suits" accept the law enforcement positions but quickly find themselves in a staff position from which they can quickly rise to the top. Many will apply for positions in Washington, where the positions are higher grades and, upon reaching the higher grade, they can then transfer back out to the field in a management position. They find themselves supervising law enforcement positions they have never performed. They can talk the talk, but they have never walked the walk. Barry was one of these types. There are those who have retired from a long law enforcement career with a law enforcement retirement without ever having worked a case or made an arrest.

Returning to Las Vegas

In 1986, the Las Vegas office, like Memphis, was also a three-man office with an agent in charge and a secretary. The atmosphere was very relaxed also. It was an exciting place to work. June and I rented an apartment and began to settle in. My son would learn that because of the difference in the school credit hours between Memphis and Las Vegas, he could not graduate from high school in Las Vegas unless he attended summer school later in the year. His mother was still living in Yuma, so we checked with the school that he had attended there and found that he could finish out the school year in Yuma and graduate there. So, he moved back to his mother's house for the spring semester.

The casework was varied in Las Vegas: child pornography cases, drug cases, air smuggling cases. However, I would come to hate the child pornography cases. The people involved in that stuff are sick individuals and cannot be rehabilitated. Almost immediately, I stumbled into a career-making case, which almost became a career-ending case. In law enforcement, you can go from hero to zero in a New York minute.

Shortly after my arrival in Las Vegas, my brother, Eddie, contacted me. He said he was in Las Vegas to get married to his long-time girlfriend. They had already had a child together, his second.

Eddie had divorced his first wife after they lost their house in San Diego. June and I attended the wedding ceremony, then made plans to join them for dinner later that evening. When I called their hotel to arrange a meeting time for dinner, I learned that they had already checked out. I would not hear from Eddie for another two years, after he and his second wife were arrested for possession with intent to distribute methamphetamine.

In time, June and I started looking for a house. But it would soon become apparent that she and I were on different sheets of music when it came to the price range of the houses we were considering. We looked at many houses in a range of prices, some out of my budget. June found one in "The Lakes" development that had a lap pool. It would have been a stretch to afford it. Andre Agassi owned a house at The Lakes at that time. I told June I did not want to put myself in a position of having a house payment that I might not be able to afford. June's response was, "If we can't buy a house in The Lakes, then we won't buy any." That was the wrong thing to say to me. I had put up with a lot of condescending things from her due to feeling guilty about her quitting her job and moving to New Orleans. Now we were back on her turf where she had her old job back with a raise. I once told her, "When you are at work, you have the clout of Wayne Newton behind what you say to people, but here at home, you do not." One of the aspects of living with June was that at 7:00 p.m. she liked to retire to the bedroom to do her nails and ready herself for work the next day. She liked to have her lapdog, me, next to her. I felt that so confining. It was time to make the break and correct the mistake I had made.

Marriage is about common values and common goals. June and I had neither. I would take a page out of her play book and use a line that she said she had used on her second husband. When June ended her marriage to her second husband, she said she told him that she did not love him and she was doing him a favor by telling him the truth and would not continue to waste his time. So, I told June the same thing. It sounds cruel, but it was the right thing to do. She took it very well. She only asked that I help her financially until she could get established. Little did I know that she had stayed in touch with an old boyfriend and would soon rekindle that relationship. Two years later, she would take a parting shot. June liked to spend most of what she made, so she had some bills she needed help with. Fortunately, we had kept our finances separate and I was not burdened with any of her debt.

I soon inherited an air smuggling case, the Bert "ET" (Extraterrestrial, a nickname given to him by his paramour) Williamson case. I presented the case to the Organized Crime and Drug Enforcement Task Force (OCDETF) for approval. It was unanimously approved by all agencies. The purpose of submitting a case to OCDEFT was to provide additional manpower and resources to investigate the case. The operation was named "Requiem to a Queen." Within a few days, Don Ware showed up at my office. He told me he had been assigned to the air smuggling case with me. We would also have an IRS agent assigned to us. The FBI never did assign anyone to the case. I hadn't been popular with the FBI since they found out that I was prosecuting an aircraft broker for the four stolen aircraft. Normally that case would have not fallen under my jurisdiction, but since the four aircraft were used to smuggle narcotics, and I had authorization from the U.S. Attorney's Office to utilize a cooperating defendant in the case, I continued to handle the case. FBI Agent Jackson called several times demanding that I return his calls, insisting that I turn over Darrell, the cooperating defendant in the case. I never returned his calls.

There was a downside to presenting the case for OCDETF funding: the case would now be supervised by an Assistant U.S. Attorney, which meant he could disapprove of initiatives that I or Don might attempt to keep in developing the case. Jay Angelo was the attorney assigned to the case. Jay was a former Marine Corp JAG (Judge Advocate General). More than once, Jay would chew my ass over me taking calculated gambles developing a cooperating witness. We eventually identified the new pilot for the organization, Mike Edmonton of Lake Tahoe, NV. Through Mike's telephone records, we identified one of his ground crew, Danny Mensinger of Lake Havasu, AZ. On a long shot, I placed a cold call to Danny's number, hoping to get him talking before he hired an attorney. It worked; Danny was willing to travel to Las Vegas to meet with Don and me. The next day, Danny and his attorney did arrive at the U.S. Attorney's Office. Jay was not pleased that I had made the cold call without consulting him. But Danny did become another cooperating witness.

I described my approach to moving a stalled case along as "shaking a tree" to see what would fall out. True, at times, something would fall and hit me on the head. But many times, some-

175

thing would fall from the tree that I might develop into a lead that could be beneficial to the case. The cowboy in me preferred to make my own developments.

Later, when we convinced Mike Edmonton to cooperate in exchange for leniency, Jay, Don, and I were debriefing him. Jay took exception to my approach at extracting particular points of Mike's criminality. At one point, Jay stepped toward me and raised his right hand in a back-handing motion to deter me from continuing the particular question. I let the incident go for then, but when Jay and I were alone, I called him on his action. I told him if he ever did that again, one of us would be getting our ass kicked. He denied that he had motioned to back-hand me, so I let it go. But it did create a rift between us.

When Don showed up at our office, I told him, "I don't believe in the turf battles that the different agencies get involved in. Whatever I have on this case is available to you. The entire case file is in the file cabinet, and you are free to view it anytime you like." We never had issues about turf but, unfortunately, our different agencies were not so accommodating. That "turf" issue would cost me dearly in the next two years. We would spend the next three years working on that case, eventually indicting 20 people in the organization. It took the resources of the three agencies.

Customs soon hired another agent to increase staffing at the office. Jeff was a DEA agent in Detroit. I did his initial interview before he was selected. Jeff struck me as someone that would say whatever he thought the interviewer wanted to hear. Or, as I described it, "He will respond favorably to whoever is asking the questions." Soon after he was hired, it became obvious that he was a "case killer." Whenever he was assigned a case, initially he would open a formal investigation into the matter. But in time when you asked him what he has developed in the case, his response was, "Oh, that case was not going anywhere so I closed it." I never knew of him ever presenting a case for prosecution or having any self-initiated cases. Jeff had one goal in life: to retired with 20 years' service and go to work for Major League Baseball in their Security Department. We referred to Jeff as a "Terminal Twelve," and he never aspired to become a Senior Agent.

One night, I was doing surveillance at Las Vegas executive aircraft terminal on an aircraft that was being readied for flight. I had been asked by another office to report its departure from Las Vegas. The aircraft mechanic asked me what I would think about a Pressurized Cessna 210 aircraft that had a "T-splice" in the fuel system, allowing an additional internal fuel source to be connected to the fuel system. The additional fuel source would allow the aircraft to stay airborne longer. I told the mechanic that, without the proper FAA documentation for the modification, the aircraft was probably being used for smuggling narcotics. The mechanic said, "That one right there has one." He showed me the aircraft and the modification to it. At the conclusion of the case, I paid the mechanic $25,000 for providing the information.

The next morning, I opened a case on the aircraft and contacted the FAA about the aircraft registration and the fuel modification. I learned that the modification had not been done legally. Over the course of the next few months, I documented the sale of the aircraft with all cash payments and identified the owner. The owner was also making multiple $5000 cash payments for the repairs to the aircraft. I learned that the owner/pilot of the aircraft had made a "gear up" landing at the Las Vegas airport a few months earlier. The aircraft owner, Mathew Trevino, was flying into Las Vegas from his home at a residential airpark in Sandy Valley, Nevada, with three friends for a night on the town. In his approach to the airport, he forgot to switch the fuel selector lever from the right-wing tank to the "both" position. As he banked the aircraft to the right, elevating his left empty wing tank, his engine was starved of fuel, causing the engine to quit. He immediately realized his mistake and restarted his engine. But in the excitement of the moment and all his passengers screaming, "We are going to die, we are going to die!" the pilot forgot to extend his landing gear. He made a perfect gear-up landing, but the aircraft would require extensive repairs to the underbelly.

As the aircraft was repaired for flight over the next few months, I prepared an affidavit supporting a request for the installation of a law enforcement transponder in the aircraft, which would allow me to track the aircraft's movements. Or so I thought. The court order was approved, allowing a certified technician to install a law enforcement transponder in the aircraft. After the aircraft was released from the repair shop, I discovered that the transponder was not working, although I later learned this would be to my benefit. Now I had to locate the aircraft and arrange for the installation to be fixed. The repairs to the installation were completed at zero-dark-thirty one night at the executive terminal. But one of the employees observed us entering the aircraft and reported it to the pilot. I thought the case had been blown, but not so. I would later learn that the employee told the pilot that "the FBI was in your airplane." Fortunately for me, he did not take the information seriously. As it turned out, the law enforcement transponder still was not working. When it was ground tested, it worked, but due to a faulty antenna connection, when it was airborne, it did not. I would have to resort to lengthy fixed surveillance to catch this guy.

On June 12, my birthday, I arranged to use the residence of a winter visitor in Sandy Valley, Nevada, as a stationary surveillance post. The house was across the street from Trevino's house. The winter visitor was at his summer home in Idaho. Another agent and I planned to use the house for as long as it took to catch the pilot landing his aircraft loaded with narcotics. We thought we might be in for a long wait. We had just arrived at the house at dusk and unloaded our equipment from our old Ford 150 undercover pickup. I began removing the protective covering from the windows of the closed-up house. No sooner had I taken the covering down from the west window than the aircraft landed with his landing lights on. I hurried to the back and cracked the back door open to watch the activity. The aircraft taxied up to the house and the pilot jumped out, carrying a bundle in his arms. He handed the package to an associate standing in the illuminated doorway of the residence. The pilot went back to the plane for another bundle. I watched as the two men made 13 trips to and from the aircraft. At one point, I saw a young woman standing in the doorway also. Did I really see what I think I saw, I thought. We needed reinforcements fast. We would need a posse, in fact. I was finally able to get a cell phone signal and make a call to another agent in Las Vegas. He rounded up a replacement to relieve me so I could go back to Las Vegas and obtain a search warrant for the house. After the judge read the affidavit, he commented, "Someone has done their homework" and signed the search warrant. We joined up with a narcotics squad from Las Vegas Metro Police Department, heading back out the Sandy Valley to execute the warrant. At 10:30 a.m., 12 hours after the pilot had landed, we kicked in the door, overwhelming the occupants. Police were everywhere. I got the pilot off to a separate room and started debriefing him when someone from the search team told me they had found a kilo of cocaine in the dresser in the master bedroom and 13 bundles of narcotics in the closet. A few minutes later, another officer entered the debriefing room and told me all the bundles contained cocaine. The whole time I worked the case, I thought it was a marijuana operation. Mr. Trevino was looking at a long prison term of 20 years. He was motivated to cooperate in furthering the investigation. The closet contained 300 kilos of cocaine, weighing out at 660 pounds, the largest drug bust in the history of the state of Nevada at the time.

Trevino agreed to cooperate and assist in apprehending additional individuals. We contacted agents of the Drug Enforcement Administration and formulated a plan to deliver 100 kilos to an accomplice in the Los Angeles area. Normally, you try to get a higher-level violator with such an operation, so you can work your way up to the main violator. We flew 100 kilos of the cocaine in

Trevino's aircraft to Los Angeles. There we hooked up several more DEA agents, one of whom would serve as an undercover agent, posing as Trevino's associate. The 100 kilos were loaded into an undercover Mercedes sedan. Contact was made with the associate. The plan was to let the associate load the cocaine into his vehicle then allow him to leave the immediate area and have a marked police unit make a routine traffic stop on the vehicle. That was the plan, anyway. Well, as soon as the loaded vehicle started to move, the shit hit the fan. Cop cars came from out of nowhere with lights on and sirens blaring, stopping the loaded vehicle in a major intersection in Huntington Beach, California. The loaded vehicle was surrounded by about 20 officers with guns drawn, some with AR-15s. What an embarrassing debacle. When I learned that the DEA Group Supervisor from LA wanted to re-seize the 100 kilos and claim it as a statistic for his office, I just went and sat in the loaded van, not letting anyone get near it. It was going back to Vegas with me. By now, I had been without sleep for close to 48 hours and I was not thinking too clearly. I needed some sleep. Then I heard some radio traffic that Trevino had escaped from the undercover agent. Unbelievable! What a keystone cop operation this became. The major player got away and, as it would turn out, we were left with one of his low-level helpers. I needed a beer. The military term, SNAFU – Situation Normal, All Fucked Up—applied. The undercover agent originally told everyone that Trevino jumped out of his car at a stop light. That statement would come back to bite both the undercover agent and me in the ass a couple years later.

The next afternoon, we were back in Las Vegas and the front-page headlines in the Las Vegas Review Journal screamed "LARGEST DRUG BUST IN STATE HISTORY, 660 POUNDS OF COCAINE SEIZED." My stock was pretty high, and the Las Vegas Office's stock was pretty high. The agent in charge was eventually promoted to a supervisor position in Los Angeles, the senior agent in the office was promoted to agent in charge, and I was promoted to senior agent.

I spent the next few months tracking down every lead I could trying to locate Trevino, but I was always a few days behind him. Then the trail went cold. The two individuals that were in Trevino's house the night of the raid were convicted. The guy claimed he was the gardener and the young girl claimed she was the housekeeper. The presiding judge, however, overturned the girl's conviction because of her age. She was only 19 years old and she had no criminal record. She was a Russian Jewish girl who had just immigrated to the U.S. with her family. If she had appeared at the sentencing when the judge overturned her conviction, she would have gotten off Scott free. Since she did not appear, there was a warrant out for her for failure to appear. I heard later that while she was on the run, she had gotten pregnant and was thinking about surrendering. It was time to tie up the loose ends and move on to other cases. Big cases—big problems, little cases—little problems, no cases—no problems. I just wished that was not true.

One of the agents in the office, Lee, had been accepted for an Internal Affairs position in Philadelphia. When he left, I ended up inheriting two of his informants and one of his stalled cases. It would take me three years to indict 20 people in that case and another year to prosecute it. The informants could have cost me my job. As the saying goes, you are not going to find good informants in the church choir. Many are involved in the criminal activity or live on the fringes of the criminal life. In this case, they were running their own criminal enterprise right under my nose while working for me.

One of the informants was an aircraft broker in Las Vegas who was also a pilot. His partner, Darrell, was also a skilled pilot. The aircraft broker, Aaron, was a Jewish immigrant who had no hands. He had prosthetic hooks to replace them. Aaron was married to a young Jewish girl through an arranged marriage, with whom he had just had a child. One of the stories I had heard was that, as a child in Israel, he had been playing with blasting caps, which cost him both his hands. He also had a large scar on the left side of his face. The other story I heard was that he was an F-16 pilot in Israel and had lost his hands in a battle. I never believed the F-16 story. Supposedly, his sister was at one time Miss Israel and was then married to a wealthy physician in California. In time, I would interview the doctor and learn that the brother and sister were quite the pair.

The partner, Darrell, made his living playing poker in the downtown casinos. He made a substantial living for himself, his wife, his stepson and their young son. He was a very soft-spoken, likeable guy. I liked Darrell and respected him as a skilled pilot. But as I was soon to find out, Darrell could easily be lead astray with the promise of easy cash.

Documented informants could occasionally be paid for information pertaining to suspicious aircraft sales. The smugglers liked to use cash to make undocumented purchases of aircraft for their operations, making it hard for law enforcement to trace the aircraft to their operation. Aaron would make the sales and then report the transaction to me. One day, Aaron informed me that he obtained the signed Bill of Sale for an Israeli Westwind Aircraft that was in the repair shop at an Ontario, California airport. Supposedly, he had obtained the Bill of Sale from the two owners prior to their arrest for narcotics smuggling in Mexico. Now, this was where it got complicated. Why did I not just rest on my laurels from the previous case? Why couldn't I be satisfied with being a one-case-wonder like so many in law enforcement? Maybe my mother was right after all. I had to learn things the hard way.

I saw an opportunity and so did the informants, but we were not on the same sheet of music. My plan was to initiate an under-cover operation using the Westwind aircraft as a prop to convince a smuggling organization out of El Paso to hire the two infor-mants to fly narcotics out of Mexico right into Las Vegas. What a brilliant plan! I was a genius!

Wrong!

The first stupid thing I did was to call the FAA in Oklahoma City to get the transfer of registration expedited from the previous owners into Aaron's name so I could implement the undercover operation. I would later learn that the bill of sale was forged. As I would soon learn, the mechanic shop in Ontario had an $8000 lien against the aircraft. Aaron and I visited the shop and were told that they would not release the aircraft to the new owner until the lien was paid. It would take time for Aaron to raise the money. It seems the mechanic saw an opportunity to keep the aircraft for himself. When Aaron had raised enough money for the lien, he and I went back to the Ontario airport to pay the lien and take possession of the aircraft. We were shocked to find out that the lien was now $15,000. What in the hell happened? Who authorized the additional repairs? The shop owner showed us the signed original work order for the repairs with the clause, "and other repairs as necessary." They supposedly had done additional repairs to the aircraft after our last visit. The next stupid thing I did was to persuade Aaron to pay the lean. Aaron reluctantly paid the $15,000 in cash and we took possession of the aircraft. Neither Aaron nor I were rated to fly that type of aircraft, so we had to leave the aircraft at Ontario. We had just obtained a several hundred-thousand-dollar aircraft for $15,000. How I would come to regret that day.

My plan was to hire a pilot who was rated in the Westwind aircraft, then have him and Aaron fly the aircraft to El Paso airport, where we could show it to the smuggling organization, hoping to convince them to use our aircraft for smuggling. Well, that was not Aaron's plan. Without my knowledge, he hired a 72-year-old pilot who claimed he was rated in the Westwind aircraft. He and Aaron traveled to the Ontario airport to fly the aircraft to El Paso. Upon departing Ontario airport, they were given departure instruction to "climb to 5000 ft, do not exceed 5000 ft" in order to keep them under arriving and departing LAX traffic. Evidently, the aircraft was too fast for the old pilot. On the ascent after takeoff, the aircraft got away from the pilot, soon busting the altitude restriction. After an unpleasant exchange with air traffic control, they got the aircraft under control and made it to El Paso. I found out about it after Aaron returned to Las Vegas.

My plan was to travel to El Paso with both informants to conduct undercover meetings with a contact from the Mexican smuggling organization. Again, that was not Aaron's plan. Once in El Paso, I planned to hook up with a local agent and place a concealed body transmitter on Aaron, so we could record the meeting with the local contact. Aaron did not like wearing that hidden transmitter, but it would be months later before I found out why. I could never get a clear transmission from the transmitter. I thought maybe it was the building they were in, or maybe it was because we were too close to El Paso airport.

Throughout the next few months, both informants and I travelled to El Paso, where we conducted several undercover meetings with the local contact. I used government funds to pay for their air travel to El Paso. I never was able to obtain any incriminating statements from the local contact using the transmitter. I then started pressing the informants to get some "front money" to finance the smuggling operation. On one trip, Aaron managed to come up with $5000 that was supposedly "front money." He knew I would seize "front money" and he could only be awarded 25% of the amount seized. The undercover operation was not coming together. I would soon find out why. It would take me weeks to sort out what was really going on.

My brother-in-law and sister, Will and Sadie, had come to visit me at my home in Las Vegas. It was the only time Will would ever visit my home. Will and I were sitting around that evening drinking beer when the phone rang. It was a good thing I had already had a couple beers when I answered the phone, but even then, I was not prepared for what I was about to hear. As I picked up the receiver, a voice screamed at me. It was the agent from El Paso.

"You motherfucker! Your informant just tried to kill me! He just tried to run me down with an airplane!" he yelled.

"Calm down," I said, "What in the hell are you talking about?"

"Your informant, "Hooks," just tried to kill me," he insisted.

My initial instinct was to be defensive and ask how he knew it was my informant. His response was that he had seen the individual in question getting in the airplane and he had hooks for hands. I reminded him that one of the El Paso's city representatives had hooks for hands also, but he did not like that statement. His response was, "I know Jay, and it was not Jay Armes. It was your fucking informant!"

Detective Jay Armes of El Paso rose to fame when he recovered Marlon Brando's kidnapped 13-year-old son, Christian. Ironically, he was called "Detective Hook." He also supposedly lost his hands playing with explosives as a child. Christian's mother hired a band of hippies to kidnap Christian. She paid the hippies $10,000 to kidnap Christian because of a custody dispute with Marlon. Armes located the hippies and Christian in a cave in Mexico.[5]

I finally got the agent to calm down to the point that he could tell me what had happened that night in El Paso Airport. I would need a couple more drinks after that conversation. Earlier in the day, the agent had observed a Beechcraft Bonanza aircraft in the tie-down area of Cutter Aviation's tarmac. The aircraft had newly painted tail registration numbers, but the old registration numbers were still visible through the new paint job. The agent ran the old registration numbers. He discovered that the aircraft belonged to a doctor in Las Vegas and that the aircraft had been reported stolen. The agent decided to establish surveillance on the aircraft in hopes of apprehending whoever was operating it. Later that evening, the agent observed Aaron enter the office at Cutter Aviation, then leave the office, heading out on the tarmac toward the aircraft. After stepping out the office door, Aaron broke into a dead run toward the awaiting aircraft, which had the engine running. Someone had already entered the aircraft and had it ready to go. Darrell was at the controls of the aircraft. The agent was in hot pursuit, commandeering one of Cutter's courtesy vans and pulling it in front of the aircraft, attempting to block its departure. Darrell and Aaron would not be deterred. The aircraft rammed the van with the left-wing tip, hence the agent's statement that "Hooks" trying to kill him. That got the agent's attention. The young Cutter employee driving the van wanted no part of this action. Darrell and Aaron forged on, fast taxiing across the tarmac without departure clearance, taxi clearance or takeoff clearance. It was full throttle across the taxi way with no regard for other traffic. By some act of superior piloting skills, or just dumb luck, Darrell sped the aircraft across the taxi way and got the aircraft airborne momentarily. But then it stalled back down into the dirt medium between the taxi way and the runway. Still undeterred, he got the aircraft airborne again and successfully executed a cross runway departure, then turned south toward Mexico to deliver the aircraft.

That was all I needed to hear. I would need a beer. In fact, I would need several beers to sleep that night. I saw my rear end, my career, and my retirement hanging out there on a very thin limb. Aaron could claim as a defense that he was operating per my instructions. It was not a good situation for a worrier, a fretter like me, to find himself in. This situation would require some patience on my part before I could dig myself out of this mess, and patience is not one of my strong suits. But I could not tip my hand. For the next several days, I felt gut-shot worrying about the outcome. In the words of actor Chief Dan George in the movie Outlaw Josey Whales, "we must endeavor to persevere." And so, I did.

The next day, I started doing periodic surveillance on Aaron's and Darrell's homes, just waiting for them to show up. A couple days later, Darrell's vehicle was observed at his house. I called another agent to assist me as I approached Darrell's house. I wanted to have a witness with me from here on out every time I talked to Darrell. It would be critical if Aaron would claim I was involved. When we knocked on the door, Darrell opened the door and invited us in. He knew why we were there, but I did not know the extent of what they had been up to. I maintained my professionalism despite the fact I was madder than hell over his betrayal. I told him to summon his wife, so we could sit down at the kitchen table and have a talk. I started the conversation by telling him in front of his wife that I could arrest him right then and haul his ass off to jail, but I was going to give him a chance to help himself out of this mess. I needed his help to get out of this mess myself. I then told him that there is a very crude saying in situations like this: "The first hog to the trough gets the best deals." In other words, the first person that cooperates in an investigation gets the best deal. That being said, I told him that I would not arrest him that night, but if he would show up at the U.S. Attorney's Office the next morning, we could work something out. If he was not there in the morning, I would be back to arrest him. He agreed, and the other agent and I left. I knew only too well what it would be like for Darrell to worry about something like this for the next 12 hours.

Bright and early the next morning, Darrell showed up. He and I met with one of the Assistant U.S. Attorneys. The Assistant Attorney offered Darrel a sweetheart deal: immunity from prosecution in exchange for full and truthful disclosure of all crimes. He had to agree to further cooperate by flying in a load of narcotics for the organization in El Paso. Oh geez, I thought to myself, not another undercover operation. That is how this mess got started. Darrel accepted the deal.

I spent the next three days debriefing Darrel in detail. I was assisted by our office secretary, who would serve as my witness as well as note-taker. I read Darrel his Miranda rights and told him that would be granted immunity for any crimes he had committed except murder. I told him that if he had committed or participated in a murder, he needed to tell me then and there, and the debriefing would stop. Darrell gave me a startled expression, paused, then he said he had not murdered anyone. As the debriefing continued, I learned that he and Aaron had stolen four aircraft out of Las Vegas and had sold them to the organization in Mexico. To add insult to injury, I learned that the $5000 that I had seized as "front money" was partial payment for one of the stolen aircraft. In addition, some of the money that was used to pay off the mechanics lien on the Westwind aircraft was also proceeds from selling the stolen aircraft. On one of our trips to El Paso, Aaron had collected another $5000 partial payment, which he had hidden in his boot on the return trip to Las Vegas. Darrell informed me that he had forged the "Bill of Sale" for the Westwind aircraft. What a dumbass I was! I had helped them steal an expensive aircraft, on which I would be answering questions years later when the real owners tried to get it back.

I had to ask Darrell the $64,000 question. This was critical, where I most needed a witness. If he answered this question wrong, my future would not be pretty. My stock would be in the toilet. "At any time during the criminal activity that you have just described, did you do any of the criminal activity at my direction?" I asked and held my breath. Darrell hesitated, as though he did not know what I was asking.

Then it dawned on him and he said, "No." Holy sweet Jesus. That was the right answer. Had he answered to the affirmative, my career would have been finished. I knew the answer, but some criminals would have accused me of being involved as a defense against a successful prosecution. I was sure Aaron would have done just that.

I called the agent in El Paso and had him seize the Westwind aircraft. I then got an arrest warrant for Aaron and his contact in El Paso. We were not going to arrest the contact in El Paso because we would need him later. Now I just had to wait for Aaron to show up. It would not take long. Two days later, I was heading home when I encountered Aaron approaching the intersection, headed in my direction. My first impulse was to run him off the road and arrest him right there, but I restrained myself. I wanted to do this right. Seems Aaron had been hiding out at his sister's house in Palm Springs, California. So, the next day, I devised a ruse to lure Aaron to the office. I contacted the agent in El Paso and had him travel to Las Vegas to assist in Aaron's arrest. I felt that was only right, given the agent's experience of nearly being run over in El Paso. I would lure Aaron to the office with the promise of a $25,000 check as payment for information relating to another aircraft sale he had provided us information on.

I called his house and his wife answered. She said that Aaron was in the shower. I asked that he return my call when he finished with his shower. Aaron called back, and I told him about the check. He said he would be over in about an hour. My plan was to lure him into our smallest office, which would be more confining. My concern was that if things went bad when he was told he was under arrest, he could start to swing those hooks around, possibly cutting someone up severely. I wanted to be able to restrain him before he knew what was happening. I positioned a chair right against one of the office walls, so the other agent and I could have access to both sides of the chair when Aaron arrived. I put the arrest warrant in a government franked envelope and sealed it.

About an hour later, Aaron arrived and sat in the chair against the wall. I handed him the franked envelope, telling him that it contained the $25,000 check, but he nonchalantly tossed it back on my desk. I handed it back to him, saying, "Damn, Aaron! I went to a lot of work to get that for you! Aren't you going to at least look at it?" He then started fumbling with his two hooks to unseal the envelope. At that moment, the other agent grabbed one arm and I grabbed the other arm, pining his arms to the chair. As I handcuffed him, he was looked up at me, saying, "But Gil, it's me, Aaron, it's me, Aaron."

With the adrenaline flowing, I lost it right then. I heard myself saying, "Ya, I know who the fuck it is, and this is Gil, and I am arresting your ass." Then I picked up the envelope. I said, "You want to see what is in that fucking envelope? There is no check! This is a warrant for your arrest. How do you like being played for a sucker, asshole?" We hauled him off to jail. But he would have the last laugh.

It would take a few days before a bail hearing was held. In the meantime, I noticed that Aaron's house was up for sale. His sister held a yard sale, selling off all their furniture. I learned that his wife had cleaned out their bank accounts and travelled back to Israel with the baby. I did not think the judge would give him bail. Was I mistaken? At the bail hearing, a member of Aaron's temple showed up, offering to allow Aaron to stay at his house as well as putting his house up to secure the bail. Bail granted. I protested that Aaron was an Israeli citizen and so could not be extradited from Israel. I pointed out that his wife and child had already gone to Israel, that they sold their house and belongings and cleaned out their bank accounts. Then I heard, "This hearing is adjourned!" But Your Honor!

Two weeks later, I learned that Aaron had borrowed his friend's car, driven to LAX, and boarded a flight to Israel, leaving his friend's car at the airport. Sometime later, I learned through INTERPOL that Aaron was living in Haifa, Israel, where he owned a jewelry shop.

I subsequently interviewed Aaron's brother-in-law, the doctor. He told me that, while married to Aaron's sister, he had purchased a lot of expensive jewelry for her, but it had been stolen from their house. His wife then filed an insurance claim on the jewelry, collecting handsomely. The doctor believed that Aaron was the one that stole the jewelry. When the doctor and Aaron's sister divorced, she got the 1.2-million-dollar house in Palm Springs. Later, there was a suspicious fire at that house, which resulted in another insurance claim payoff. The doctor believed that Aaron set the fire. I always wondered if all the jewelry that was supposedly stolen from the doctor's wife was how Aaron opened his jewelry shop in Haifa.

I did not want to do this undercover operation, but it was part of Darrell's plea agreement and, worse yet, it would have to be conducted in west Texas and southern New Mexico. This meant that it would be under the control of the office responsible for that area. As it would turn out, five different federal offices and a state and local agencies would get involved. This was going to become another disaster I would regret.

It started out well in Las Vegas. Darrell placed consensually monitored recorded telephone calls to the contact in El Paso. The contact, Mike, would serve as the middle man between Darrell and the head of smuggling organization in Mexico, Carlos. Through Mike, Darrell was letting Carlos know that he was interested in working for him. Delivering the stolen aircrafts to Carlos had cemented Darrell's credibility with Carlos. I could have never planned it that way. After several calls to Mike, Darrel finally got a page from Carlos, but he had to go through Mike to learn what Carlos wanted. That recorded phone call would start a chain of events that would have cost Darrell his life if not for some quick thinking on his part. During that phone call, specific words became critical to the prosecution of the case. I needed Darrell to inject into the conversation what Carlos's specific wants were and have Mike acknowledge the specific wants. Normally these conversations were in code, never using specific incriminating words in the conversation. In the scripted conversation, I wanted Darrell to slip into the conversation, "I got a page from Carlos, I think he wants me to come down and do a load."

To my surprise, Mike responded "That is what he wants." Damn, did he really say that? Did I get it on tape? When I checked the tape, it was there. We were off and running on yet another "keystone cop" operation.

Darrell and I hopped a Southwest Airlines flight to El Paso and hooked up with the agent who Darrell had "tried to kill" a few weeks earlier. The agent was not pleased when he learned that Darrell was at the controls of the aircraft that night, not Aaron. But he had to bite that bullet. We dropped Darrell off at the bridge to

Mexico and he walked into Mexico. The other agent and I hauled ass to the State Police Headquarters in Socorro, New Mexico, for an operational briefing. The other agent was wrapped pretty tight on a good day, but tonight he needed some meds. He drove a government 1987 yellow Chevrolet Camaro IROC-Z, which he usually drove at 110 mph. For the next three nights, he would drive the trip between El Paso and Socorro at 110 mph. I sure could have used a beer, but for the next three days, that was out of the question.

For the next three nights, over the Thanksgiving holiday, we would drop Darrell off at the bridge to Mexico and then head back to Socorro to attend an operational briefing. Through information provided by Darrell, we had identified the makeshift dirt airstrip south of Socorro, New Mexico. The first two nights were a "no-go" due to the airstrip in Mexico being used by some Mexican police to offload shipments of narcotics they were bringing from South America. Also, supposedly Carlos's Socorro ground crew had gotten drunk and he could not contact them.

The operational briefing was conducted by a supervisor from the Customs Albuquerque Aviation branch. Plan "A" was to execute the bust of the ground crew and aircraft crew as soon as the aircraft touched down and was on its landing roll out. The air crew would not be able to abort the landing and takeoff again. However, if Plan "A" could not be executed, Plan "B" would be implemented. Plan "B" was to allow the aircraft get airborne again and return to Mexico with Darrell so he could make a second run that night. The first run was to be Darrell's training flight. The ground crew would be busted after the aircraft was safely out of the area. Everyone was to maintain radio silence until the bust signal was given. The bust signal would be "Mustang, Mustang." We were extremely concerned about law enforcement radio traffic due to the remoteness of the area of operation. Even though it was not likely the ground crews could monitor our frequencies, if they had a police scanner, they would know law enforcement was in the area if someone was 'breaking squelch" on the scanner. Everyone was to get in position and stay in position until the bust signal. I told the other agent that we should not be running up and down the highway at a high rate of speed in his yellow Camaro drawing attention to us—a lot of good that did. He would not stay in position.

In addition to all the ground law enforcement units, we had a Customs Blackhawk helicopter with airborne bust crew and a state police helicopter with a bust crew. Additionally, we had a Customs radar equipped aircraft overhead flying surveillance. The helicopters were staged several miles to the northeast out of the operational area. I was unaware that one of the Albuquerque agents had sneaked into the operation area on foot and had taken a position on a small mountain overlooking the airstrip. He had a law enforcement radio with him, which would prove to be a crucial mistake.

We were all in position and everyone was keeping their mouths shut for the time being. Then we got word from the airborne Customs aircraft that was overhead to "expect Mustang in 10 min." One of the ground units monitoring the citizen band channels heard the ground crew tell the income smuggling aircraft, "All clear, come on in, it is so quiet down here you can hear a fish fart."

Damn, I thought, this is going to go down like we planned it. But I thought that too soon. Within a few minutes, the motor mouth on the mountain started giving the world a blow by blow account of what was transpiring out in the dark of night. "Ok, he has just turned final approach for the airstrip, ok, now he is touching down, he is on his landing roll out, now he is at the end of the strip turning around, they are kicking the load, the aircraft is starting his takeoff roll, ok he just lifted off." A smuggling aircrew will only spend minutes on the ground as they kick the load out while the engine was still running, then leave quickly.

By now, listening to that radio traffic, I was wrapped as tight as the other agent in the car with me. We both were fighting over the police radio microphone. I grabbed the microphone from the other agent. Keying the mic, I yelled, "Shut the fuck up, Mustang, Mustang!"

The other agent grabbed the mic back and yelled, "Mustang, Mustang!"

Now all I could do was yell, "Mustang, Mustang!" into the night. No one heard us. What motor mouth did not realize was that by having his mic keyed and being at a higher elevation, he prevented everyone from transmitting. Finally, "Mustang, Mustang" Plans "A" and "B" were down the toilet. Then the shit hit the proverbial fan. Or, in this case, it hit the helicopter rotors. Both helicopters launched at the same time from just a few miles away. The Blackhawk sounded louder than a freight train coming.

The ground crew ran like scared jackrabbits. As the two helicopters approached the airstrip, the powerful down draft of the
Blackhawk almost forced the smaller state helicopter to the
ground. Fortunately, the pilot recovered. Two of the ground
crew made it to their cars, but one poor soul was left on the
ground trying to outrun the Blackhawk. He was beat into submission by the rotor downdraft. One of the ground crew that
made it to his car was heard over the citizen band radio yelling,
"Abort, abort! Don't come back!" The fleeing aircraft had been
warned.

It was all chaos in the area, vehicles going in every direction,
some with their lights turned off in an effort to stay undetected.
The two fleeing ground crew vehicles sped with lights out, trying
to flee the area. One of the Customs ground units running with
no lights went off in a ditch. One of the fleeing ground crew vehicles running lights out encountered a DEA vehicle across the road
and spun out, but regained control. As he floored the vehicle in a
further attempt to flee, he showered the DEA vehicle with gravel,
knocking out all the lights on the front of the vehicle, thus disabling it. "SNAFU" best described the situation.

My only concern at that time was that Darrell was on that
airplane heading back to Mexico and the pilot was aware that the
load had been busted. What would Carlos's reaction be when he
heard? We may have just gotten Darrell killed. How would I tell
his wife? At daylight, I searched out the operational supervisor. I
found him sitting in his car at a nearby gas stop. I walked up to his
car and told him that if Darrell did not come back from Mexico,

he would be the one to tell his wife why. I turned and walked off. It was a good thing I could not find that motor mouth.

It was three days before I heard from Darrell. Carlos had held him hostage until he could figure out what happened. Darrell's own quick thinking saved his life. As soon as the aircraft landed in Mexico, he got in Carlos's face, yelling at him, "What in the fuck kind of operation do you have? The cops were waiting for us." Carlos was caught off guard. But Carlos told Darrel that he would be staying there until he could figure out what happened. Some days later, Carlos assumed that the ground crew was responsible for the bust and let Darrell go.

We only caught one of the ground crew that night. The other two fled in their vehicles into the night. We identified a fourth person who was sitting in the rest area nearby monitoring a police scanner and citizen band radio, but that was not enough to arrest him. Mike was also arrested and convicted. Darrell was a free man without a criminal record. He had done his part.

During the three-day debriefing of Darrell, our office secretary and I developed an attraction toward each other. She had just ended a relationship with a guy she was dating. Lucia was a financially struggling single mother of two daughters, eight and eleven years old. Before long, she and I would be dating. After she received her college degree at UNLV, she was selected as a Special Agent in the Las Vegas office. After she had attended the Federal Law Enforcement Academy in Glynco, Georgia, she and the two girls moved in with me. It would be a hard transition for the three Hispanic females and the "old gringo." The youngest daughter was a sweetheart, but the oldest daughter was her daddy's girl. The transition for us would take time. At eleven years old, she was becoming the dominate female of the three and would resist the old gringo's authority. It would take years for her to accept me. As I have learned with animals, you cannot force them to accept you. You just must earn their trust and let nature take its course, like the wolf in the movie Dances With Wolves. Later, I would wonder what I was thinking. But by the end of that year, we were married in Las Vegas.

I believe there are those of us that, when seeing someone struggling in life, naturally want to provide them a "safe harbor," especially those of us that have experienced life's struggles growing up as I had. Maybe we believe that by providing them a safe harbor, they will endear themselves to us and love us. That may work in the beginning, but when the winds of life's struggles subside for them, they may want to venture outside that safe harbor on their own. In hindsight, I came to realize that was the type of relationship Lucia and I came to have. I also realized when they decide that they want to venture outside the safe harbor and you try stopping them, they will resent you, maybe hate you. I am embarrassed to admit that I was crazy about Lucia and lusted after her in the worst way. But nothing lasts forever. It would soon be evident that the level of endearment was not shared by Lucia. In time, I would realize that marrying her was the biggest mistake I ever made. At 42 years old, I was acting stupidly.

Over the years, I had successfully extradited myself from the chaos of my own family, but I could not have foreseen the chaos I was about to bring into my life by marrying into an extended Hispanic family. My first rude awakening came shortly after Lucia and I married. One evening at home, we received a call from Lucia's middle brother, Eddie. Lucia and he had never had much to do with each other after leaving home.

In fact, she said, as children they hated each other. Eddie and a nephew of his had just arrived in Las Vegas from El Paso unannounced. It seemed he was calling Lucia, hoping to be offered a place to stay. I was aware that Eddie had had prior drug arrests, so I informed Lucia that he could not stay with us. Three days later, I would learn that I had made a very wise decision. Through other family members, we learned that Eddie had recently been released from jail after being arrested for distribution of narcotics from the apartment located at the back of his mother's house. According to other family members, Eddie had just spent three days in jail before his common-law wife could raise the bond money. Eddie was so furious with his common-law wife for not being able to raise the money sooner that he beat her to the point of breaking her arm. To avoid being arrested again, he fled El Paso for Las Vegas.

Approximately two weeks later, I encountered Eddie driving his bright red Cadillac convertible in the downtown area of Las Vegas. I began to follow him, hoping I might encounter a Las Vegas Police Officer and report Eddie as a fugitive. I did not want to communicate over the law enforcement radio that I was following a fugitive. I feared that Lucia may overhear the report and intervene. I continued to follow Eddie, but after a time, he noticed I was following and decided to flee Las Vegas. As he continued south out of Las Vegas through Henderson, NV, into Boulder City, I finally encountered a local police officer and reported him. Eddie abandoned his vehicle and fled on foot, evading the police officer. Three days later, he and his nephew were arrested while burglarizing a local home. Initially, he told family members that I had him arrested, causing family members to vent their anger toward me. In time, they learned the truth. Other such incidents over the years would create friction between Lucia and I, as well as other family members.

Eddie was returned to prison in El Paso to serve out the sentence he received for distribution of narcotics. Not long before he was to be released, he was caught having anal sex with another male inmate. His prison sentence was extended by six months for violating prison rules. After he was released, he learned that he had contracted AIDS. Even knowing that he had the AIDS virus, he married a local woman and fled El Paso to avoid complying with the conditions of his probation. Family members initially were unaware of his whereabouts, but they eventually learned that he was living in San Jose, CA. Lucia also learned of his whereabouts but made a point of not informing me for fear of me notifying the U.S. Marshals Service. Against my advice, she traveled to San Jose to visit Eddie. When she returned to El Paso, she visited the Marshal Service to arrange for her dying brother to return to El Paso to live out his final days without fear of being arrested. He died not long after returning to El Paso.

Sometime later, family members discovered that Eddie had fathered an illegitimate child with a woman from El Paso. No one in the family even knew that the child existed. I soon learned that Lucia was in the process of getting custody from the child's foster mother in Phoenix, AZ. It was not clear as to who in the family would be accepting responsibility for the ten-year-old girl. Lucia did tell me that if she was not married to me, she would have adopted the girl. Lucia did arrange for the girl to stay at our home for two weeks, so the child could meet the many extended family members. Fortunately, the foster mother had already started adoption proceeding for the child. As a state educator, the foster mother had done an exemplary job of raising the young girl. Academically and socially, the child stood head and shoulders above her maternal siblings. The child obviously preferred her life in Phoenix to the one she faced in El Paso. The child never furthered her interaction with her El Paso family members after she returned to Phoenix.

When Lucia's ex-husband learned that she had remarried, he informed her that he did not feel he had any fiscal responsibility to his two daughters. He was paying court-ordered child support but decided he was moving back to Mexico to work for his brother, so he would not have to pay child support. For the next ten years, he did not contribute to the girls' support, nor did he send them birthday cards/presents or Christmas cards/presents. Initially the girls visited him during the summer, but that only lasted one year. We soon discovered that they would only stay at his house on the first night in El Paso, and the rest of the time, they stayed at their grandmother's. The summer visits were discontinued.

Marrying the only woman in a small, mostly male office creates a whole new set of dynamics for the work place. Some of the other males, married or single, become uncomfortable with a married couple in the office. Being the senior agent would sometimes place me in the position of being Lucia's acting supervisor when the agent in charge was absent from the office. I was very careful not to create the perception of any improprieties during those absences; however, some "macho males" have difficulty with a female in their ranks. I would learn to despise the term "perception is reality." Many times, a person's reality is not perceived, it is fabricated. To those people, I would say, if you think perception is reality, then you need a reality check. Reality to me is what I live, not what some other person perceives or fabricates; it is not what someone sees in a "reality show" on TV. A fabricated perception by a macho Hispanic manager would be used in an attempt to split up a newly-created family, transferring Lucia and me to two completely different offices in southern California. A ten-month nightmare would soon begin.

My most embarrassing law enforcement moment happened while walking through the main lobby area of Caesar's Palace Hotel and Casino. Weeks before the incident, I had delivered a cocaine sample to a dishwasher working at Caesar's. We were trying to interest the individual in purchasing a larger amount and then arresting him for possession with intent to distribute. The individual never did reestablish contact, so we decide to arrest him hoping to solicit his cooperation in identifying others. We planned to go to his place of employment—Caesar's—where he worked in the kitchen. Accompanied by hotel security, we were headed through the main lobby to the kitchen. As we walked through the lobby, my Walter PPK 380 semi-automatic handgun slipped from my pants waistband down my right leg. The handgun then bounced off the top of my right foot and slid across the polished marble floor ten feet out in front of us. Not wanting to create a scene, I kept walking and bent down, casually picking up the handgun, then stuck it back in my waistband and kept going as if nothing had happened. Of course, I was regularly reminded of the incident. In life, I have learned that when you screw up, keep your head down and pray for someone else to screw up so you are not visible on the "radar."

Easter 1955, Sadie, Gil, Darla, Paula, Darlene, and little Eddie

Gil and Eddie, ages 15 and 8

Tom

Naomi

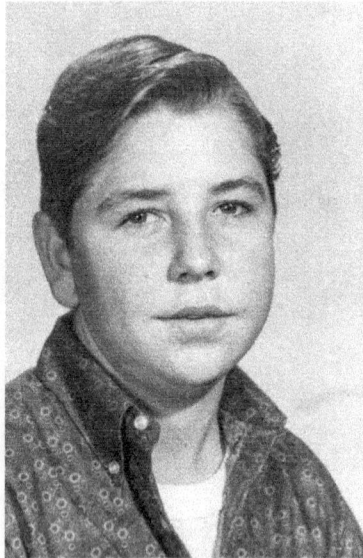

Gil, age 14 and 15

Eddie

Eddie and family

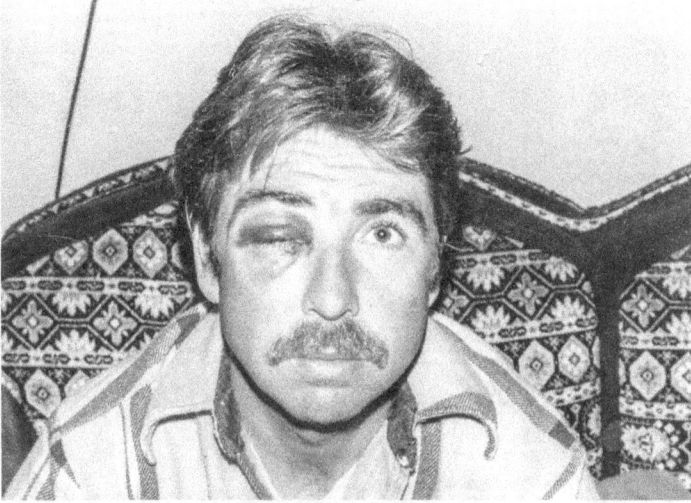

New Years '79

New Orleans, 1985, Gil and son.

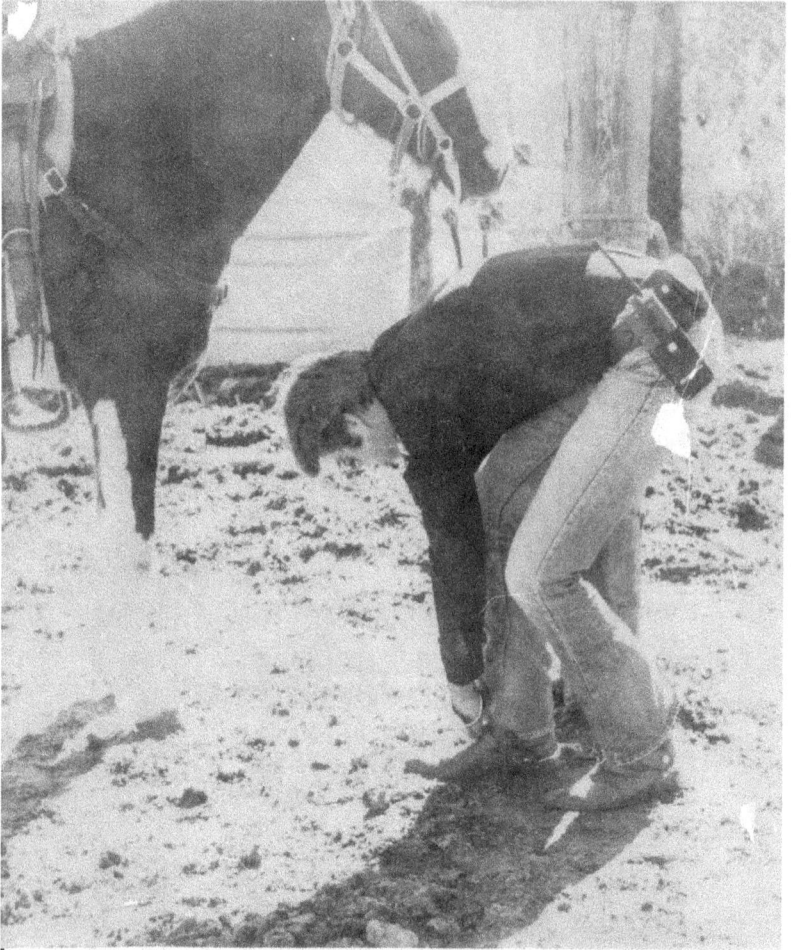

Heading for the telephone pole

Westwind aircraft

Aircraft that was used to transport 660 pounds of cocaine in to Nevada

America's Most Wanted

Some would soon ask, "Why didn't you leave well enough alone? Why didn't you just let sleeping dogs lie?" In time, I would ask myself the same questions. In time, I would ask myself why I didn't just keep my mouth shut. I was up to my neck in the three-year "Requiem to a Queen" case. I had my hands full because the case was just breaking open. Why did I add a new marriage, with two step-daughters? But no, I couldn't leave it alone. I was about to learn another hard lesson.

That year, I got the not-so-bright idea that I would submit the Matt Trevino case to the producers of the TV program AMERICA'S MOST WANTED in hopes that I could locate the two-year fugitive. First, I would have to write up the proposal and get agency approval. That turned out to be easy. To my surprise, the producers readily accepted the case. Next, I would have to assist the producers in reenacting the development of the case, the surveillance, the takedown, the delivery of the 100 kilos of cocaine, and Trevino's escape. The case was presented on national TV on July 29th, 1989. I was in the program's studio in Washington the night it aired, fielding leads to Trevino's whereabouts. I received some promising leads, but they were cold. I even learned from an ex-wife that Trevino was not his real name. His real name was

Ernesto Translavina. The next day, I was on a plane back to Las Vegas to follow up on the leads. A couple days later, I got a call from the FBI in New York advising that they had been contacted by an informant providing the whereabouts of Trevino. He was thought to be in Queens, New York, of all places.

However, his employer reported that Matt had left the country the day before the program aired for a business trip to Mexico City. Damn, seemed like a break always was always just out of reach. Now it would be a waiting game to see if he would come back. As it turned out, he had been tipped off by a girlfriend. After about 30 days, Matt contacted his girlfriend in New York. He asked her to bring him some money and his stereo equipment. It sounded like he was planning to stay in Mexico. I then got word that the girlfriend and her mother would be departing New York for Mexico City to visit Matt. So, I requested that agents in New York follow them to the airport and make sure they got on the plane. That was accomplished. I was told that the Agent in Charge in Los Angeles had given me carte blanche to do and go wherever I needed to go to pursue Matt. As soon as I got identifying data and confirmation that the two females were on their way, I hopped on a plane to Mexico City. I needed to be there before their flight, so I could identify them to Mexican Federal Police.

Again, the plan did not go as thought. I got to Mexico City on time. However, when the ladies arrived, they were not met by Matt, but by a cab driver. The Mexican Feds began following the cab as it left the airport. After a while, the cab driver made the surveillance and attempted to flee. That was a big mistake. The Mexican Feds ran the cab off the road and, after a little "attitude adjustment," the cab driver agreed to take them to where Matt was. Ironically, he was found about a block from the American Embassy. When approached by the Mex Feds, Matt denied his identity, claiming. "Me llamo Rodrigo, me llamo Rodrigo." After a little more of the same brand of "attitude adjustment," he remembered his name. He was hauled off to police headquarters.

I did not get to see Matt until 1:30 in the morning. By then, he had gone through a significant attitude adjustment. As I walked into the office where he meekly sat erect at a desk, I noticed that he had a big red whelp on the right side of his forehead, there was a spot of blood in his reddened right ear, and I noticed some blood-stained Kleenexes in the trashcan next to the desk. I walked up to him and asked Matt if he remembered me. His eyes lit up and he said, "Gil, am I going back with you? Am I going back with you?" Seems he was glad to see me and wanted to go back to the States with me. I was told to come back to the jail later that morning when he would be released to me.

When I showed back up the later that morning with two agents from the Mexico City office, I was kept waiting the entire day and finally told to come back the next day. Well, the next day, the same thing happened. On the third day, we waited all day again. Finally, one of the agents from Mexico City had had enough and demanded to see the commandante, which got their attention. The immigration officer started processing Matt for release. He did not want to have to explain to the commandante why we had been kept waiting three days.

Unfortunately, the only flight out to the States that night was to Chicago. I did not want to go to Chicago, but I was getting the hell out of Mexico. We proceeded to the airport and were met by the Mex Feds with Matt in tow. I put the handcuffs on him and we boarded the flight. En-route to Chicago, I telephonically contacted the America's Most Wanted representative and advised her that we were en-route to Chicago with Matt. On the flight, Matt said something very disturbing regarding his escape. At first, he said that he did not escape but that the DEA agent had let him go. Then he clarified it by saying the DEA agent had stopped to use a pay phone and while the agent was distracted on the phone, he just walked away. That contradicted the agent's version and what had been portrayed on America's Most Wanted. I would have to leave it for the moment. It was Matt's word against the DEA agent's. But that issue would come up again. We were met by the film crew in Chicago to record Matt's capture. My stock was high again, but not for long.

As we walked through the Customs area at Chicago's airport, the film crew followed us, filming as we walked. Matt was upset with having the lights and camera in his face, saying, "I can't help you anymore if you put this on TV." I just told him to smile because he was on national TV. Did he really think I was dumb enough to fall for that again? In time, Matt was extradited back to Las Vegas to stand trial.

Matt was looking at 20 years in prison for the 660 pounds of cocaine and another 5 years for the escape. It would take a week to present all the evidence and witnesses at the trial. Matt would be the defense's only witness. The prosecution had completed its case by Thursday morning. Matt took the witness stand Thursday afternoon. He claimed that, at the time of his arrest for the cocaine, he was doing an impromptu undercover operation for law enforcement. He was forced to do this by the smuggling organization and had attempted to contact law enforcement but was unsuccessful. Matt revealed what we had already discovered: that he was a fugitive from state narcotics charges out of Texas. That case was still pending against him and I would be subpoenaed to testify in that case. He also claimed that he did not escape, but that the DEA undercover agent had let him go. Critical to his claims was that, in cooperating with us in the controlled delivery of the 100 kilos of cocaine to his accomplice in Los Angeles, the government, meaning me, had made a lot of promises in exchange for his cooperation. According to his testimony, I had promised not to seize his aircraft. Fat chance of me not seizing his $240,000 aircraft, I thought, which he had purchased with drug proceeds. Supposedly, I had promised not to seize his home in Sandy Valley, Nevada, which was also purchased with drug proceeds, and that he would be allowed to assist the government in apprehending members of the organization, thus reducing his prison sentence. While still on the witness stand, Matt testified that his debriefing was recorded, and the promises were recorded. Matt stated while he was being debriefed that he kept asking, "Can we speak off the record, can we turn that thing off?" A faint bell went off in my head. Damn, where have I heard that statement before?

During the weeklong trial, all agents present during the debriefing, including me, testified that no promises were made, nor was the interview recorded. I testified that I took notes and used them to prepare my reports. Agents are not allowed to make any promises to defendants. Only the U.S. Attorney's office has that authority. There were only four agents present during the debriefing: myself, my supervisor, a senior agent, and a new hire agent that had just transferred over to our Customs office from the IRS office in Las Vegas. The new hire was in and out of the debriefing room during the lengthy debriefing. He had the perfect initials to fit his personality: "B.S." The undercover DEA agent testified that Matt jumped out of the undercover vehicle at a stoplight and he "had chased him."

As I left the courtroom on Thursday afternoon, I was troubled by Matt's statement. "Can we speak off the record, can we turn that thing off." Things were going to get more troubling that evening during a few beers at the Golden Nugget Casino.

At dinner and drinks that evening at the Golden Nugget Casino, the two Customs Agents—one being an internal affairs agent and the other a DEA undercover agent—and I began discussing Matt's claims. It is amazing what a few drinks can do to someone's memory and tongue. During the discussion, the DEA agent said, "The reason I didn't chase him was because there were still some kilos of cocaine left in the undercover vehicle and I did not want to leave it." One thing you acquire during a 29-year law enforcement career is a built-in bullshit meter, and my bullshit meter just registered 10 decibels. I called him on it, telling him that was bullshit because I had all the 100 kilos with me in my vehicle and I was sitting on it like a mother hen. Then he said, "Why should I chase him? You guys fucked that deal up." Now a big church bell was going off in my head. My built-in bullshit meter just went off the scale. Did he realize that he was admitting that he had committed perjury when he testified? Originally, he claimed that, as he stopped at a stoplight after the delivery of the cocaine, Trevino jumped out of his car and ran. He also claimed that he had chased Trevino but could not find him. His statement could make a difference in the escape charges, which carried a five-year prison sentence. I reminded him that the delivery portion of the case was a DEA Los Angeles operation, not a Customs Las Vegas operation. That shut him up.

He had just put me in a bad position. There were two other witnesses to what he had just said and, unfortunately for me, one was a Customs Internal Affairs agent. I had to report this to the U.S. Attorney's office. It was a bad position to be in, to have to rat out another federal agent. But it could cost me my job if I did not report it.

The next day was Friday and the last day of the trial. The jury convicted Matt on all charges. He was sentenced to 25 years to be served. I just wished that would have ended it. But that was not to be the case.

On Saturday, I found myself assigned to a stationary surveillance, watching a residence that another agent was attempting to obtain a search warrant for. I sat most of the day watching the house and thinking about that phrase, "Can we speak off the record, can we turn that thing off?" Then it hit me. Matt had said that. Agent B.S. did have a micro cassette recording in the debriefing room. Then I remembered the rest of it. I needed to speak to the Assistant U.S. Attorney first thing Monday morning. I did not realize the far-reaching implications of what I was about to do.

When I met with Assistant U.S. Attorney, Ben Little, I prefaced the conversation with, "I don't know if I should tell you this now or wait until after the appeal." His immediate response was, "You had better tell me now." I told him about the disturbing conversation with the DEA agent. I told him that Agent B.S. did have a recorder in the debriefing room that day. I also related what Agent B.S. told me about what he did with the tape and why. B.S. originally told me that he had destroyed the tape because there was nothing of importance on it. Ben was in the middle of preparing documents for another case and told me to come back later so I could give a sworn statement that would be forwarded to the presiding judge in the case. Later, my sworn affidavit was forwarded to the presiding judge. Ben took it much better than I expected.

Months earlier, the "Requiem to a Queen" case had broken wide open when Don and I rolled one of the co-conspirators in the case. George was a good man who'd been tempted by substantial amounts of cash to step across the line into the criminal life. Maybe it was his wife's advanced cancer that forced his hand. George was, like me, a worrier, a fretter and he could not handle what we had done to him. He had to come clean. He had to spill his guts. Through information provided by George, we finally identified the "father of the conspiracy," Will Hodges. Will owned and piloted the original smuggling aircraft that had crashed in Mexico with the heir apparent to the organization with him. Now Don and I were hot on his trail. We soon found the old desert rat.

Actually, he looked more like a desert weasel with his beady eyes and coke-bottle glasses perched on his chinless face.

We learned that Hodges had had his current aircraft seized by U.S. Customs for improper documentation when he entered the U.S. and he was petitioning to have his aircraft returned. We contacted the agent in Los Angeles who was handling the case to get his help in locating and meeting Hodges. The first couple of requests for assistance were unsuccessful. Finally, on the third attempt, the agent admitted that he had "kinda" dropped the ball on locating Hodges but he would now renew his efforts. He admitted that he had not returned Hodges's calls. He finally called back, stating that he had located Hodges and had scheduled a meeting with him. The agent understood that Don and I, Task Force agents, intended to meet with him and Hodges. The meeting was scheduled for a future date. We knew we had to get Hodges to cooperate.

As it turned out, on the scheduled date of the meeting with Hodges, I was assigned a Civil Air Patrol flight from Las Vegas to Lake Havasu, Arizona, to pick up blood from a blood drive there and transport it back to Las Vegas. Also, the Agent in Charge of our office was absent, so I had assumed his duties for the day. Don and I decided that Don would attend the initial meeting with Hodges: my first mistake. The meeting was scheduled for later that day in Yucca Valley, California. About mid-day, I received a call from the agent in Los Angeles asking about my arrival time. I informed him of my situation and that Don would attend the meeting. The agent went ballistic, shouting at me and telling me, "Don is not going to meet Hodges and for me to 'turn him around.'" I explained that I couldn't, and Don was already en-route. The agent hung up on me.

I contacted the agent's supervisor in Los Angeles, asking him to intervene. Apparently, that did not happen. My concern was how unsuspecting Don was going to be treated as he arrived at the meet location. I would learn the next day what had transpired. Hodges had already arrived at the meet location. Don got there shortly thereafter. Don approached Hodges and introduced himself. Don and Hodges sat down to talk when the Los Angeles Customs agent walked in, walked up to their table, and, pointing a finger at Hodges, said, "If you planned to talk to him—" pointing a finger at Don "—then I am leaving." He walked out the door, got in his car, and sped off. But Don and Hodges connected. The following week, Hodges was in our office being interviewed by both Don and me.

The next day I was told by my supervisor that the assistant agent in charge in Los Angeles who had oversight of the Las Vegas office had ordered me to write a memo about the incident. I tried to talk my way out of it, explaining that I was not even there and did not know what had happened. I was ordered to write the memo. I agreed to write the memo as directed, but I pulled no punches: my second mistake. I wrote a "tongue-in cheek" sarcastic memo blasting the unprofessional conduct of one federal agent toward another. Some of my comments were edited out before my memo got out of the office. But I think the phrase, "had someone taken the bull by the horns, or in this case, the rabid dog by the tail, the incident could have been avoided," may have been the slap in the face to the new short Hispanic manager, Adolph Rivera.

The next day, Adolph, accompanied by another manger, was in our office to have a talk with me. I was summoned to the conference room and sat in front of the two managers. Adolph slid a memo across the table to me, which informed me that I was to "receive punitive action" for my part in the incident. Hell, "punitive action?" He obviously did not know the agency disciplinary procedures yet. It was only a matter of semantics, but it was a mistake on his part. I was not going to make a third mistake now that I saw that Adolph did not appreciate my sense of humor. When Adolph saw that I was not going to be confrontational, he seemed to relax.

As the meeting ended, I asked, "What is the range of discipline that I might face?"

He responded, "Well, you aren't going to be transferred." I asked if he was seriously thinking about transferring me over this. He said it was considered. Hell, that was not even on the table of discipline for a first offense. According to Adolph, I should have never allowed an agent from another agency to participate in "an informant development meeting." What the hell was he talking about? I had never heard of it being a violation of procedure to allow another Federal Agent to meet with a potential Customs informant. Hodges was either going to be an indicted coconspirator or an unindicted coconspirator, his choice. Again, it was matter of semantics. Don had gone to "seek the cooperation" of Hodges in the conspiracy investigation. The matter seemed to have pushed to the back burner. I went back to work on the Requiem to a Queen case and the Trevino case.

We indicted 20 people in the Requiem to a Queen investigation, including the second heir apparent, pilot Bert Williamson, who was extradited from the Philippines where he was hiding. The indictment was then unsealed. It became apparent to the organization that George was cooperating since he was not an indicted coconspirator. One of the members of the organization put out a "contract" on George. To ensure his safety, I hid him at a secret location in Las Vegas. Each day, it was my responsibility to pick him up and transport him to the U.S. Attorney's office, where we debriefed him. On one Friday morning, I arrived at the location to pick George up.

As George sat in my vehicle, he said, "I have been reading about you in the paper, and you were on TV also."

"What are you talking about, George?" I asked. He told me it had something to do with a judge overturning a conviction in one of my drug cases because of a missing tape. Oh shit, I knew what he was talking about. My stock just went back in the toilet again. By Monday morning, my stock would be in the septic tank. There was a 10-month storm a-brewing.

When I got to the U.S. Attorney's office, I learned that the presiding judge had overturned Matt Trevino's conviction because of the infamous missing tape. The attorney, Ben Little, did not seem to be concerned. He just said he should have requested a hearing on the matter when he submitted my affidavit. He would now request a hearing on the matter. That was some temporary relief. Monday morning, it would not make a difference. Meanwhile, my supervisor had faxed a copy of the Las Vegas Review Journal Newspaper article to Adolph in Los Angeles regarding the conviction being overturned due to the missing tape recording.

Monday afternoon, I was summoned to my supervisor's office, where Adolph was seated at the supervisor's desk with my supervisor seated off to the side. Adolph prefaced the conversation with, "I have bad news for you, Gil. You are being transferred to our office in Terminal Island, California. We will do what we can to accommodate your wife, Lucia." I felt like Steve McQueen's character in the western movie Tom Horn when he was called to the witness stand to testify at his murder trial.

I thought to myself, You are going to say what you are going to say, you are going to do what you are going to do, and I am not going to give you the satisfaction. I was not visibly upset, but in my mind, I was thinking, You pencil dick little man, you puss of an excuse for a man, I will not give you the satisfaction, you would not make a pimple on a real man's ass. Adolph attempted to bring up what Lucia's intentions might be. I was thinking, You dumb ass, you can't discuss another employee's options with me, you have to discuss them with that employee. Adolph then informed me that I was a good investigator but a poor agent. He said that the U.S. Customs Service was like the military, and he was my sergeant. After Adolph left, my supervisor told me that I handled that very well. Never telegraph your intentions, I thought.

I later learned that Adolph had been to the U.S. Attorney's office that morning to discuss my transfer, which would impact the

Requiem to a Queen investigation. Adolph asked the supervising attorney if the case could be prosecuted without Gil. The attorney responded, that, short of him dying, no. Adolph informed that him he would do what he could to accommodate the attorney in the prosecution of the case. Adolph and I were about to enter a 10-month legal battle that would cost the government $23,700 in attorney's fees and tens of thousands of dollars in moving expenses.

In my experience, "suits" rise quickly to the top in government service on the back of others. Many times, the "suits" are motivated not by a sense of job performance but by a quest for power over others. The "suits" recognize that "fast tracking," sucking up to a person in a position of authority, is a faster way to rise to the top of the ladder than doing the job. They might also recognize their own inability to do the job that they were hired to do. They have no shame nor see any indignity in their actions. They have no empathy for their fellow workers. Throughout the next few years, I would receive bits and pieces of information about the rise and fall of Adolph Rivera. I met him on his second rise after he had hidden his first fall by changing agencies. Many of those with his type "A" personality shine in their first year, but in their second year, their actions are questioned, and in the third year, they are finally muzzled, but only after they have done harm to many good people who just want to do their job. I always referred to this as the 'three-year cycle." In my 40-year career, I saw so many of these types quickly rise to the top and then crash and burn, to just finish out their time to retire. Some are what I call "one-case-wonders." They develop one major case, participate in one major case, or take credit for involvement in one major case, then rest on their own or someone else's laurels. In their quest to quickly rise to the top of the ladder, they must climb over others as they work their way to the top.

It was reported to me (but never proven) that as an FBI agent, Adolph's first rise came when he joined a Hispanic class action against the FBI, claiming discrimination. It was alleged to me also that Adolph joined the class action suit after it was originally filed. When the suit was decided in the Hispanic agents' favor, those participants were promoted to management positions within the FBI. Allegedly Adolph received a promotion to a management position in a small FBI office in the Indianapolis area. The story goes that as a manager of this office, he started "keeping book" on his subordinates. The subordinates, including the office secretary, in turn started "keeping book" on Adolph. What goes around comes around. They would allege that Adolph had submitted reimbursement vouchers claiming lodging expenses he had not incurred. Supposedly, an FBI inspection revealed that the subordinate's allegations were true. Payback is a bitch. According to the information I received, Adolph was demoted and transferred to New York City. These allegations would become critical to Adolph's career several years later.

In the mid-1980s, Adolph and several other FBI agents from the New York City office were hired by the U.S Customs Service Office of Investigation to staff positions on the West Coast. Adolph quickly worked his way into a staff position then into management. Another thing I have learned over my 40-year career is that when employees "jump ship" from a prestigious agency like the

FBI to a less prestigious agency, those employees may have issues within their agency. Such would be the case with Adolph. The FBI has always been recognized as very professional law enforcement agency (until the Obama era). That is why I later recommended that my son accept a Special Agent position with the FBI over a position with Immigration and Customs Enforcement (ICE). I am very proud of him being an FBI agent.

I was soon notified in writing that I was being force transferred to the Terminal Island office. In the notification letter, I was given the choices of accepting the position, resigning, or being terminated. The letter further stated that the reason for my transfer was that "I had been determined to be an expert in narcotics investigations and my expertise was needed in Los Angeles" but I would be assigned to a financial investigations group upon my arrival in Los Angeles. There went my bullshit meter again. I contacted the manager in charge of the financial group in Los Angeles, telling him about my transfer and the reason. His response was, "That is hogwash." This was a classic example of the "power theory." If someone becomes knowledgeable in a particular endeavor, they gain power and, therefore, they must be removed from that endeavor and placed in one in which they have no knowledge, thus removing their power.

I would have 15 days to make my decision. On the 13th day, I accepted the position. My plan was to leave Lucia and the daughters in our new home in Las Vegas while I found temporary lodging in the Los Angeles area. I had a class "A" motor home that I intended to live in during the work week, returning to Las Vegas on the weekends. This was not an effective way to start out a new relationship with anyone.

Soon after that, U.S. Attorney Ben Little requested a hearing before the presiding judge in the Trevino case. On the way to the courthouse to testify at the hearing that day, I saw my ex-wife, June, walking down the street toward the court house, but I never gave it much thought. In hindsight, when you see your ex-wife in the vicinity of the courthouse, just figure you are not going to have a good day. Evidently, she had contacted Matt's defense attorney, informing him that I routinely carried a micro-cassette recorder in my briefcase. Matt's attorney knew the judge would never let an ex-wife testify in the hearing, but the attorney obviously wanted June there for the "shock effect" just to intimidate me. I testified at the hearing regarding the missing tape. I did remember Trevino making the statement about speaking off the recording and turning the recorder off. I further remembered that Agent B.S. was the one who had the micro cassette recorder. He kept trying to record the debriefing, but Trevino kept asking to turn it off. Three days after Trevino's arrest, Agent B.S. handed me some notes saying that those were the notes he transcribed from the tape before he destroyed the tape. There seemed to be little interest in the DEA agent's contradictory testimony. Within a few days, the presiding judge had reinstated Trevino's conviction. The judge actually stated in his decision that Agent Andrew's actions of coming forward were "laudable." I had hopes that the conviction being reinstated would change Adolph's mind, but I was mistaken. He would still come after me with everything he could fabricate. The lines had been drawn. The issue over the missing tape was also investigated by Internal Affairs, which exonerated me.

I immediately filed an agency grievance claiming that the forced transfer was "punitive" in nature as cited in Adolph's original memo. According to the agency disciplinary procedures, disciplinary action is to be corrective in nature, not "punitive." I also contacted attorney Susanne Lawrence in Washington D.C. Susanne's firm specialized in adverse personnel actions against government employees. After reviewing my case, she filed a Merit System Protect Board case against the agency, citing protection under the Whistle Blower Protection Act. Neither disclosure to the U.S. Attorney regarding the missing tape issue, nor the contradictory testimony of the DEA agent could be used to take disciplinary action against me. It would become critical to the issue as to when and who decided to transfer me. Adolph and my immediate supervisor were subpoenaed by my attorney for depositions. Lies are hard to remember, as Adolph would soon discover. My supervisor testified first, stating he was contacted by Adolph on Saturday after the newspaper article was faxed to Adolph. He further stated that Adolph told him that he would have to discipline me for the issue. My supervisor also stated that he did not want to transfer me. He also did not want to lose Lucia or me because we "hit the ground running" when it came to doing our jobs. Immediately afterwards, Adolph testified that he had made the decisions to transfer me on Thursday, the day before the news article came out. That was a contradiction between the two government's witnesses. My attorney never caught the contradiction, but I did, and so did the government attorney. Someone was lying, and it wasn't me.

My case was reviewed by a federal judge in Denver, Colorado. Before my transfer was to take effect, the judge issued a court order against the agency, preventing them from transferring me until the matter was settled and further ordering the agency to negotiate with me to settle the matter. Effectively, he was saying he believed that the plaintiff had a valid case and it would be in the government's best interest to settle the case. That sent shock waves throughout the agency. Susanne was stunned. Her stock in her firm skyrocketed. It was the first time anyone had gotten such an order in a Whistle Blower case.

Now the agency gloves were about to come off. Now they were to contradict themselves again. I was no longer being transferred because I was an expert. Now it was because I was a worthless piece of crap. The agency even had a statement from Barry Grisham in Memphis stating that I was a poor agent. I reminded the agency that Barry had been demoted two grades from his Agent in Charge position and forced transferred to a three-man office. They were now saying I was being transferred for the "totality of the circumstances." They were even then saying that because I at times found myself in a temporary management position over Lucia, which could create a conflict of interest. They did not cite any specific instance where I had acted inappropriately, but employees "could perceive" that there could be a conflict. There is that word "perceive" again.

Then the agency, mainly Adolph, started the time proven harassment campaign. On Fridays at 4:30 p.m., I would be called back to the office for some drummed up counseling session. My supervisor actually came to my house on a day off to issue me a letter of reprimand for accepting a call from an agent in Tucson, Arizona. That was a calculated plan to demoralize me, to break me, so I would throw in the towel and accept one of the agencies' offered compromises.

From the beginning, I told Susanne and the agency that I would only accept a transfer to another state, like Nevada, that did not have a state income tax. Accepting a transfer to state with an income tax would mean a significant reduction in take-home pay. I offered to take a transfer to El Paso, Texas, the home town of Lucia and her daughters. I felt that by them relocating back to El Paso, it would be less disruptive for the two daughters. Initially, that was rejected, citing that it would create the perception to other employees that "I had won." I also offered to take a voluntary reduction in grade back to journeyman agent, thus eliminating any perceived conflict of interest if that was "truly a matter of concern." Initially, the agency did not respond to that offer. In time, I was offered a position in Riverside, California, but I knew that was a trap. If I had accepted that position, I could be transferred to Terminal Island in short order. Because of the proximity to the Terminal Island office, that would not be deemed an adverse action. In short order, I was offered transfers to Laredo and McAllen, Texas, which I rejected. Then, out of the clear blue sky, they decided to accept my offer to take a voluntary reduction in grade and remain in Las Vegas. It was settled, or so I thought. A few days later, I was returning from testifying in a case in Flagstaff, Arizona, when I received a call from Susanne. She had been trying to reach me all day. The agency had reneged on the offer for me to take a voluntary reduction in grade, but they were now offering, after a 10-month emotional battle, transfers for both Lucia and me to El Paso, Texas. They would also pay all my $23,700 in attorney's fees. The agency was now offering paid moves for us both as separate employees, to include 60 days of lodging and meals. They would also be paying some the cost of buying a new house. What in the hell happened? I never did find out.

Susanne Lawrence soon gained a national reputation and in time stopped taking new clients. She liked to say that she had a house in Florida that the U.S. Customs service bought for her by defending their employees from adverse actions proposed by management.

Before I was to leave Las Vegas, I was subpoenaed to testify at Matt Trevino's hearing on his state charges in Dallas, Texas. Matt's public defender requested a hearing to argue dismissal of his state charges based on the allegation that I had kidnapped him from Mexico and the state had violated Matt's speedy trial rights. It was the most unusual court proceedings I ever attended in 29 years in law enforcement. The public defender called me to the stand to testify about Matt's capture in Mexico and his return to the United States. Matt claimed that I kidnapped him from Mexico, but that was quickly rejected. During the whole proceeding, the state judge read the local paper while he listened with one ear to the arguments. The public defender then did something so unusual that I could not believe it was happening. He informed the judge that he had requested that the court clerk testify about the numerous times Matt's case had been before the court but had been continued, thus denying his right to a speedy trial. The clerk had actually left the courthouse to avoid testifying. The public defender then advised the judge that since he could not locate the court clerk, he requested that the judge testify about the previous appearances and continuances. He informed that judge that he would not have to take an oath to tell the truth and he could testify from the bench. The judge agreed to answer questions by the public defender from the bench while he continued to read the paper.

After questioning the judge, the public defender informed the judge he would call himself to testify. The judge allowed him to take the oath and testify standing before the judge. The motion to dismiss was quickly denied. Before the proceedings started, I had an opportunity to talk with Matt. He was very proud to tell me that he had an excellent job in federal prison teaching English to other inmates and that he also taught classical guitar. But the highlight of the whole proceeding was when it was time for the state inmates to return to county lockup. They were all shackled together in an old-style chain gang before leaving the court room. Matt was shackled in the lead position and when it was time to leave, he began giving orders to the other inmates—"Hey guys, come on we have to go!"—and led the chain gang out of the court room. I would have given any thing for a picture of that.

I was to report to El Paso in February of 1991. However, before I got there, word got back to me that Lucia and I should buy a house on the west side of town because I was going to be assigned to work at the Las Cruces Office, New Mexico, 40 miles north. The retaliation was to continue.

During these 10 months of emotional agony, I drank frequently to self-medicate myself against all the stress. I kept the stress bottled up inside of me, and as expected, it had a significant effect on my new relationship with Lucia and her daughters. I was withdrawn, and the strain was obvious to all those around. Those four years working in Las Vegas took a heavy toll on me.

Right in the middle of all this nightmare, I got a call from my brother, Eddie. He wanted to borrow $1500. He told me that he and his wife had been arrested for dealing meth. The narcs had done a search on their house and found some meth underneath the mattress in the baby's basinet. I told him that I was unable to give him the loan. I learned later that Eddie pled guilty to the charges in exchange for the charges being dismissed against his wife. Since he had a job, he was sentenced to weekends in jail and probation. I would not hear from him again for 17 years. Things had gone from bad to worse for him.

Requim to a Queen

Before leaving Las Vegas, I was instructed to concentrate my efforts on the Requiem to a Queen case, which I did. However, Adolf would later claim that I was instructed to concentrate my efforts "exclusively" on the case. One afternoon, when I returned to my office, I found a handwritten note informing me that an agent from Tucson, Arizona, requested that I return his call. My supervisor left the message for me. I called the agent, whom I had never met. He wanted me to telephone a person living in Las Vegas to determine if the person might be interested cooperating in a narcotics investigation and becoming an informant for the government. Initially, I told the agent that I would have to refer his request to the agent in charge for assignment. The agent insisted that I make the contact with the individual. Against my better judgment, I agreed to make the contact.

The call to the individual was very brief. He informed me that he was not interested in cooperating with the government. I did not detect any hostility. I then advised the agent in Tucson of the results of the call. The whole matter took approximately 10 minutes. The next morning, I was sitting on a bench outside the Federal Court room, waiting to meet with the Assistant U.S. Attorney. My supervisor approached me, wanting me to explain my actions regarding that phone call to the individual. I unsuspectingly recounted the brief incident. He then informed me that the individual had contacted our Sector Communications Center in Los Angeles the night before, complaining about my phone call to him. The individual had threatened my life. He further informed me that Internal Affairs was opening an investigation into the matter as a result of the threat. Apparently, the phone call enraged the individual and he called our Sector Communications Center to vent his anger. I never gave the matter much thought after that.

A few days later, on a Friday when I was on a day of annual leave, my supervisor called me at my home. He wanted me to come to the office regarding the matter of the call. I reminded him that I was on annual leave. He insisted that he come to my home to meet with me over the matter. When he arrived, he informed me that he was issuing me a formal Letter of Reprimand for disobeying his orders by making that telephone call. Again, it was a matter of semantics as to whether his instructions included the word "exclusively." I always believed that Adolf put the Hispanic Tucson agent up to calling me to persuade me to make the contact with the individual, knowing that the individual was hostile. I even wondered if the agent was actually the person that called the communications center. I also believed that my supervisor was forced by Adolf to issue the Letter of Reprimand, then delivering it to me at my home. I did not protest the letter of reprimand nor show any disrespect to my supervisor. As far as I was concerned, the letter of reprimand was just something to wipe my ass with. It was just further retaliation by Adolf in his attempts to demoralize me. The letter could also be used as fodder to justify his actions. In my opinion, it was mainly about payback. From that point, on I was not even allowed to receive telephone request from other agents or agencies.

My supervisor later admitted to me that Adolf told him that if he did not follow his orders, he would be transferred as well. My supervisor was just trying to make it to retirement without being forced transferred, but Adolf was determined to "break his back" if he did not follow his orders. I found the whole incident petty and was amazed at the extent a manager in the Federal Government would go to avenge his bruised ego. Unfortunately, Adolf and I were not yet finished with each other.

Much later, I would learn that Adolph's attempt to transfer me was motivated in part by his desire to create a Senior Agent vacancy in Las Vegas, thus allowing him to transfer one of his FBI buddies from San Diego to fill my position. Supposedly his buddy got impatient due to me challenging the transfer and moved on to greener pastures. However, a female African-American former FBI agent was then transferred from San Diego to fill my vacancy. She soon became management's worst nightmare by creating multiple EEO issues.

The "Requiem to Queen" case was originally started in 1986 before I arrived in Las Vegas. An aircraft broker, Al Donnelly, from San Jose, California, had come to the attention of U.S. Customs when it was discovered that he had not properly reported the sale of aircraft to the F.A.A. Subsequently, Al and his wife, Brenda, would soon begin cooperating with Customs in exchange for leniency. Initially, he identified a major narcotics violator in San Bernardino, California, Rigoberto Lizarraga. He was having large shipments of marijuana and cocaine flown into the Las Vegas area and then driven overland back to Los Angeles, California. As was the modus operandi when building a large smuggling operation, many violators started out with shipments of marijuana, but they soon realized the bulk required to produce the same profits, which could be obtained with smaller amounts of cocaine. By 1986, Lizarraga was having multi-hundred kilos of cocaine flown into the Henderson, Nevada, and Las Vegas's McCarran Airport utilizing three different pilots: William Hodges, Harry Ashley and, subsequently, Bert Williamson.

The original pilot for the organization was a 60-year-old, down-on-his-luck pilot named William, known as Will, Hodges. "Old Will" had been smuggling narcotics in aircraft since the early 70s. His failing eyesight meant he was no longer able to pass his medical exam, thus losing his F.A.A medical certificate. In the early 70s, Will lived in Napa, California. He regularly flew his Queen Aire aircraft to Mexico to pick up shipments of marijuana, which he flew into China Lake, California, to drop off. He then would then continue on to Napa, where he lived with his wife, and later, his young daughter. As his eyesight failed him, he began wearing coke-bottle eye glasses just to get around. Will continued to operate his aircraft even though his medical certificate was no longer valid. By 1985, "Old Will" would find himself cut out of in the smuggling organization by the heir apparent pilot, Harry Ashley. It seems that Will recruited and trained retired navy chief Harry to be his copilot. Harry spent 25 years in the Navy as an aircraft mechanic. Ironically, Harry retired out of the Navy at Memphis Naval Air Station a few years before I was assigned to Memphis. One of my flight instructors at the Navy Flying Club was a close friend of Harry's. Originally, Will and Harry were using Will's twin engine Queen Aire aircraft, FAA tail registration number N911CF, to smuggle shipments of marijuana from Mexico into the Henderson, Nevada Airport, where they were off-loaded in Harry's aircraft maintenance hangar, assisted by his two sons, Bobby and Sammy.

On one of their trips to Mexico to pick up a shipment of marijuana, Will and Harry attempted to land on a dirt airstrip they regularly used. But there had been rain the night before. When they touched down, they realized that the airstrip was too muddy to land. Before they could abort the landing, the landing gear became bogged down in the mud and the nose gear collapsed, flipping the aircraft. Will and Harry were trapped inside; they had to use a survival ax to cut themselves out. Fortunately for them, there was no fire, and neither was seriously hurt. Eventually, they made their way back to Las Vegas via commercial carrier.

The organization now found itself without an aircraft. But Harry would soon remedy that by purchasing a newer King Aire aircraft. Since Will no longer had an aircraft, there was no need for his continued involvement in the operation. Besides, Harry had taken an immense dislike to Will over comments Will made about his own 8-year-old daughter. Apparently, Will and his wife had divorced. Custody of the young daughter was given to Will's wife. Not satisfied with the court's decision, Will kidnapped his daughter and fled to Yucca Valley, California, where he hid out in a "prepper type compound." They were living off the grid, with no electricity or city water accounts that could be used to trace his whereabouts. During one of their flights together, Will told Harry about bathing his 8-year-old daughter, describing how as he bathed her pubic area and thought to himself how "someday, some guy will be playing with that thing." The comment so disgusted Harry that he wanted no part of Will, especially now that they were not using his aircraft anymore. Harry started flying loads out of Mexico unbeknownst to Will. Will eventually found out about the activity when he visited his contacts in Mexico and learned that Harry was still working for the organization. Will tried to cut himself back in the operation, but Harry wanted no part of him. Will made several attempts to blackmail the organization so they would give him a piece of the action. Will had to be careful not to expose himself to any criminal liability, at least until the statute of limitations of had expired. Besides, it could be unhealthy for Will if the Mexican organization felt threatened.

Harry then recruited and trained his heir apparent, Bert "E.T." Williamson. But Harry soon had doubts about the wisdom of training Bert to fly. Early into to his flight training, Bert intended to raise his wing flaps on takeoff but mistakenly grabbed the landing gear lever instead. He raised the landing gear while the aircraft was still on the ground, causing the aircraft to settle back to the runway, damaging the under carriage of Harry's single engine trainer aircraft. Bert successfully completed his initial flight training and rapidly got his rating in multi-engine aircraft. Bert eventually became "champion" pilot to the organization. He was paid 1.2 million dollars per trip for brazenly flying his Merlin II aircraft into Las Vegas McCarran airport in broad daylight, loaded with 1500 kilos of cocaine.

In 1986, President Reagan announced that cocaine was not considered a recreational use drug. For some reason, that announcement struck a nerve with Harry. He decided he no longer wanted to participate in the smuggling operation. Harry and his two sons, Bobby and Sammy, withdrew from the criminal conspiracy. Harry then owned a pristine Beechcraft King Aire, which was his pride and joy. With his Navy retirement and his proceeds from his smuggling career, he and his wife Dorothy would live out their years comfortably. Bobby, a pilot, and Sammy, an aircraft mechanic, parlayed their money into creating a legitimate Grand Canyon scenic tour operation out of Las Vegas airport. Bobby was the chief pilot and Sammy was the chief mechanic. Ironically, they would partner up with a retired Las Vegas police officer who was also a pilot. Bobby and Sammy were never charged with a crime.

Bert then found himself in need of an aircraft to continue his participation. He needed a new base of operation as well as a ground crew. Harry no longer wanted the operation based out of the small Henderson airport near his aircraft maintenance business. Harry and his sons successfully washed their hands and money of the criminal activity.

Bert took his accumulated proceeds and convinced an old Navy buddy of Harry's, a pilot named Errol Robertson, to fly cardboard boxes of cash back to the east coast to purchase an older Merlin aircraft. Bert was not satisfied with the aircraft when it was delivered. He instructed Errol to sell the aircraft in order to purchase a newer Merlin II aircraft. Again, Errol flew back to the east coast with cardboard boxes of cash to purchase another aircraft. Bert also convinced Errol to become his "spotter" pilot, providing security for him as he crossed into the U.S. from Mexico near Calexico, California. Errol's job was to fly to Calexico airport, then wait for communications from Bert that he was nearing the U.S./Mexico border. Errol then would get his aircraft airborne and fly orbits above the border to ensure that Bert was not being followed by U.S. Customs aircraft. Once given the all clear, Bert and Errol continued to the Las Vegas airport

Errol's participation in the operation was short lived due to a fatal crash at the Reno air races. Errol was racing his composite aircraft at the races. While in a left banking turn around a pylon, Errol's right wing clipped a dust devil, which tore off the wing. Errol's plane crashed, and Errol was killed instantly. Errol's crash was caught on the "Wings of Fire" video that year.

When I inherited the case in mid-1987, the previous case agent had already established a court authorized pen register on Bert's phones. This recorded the numbers of the incoming calls as well as the outgoing numbers dialed. One thing you learn in a 3-4-year criminal conspiracy investigation is that pen registers will not prove anyone's guilt, but they sure as hell will identify those involved in the conspiracy, as well as any paramours the conspirators might have. Bert and Harry had a couple young ones, unbeknownst to their wives. Bert's would cost him hundreds of thousands of dollars of his drug proceeds and his marriage to his wife, Martha. After Bert set his singer girlfriend up in her Las Vegas night club, The Nashville Club, she would "stomp on his heart," as he put it and make fun of his weathered, wrinkled face. She always described him as resembling "ET" the Extraterrestrial. Harry would divorce his wife of 25 years and run off to the gulf coast to motor around the waters of Florida with his new 23-year-old wife, Dawn, so she could sunbathe in the nude on board their vessel.

After Bert assumed the role of pilot for the organization, he recruited two old buddies from their days of working at the Sahara Hotel Casino. George Connelly and Jack Harrison helped him with the ground operation at McCarran Airport. Bert moved to Las Vegas from Loveland, Texas. Back in those days, he went every morning to the personnel office at the Sahara until he got hired for hotel maintenance. George was a pit boss at the Sahara and Jack was a dealer. George would later tell me that it was back in the days of the "skimming" operations, when the dealers and pit bosses skimmed money from the gambling tables.

After inheriting the case, I learned through Al Donnelly that Bert was in the process of buying eleven condominiums in Las Vegas for cash through real estate broker Larry Sheeler. Subsequently, we served a U.S. Customs administrative subpoena on the real estate broker for records pertaining to the sale of the eleven condominiums. Al then advised us that Sheeler tipped Bert off about the subpoena for the records. We immediately withdrew the subpoena, informing Sheeler that we had requested records for the wrong person. We allowed the sale of the eleven condos to close. We would seize the condos later. Al also told us Jack had a cold storage unit in the back of his house where the marijuana was being stored.

Sheeler's tip apparently caused Bert to panic. He decided to move his eighteen classic cars, which he kept in a shop behind his house, as well as eight suitcases of cash he was storing under his bed at his house. Bert moved sixteen of the cars, one which was the classic Buick sedan that Tom Cruise drove in the movie Rainman, to a storage facility in northeast Las Vegas, which was rented by Jack Harrison. The other two, a Stutz Blackhawk convertible, which he had purchased at the Imperial Palace car auction, and a classic Mercedes 280SL, along with the eight suitcases of cash, he stored in two adjoining storage sheds in a large storage complex off Sahara Ave. in Las Vegas. They were also rented by Jack Harrison.

As the investigation unfolded, I learned that Bert claimed that someone in his organization had ripped him off for a large amount of cash that he had hidden from law enforcement. In an attempt to learn who had stolen his money, Bert secretly taped recorded interrogations of members of his organization and gave the recorded interrogations to an individual who had a "voice stress analysis machine." Supposedly, the voice stress analysis machine could determine if someone was lying during the interrogations. Bert was unsuccessful in determining who was lying, so he hired a Swedish Psychic, Olaf Johnson, to go to the storage location to see if he could discover the identity of the thief. Olaf also was unsuccessful in his attempts to identify the thief. Bert would not know until four years later at his trial who stole two million dollars out of his three-million-dollar stash. By a stroke of monumental luck, Don Ware and I found the career criminal in a Nevada State Prison. He did not have a single penny left of the two million dollars. As Don and I ended the interview with the individual, he asked, "Mr. Andrews, could you help get my wife get on welfare?" I could only shake my head, knowing that just a couple years earlier, he was a "tax free" millionaire. His wife, a former prostitute, was back to her old tricks.

Shortly after I inherited the case, through the pen register and through tips from Al Donnelly, we were able to identify members of Bert's ground crew as well as a Las Vegas cocaine dealer who was dealing large quantities of cocaine provided by Bert. The dealer, Bernie Friel, a quadriplegic, was then selling large quantities of the cocaine to a dealer in Saint George, Utah, named Sir Hector "Sector" Johnson. Discovering Johnson's involvement would be the break in the case that would blow it wide open. Leonard Johnson had been dubbed Sir Hector back in his hippie days when he and his wife lived in a commune. In time, Sir Hector was shortened to Sector for convenience's sake.

Fortunately for us, the subsequent cooperation of Sector would revive the stalled case after we lost our eyes and ears in the case, Al Donnelly. Al's wife, Brenda, informed us that Al had hung himself in the shower of a motel room and that she was the one who discovered his lifeless body. According to Brenda, she and Al had been to a party at a friend's house and Al had become jealous over Brenda's interaction with another male at the party. After they returned to their motel room, an argument ensued over what had taken place at the party. Brenda subsequently went to bed, but Al stayed up drinking. When Brenda awoke a short time later, she discovered Al's body. It was a significant blow to the case. Years later, when we were trying to convince Brenda to testify in the case, a slip of the tongue by Don would insure that Brenda would never voluntarily testify. We were debriefing Brenda about her knowledge of the operation with the intent of convincing her to testify. Brenda informed us that she did not want to testify but Don was trying to persuade her to do so. Without thinking, Don told Brenda, "Why don't you go back home and sit down with Al and talk it over?" Brenda lost it. Too late, Don realized what he had just said. We never saw Brenda again.

Bernie Friel was an old friend of George. At one time, he had owned a profitable motorcycle sales/repair business in Las Vegas. However, Friel was an avid motocross racer and had crashed his motorcycle shortly after leaving the starting line in a race. He was run over by several competitors. Friel's neck was broken, leaving him a quadriplegic the rest of his life. Since Friel was racing in his jersey with his business logo on it, he filed for, and was awarded, a significant workman's compensation claim. He would require around the clock care. The State of Nevada awarded him $11,500 per month for life to hire nurses to attend to him. Friel did not hire qualified nurses but instead hired two of his nieces and another down-on-her-luck woman as attendants. Friel turned the women into coke whores by paying them at times with cocaine. Sector's wife once told Lucia and me that Friel offered her $1000 to sit on his face. She said she was tempted but was afraid that Friel would tell her husband. According to her, Friel regularly paid women to do that.

Friel was married at the time of his accident, but his wife soon came to a realization about the reality of being married to a quadriplegic and divorced him. Before doing so, she made a play for her husband's friend George. George rejected her advances, but he admitted he was tempted, saying that Friel's wife was a very good-looking woman.

With Al out of the picture, we were at a loss as to what direction to take with this investigation. But a drug deal gone wrong by Sector Johnson would revive the case. Sector sold a couple ounces of cocaine to a street level dealer in Sioux Falls, South Dakota. That was a big mistake on Sector's part. When arrested, the street dealer rolled over on Sector. He was indicted for possession with intent to distribute cocaine. Due to South Dakota's strict drug laws and sentences, he was looking at some serious time in a state prison. He took little convincing to cooperate in our investigation. On the day Don and I travelled to Sioux Falls to debrief Sector, it must have been the coldest day on record. Just walking down the street a half a block for lunch made my lungs hurt so bad from breathing the cold I could not stand to be outside. I was as happy as Sector to get the hell out of Sioux Falls. We had Sector released to our custody so he could make several cocaine buys off of Friel.

The plan was to wire up Sector with a body transmitter and

have him negotiate several "buy walks" (letting the dealer and government money walk) of cocaine from Friel, hopefully facilitated by George. It was not going to be easy. George was suspicious of Sector, and Friel lived on a dead-end street just two houses from the end of the street. Maintaining surveillance on Sector during the buys was going to be difficult, especially if there was any counter surveillance by Friel's people. To put the plan in motion, we first had to convince Don's DEA management to provide "buy" money for the cocaine, money that would not be recovered after the buy. We also had to convince them to provide additional money, so we could have Sector pay Friel money owed to him for previous cocaine deals. Amazingly, DEA management went for the plan.

The first two buys went as planned. It was amazing how well the body transmitter worked. Even when Sector excused himself at Friel's house to use the restroom, the sound of him urinating in the commode sounded like a small waterfall. There were some chuckles in the court room when that tape was played for the jury. Prior to the first two meetings, Friel had had someone, presumably his attendant, place the requested amount of cocaine in a drawer under his waterbed. Once the deal was agreed on, Sector would retrieve the cocaine from the drawer and replace it with the money. During both meetings, Sector made payments toward the $13,000 he had owed Friel and insisted that he meet with George, "the bookkeeper," so he could reconcile the balance owed. Initially, Friel and George balked at the meeting. Finally, on the third meeting, Sector convinced Friel to have George meet him. Sector left the buy money with Friel and was told to meet George at the end of the street. Sector and George discussed the amount owed then George told Sector to go back down to Friel's house and retrieve an ounce of cocaine from the bed of a pickup parked in Friel's driveway. Finally, we had George on tape doing a cocaine deal. As George left the area to return home, he was followed back to his house.

The next day, we got a search warrant for George's house. That evening, Don, an IRS agent, and I executed the search warrant on George's house. George's cancer-ridden wife was present during the search. We did not find any cocaine, but we did find financial documents and a baggie full of marijuana seeds in a floor safe in a closet. At the conclusion of the search, we excused ourselves and left George and his wife standing in their living room. They must have wondered what the hell just happened. But when a DEA agent, a Customs agent, and an IRS agent show up at your house with a search warrant, you can bet your future is not bright. George knew it.

Two weeks later, we got a call from George's attorney: George wanted to meet. It would be a tell-all meeting without the attorney staying for the entire meeting. George did not feel he needed the attorney present since he had made up his mind to come clean. The attorney excused himself shortly after the introductions. Over several debriefings, George provided a genesis of the smuggling operation, including the names of many of those involved in the smuggling operation as well as those involved in the distribution of the marijuana and cocaine in the Las Vegas area. George told us that not arresting him at the time we served the search warrant on him was the worst thing we could have done to him. Like me he was a fretter, a worrier. He said that after we left, he broke down and told his wife what he had been involved in. Then he met with his adult son and spilled his guts to him. He said it was the hardest thing ever had to do. He could not stop crying during the whole confession to his son.

George identified an old buddy of his, Jack Harrison, as the individual who originally stored the marijuana for the organization in a cold storage unit he had in the back of his house. George also repeated the same story Al told us about Bert being ripped off for a large amount of cash that he had hidden in a storage shed. Bert once bragged to George that "they may get me on taxes, but they won't get me with an ounce of dope." Bert had not filed taxes in five years. George told us that Jack rented the storage shed on Sahara Avenue for Bert. But George said no one believed Bert about the theft. We all thought that it was a story made up by Bert to justify to his wife Martha where all the money had gone. He said, "We all thought Bert had spent the money on his girlfriend Jane's nightclub." George also repeated the story about the Swedish Psychic, Olaf Johnson. Don and I had to verify as much of the information George provided as we could.

As we left the interview room that day, we ran into the IRS agent who was recently assigned to the case. Larry was the third IRS agent to be assigned to the case. The first two agents had been reassigned to other cases. Don and I recounted to Larry what we had just learned from George in the interview, including the story about the money being stolen out of the storage shed off Sahara Ave.

Then Larry said, "Just six months ago, I got a call from Las Vegas Metro Police about a guy they had stopped for brandishing a weapon out of the window of his vehicle as he was travelling down the freeway." According to Larry, someone had cut the guy off on the freeway so the guy, John Bruce, brandished a semi-automatic pistol out the window to the passing motorist. Las Vegas police caught up to Bruce just as he was pulling into a small RV park just off Sahara Ave, which adjoined a large storage facility. Bruce was staying with his friend, Tom Lepeck, and Tom's wife, in their small mobile home. The police officer arrested Bruce for violation of his probation since he was a convicted felon in possession of a firearm. The police officer found "trophy photos" Bruce had taken of a large stack of cash, along with his 9mm semi-automatic handgun lying on top of the stack of money. The police immediately suspected that the stack of money was probably drug proceeds, so he contacted the IRS. Larry responded to the call to interview Bruce. Larry was also convinced that the stack of money in the photo was drug proceeds. But it was not from John Bruce's drug operation. When asked where he got the money, Bruce told Larry that he found it when he burglarized a storage shed. Larry told Bruce that he was lying, insisting that the money was drug proceeds. "No sir, I found the money in a storage shed," was his response to Larry's accusations. Bruce was hauled off to jail and Larry never pursued it any further.

Don and I immediately realized that we needed to find Mr.

John Bruce. It would not be hard, as he was back in state prison just 30 miles north of Las Vegas. Don, Larry and I immediately set up an interview with Bruce at the prison. Bruce was very candid about his story. There was just one aspect I would never accept, but I could not break him on that portion. I have always believed that he was protecting his buddy, Tom Lepeck. We would soon learn how Bruce and Lepeck became "tax free" overnight millionaires.

Bruce claimed that his buddy, Tom, rented four adjoining storage sheds at the facility and was using them for an auto maintenance operation. According to Bruce, he and Lepeck had been working on cars for three days straight and they were high on meth. Bruce said that at about 12 midnight on the third night, he was so "wired" from the meth that he just had to get out of the shed and take a walk. Bruce claimed then he walked all the way to the other end of the 884-unit storage facility, which was a quarter of a mile long. He claimed that when he got to the other end, something happened that he could not explain because, "It was like a bolt of lightning hit me." He said, "You have to understand, Mr. Andrews, I have been a career burglar most of my life. Out of the last 20 years, I have been in prison 19 years." Something told him to break into the two storage sheds he was standing next to.

So, Bruce went back to Lepeck's shop to get some bolt cutters to cut the locks off the shed doors. Then he walked back to the same two storage sheds, removed the locks, and entered the sheds. Bruce said that inside the storage units was a white Stutz Blackhawk convertible and a Mercedes 280SL convertible. As he looked around the units, he noticed that there was a work bench in the back of the unit that was covered with a tarp. He lifted the tarp and discovered eight suitcases. Bruce said he opened the suitcases and discovered that they all were full of U.S. currency. Bruce claimed he got scared.

"I thought I had found some Mob money," he said. He then left the two units and walked back to where Lepeck was to get Lepeck's car. He then drove back to the two storage units and loaded up five of the suitcases, then drove back to Lepeck's shop. Bruce claimed that he and Lepeck had to wait until Lepeck's wife left for work that morning before they could return to Lepeck's mobile home. After Lepeck's wife left for work, Bruce and Lepeck took the suitcases to their mobile home and emptied them on the kitchen table. Bruce said, "There was so much money that we couldn't count it all, so we counted one stack and it contained $10,000 in it, so we just counted the stacks of money and we figured that we had two million dollars." He said that he gave half to Tom and he kept half, but they were convinced it was "Mob" money so they originally decided to not spend any of the money for a while. Bruce then said that he waited about three months, but he could not help himself. He started spending the money.

During the prison interview of Bruce, he amazingly would account for the expenditures of approximately half a million dollars of the money. He gave $10,000 to his brother to restore his Corvette and purchased a $13,000 necklace and a $13,000 engagement ring for his girlfriend, a prostitute, and so on. He also told us what happened to the remaining half a million dollars. According to Bruce, a friend of his, Robert Morris, owned a car stereo business in central Las Vegas. Morris was struggling financially and was close to losing his business. So, Bruce offered to invest some money in his business to help him out. He asked Morris how much he would need to get himself on his feet financially. Morris told Bruce that he figured that $300,000 would do the job. So, Bruce took his remaining cash over to Morris's business and gave it to his secretary. Bruce did not know how much money was in the bag he dropped off, but a few days later, Morris's secretary called him and told him that he had provided $11,000, more than the agreed-on amount. She told him he should come and get the $11,000. In approximately only one year after the burglary, Bruce was again penniless.

As we left the interview that day, we knew we had to track down Tom Lepeck and Robert Morris. Larry went after Lepeck and Don and I went after Morris. Don and I found Morris and his secretary at his business. Morris admitted that he had been provided with $300,000 by Bruce, but he claimed that there was no documentation of Bruce's investment. It was a "gentleman's agreement," just a handshake. When we interviewed the secretary, she too admitted that Bruce provided her with a hefty sum of cash in a bag. Don and I interviewed the secretary twice, but when we went back to interview her a third time, we learned that she and her boyfriend had skipped town. We subsequently learned that the bag contained approximately $511,000; $300,000 went to Morris, $11,000 went back to Bruce, and the secretary skipped town with approximately $200,000. We were never able to locate her or her boyfriend.

Larry's interview of Lepeck was much harder. When confronted by Larry about Bruce's statement that he gave him $1,000,000, Lepeck said that Bruce was lying. Lepeck said that the Bruce at one time did give him a brown paper bag containing money, but Lepeck said he gave it back. Who would a jury believe, Lepeck or a career criminal that was a meth freak? Lepeck was never charged with a crime. Larry did later learn that Lepeck had come up with a clever scheme to launder the $1,000,000. Many afternoons, he would take a large sum of currency to the Palace Station casino, where he would exchange the bills for an equal amount of silver dollars. Lepeck would then play the five-dollar slot machines until the girls in the change booth changed shift. After the shift change, Lepeck would take the silver dollars back to the change booth and cash it in for bills. At that time, if someone claimed he had over $3000 in gaming winnings, he would be required to complete an IRS form reporting the winnings. That was exactly what Lepeck wanted: to pay taxes on the some of the laundered money. One of the girls in the change booth told Larry that "Mr. Lepeck was one of the best five-dollar slot machine players she had seen." She was not aware that Lepeck had purchased most of the silver dollars not long before she started her shift. When Lepeck bought his 100+ acre ranch in southern Utah, he claimed he bought it with his gaming winnings. Larry could not prove otherwise.

The part about John Bruce's story I will never believe is that part about the burglary being a random "bolt of lightning." I believe that Lepeck's auto repair operation was actually a "chop shop." The units Lepeck rented were not equipped for a commercial auto repair operation. Adjacent to the storage facility was a Chevrolet dealership, which reported that some of their new vehicles had been broken into and the stereo systems removed. I also believe that either Lepeck or Bruce saw Bert when he stored the two vehicles in the sheds, and Bruce intended to burglarize the vehicles when he broke into the sheds. The car stereo thefts could explain the connection between Bruce and Morris, but Bruce would never admit to the chop shop operation.

After George provided us with Jack Harrison's name, we located him and went to interview him. During the interview, we asked Jack about the cold storage unit at his house and renting the storage sheds for Bert. He acknowledged that he had rented several storage sheds at Bert's request. We then asked if we could look in his cold storage unit. Jack readily agreed and opened the unit for our inspection. As I stood in the opened door way, the smell of marijuana overwhelmed me. There was no marijuana in the unit because it had been cleaned out, but visible in the sunlight shining through the opened doorway were several marijuana seeds. I think George had tipped off Jack before our visit. I collected the seeds in view of Jack, who was visibly shaken. Jack agreed to cooperate and took us to the two storage sheds he had rented for Burt.

We also wanted to locate Olaf Johnson, the Swedish Psychic, to verify that part of George's story. We located an address for an apartment complex in Las Vegas, so Don and I drove to the location to interview Johnson. There was no one at the address. We decided to leave and come back another time. As we drove down the street to leave, we saw an older male walking down the street toward the complex.

Don said, "That looks like an Olaf Johnson, let's ask him." Damn, it was Olaf Johnson. Ironically, he looked so much like Don that they could have been brothers. After we interviewed Johnson, we drove him to the Sahara storage facility, where he had unsuccessfully used his psychic powers to identify the thief.

Then it was time to bring in Bert's former girlfriend, Jane, for a serious interview. By then, Bert and Harry had gotten wind of the investigation and skipped town. Bert went to the Philippines to participate in the search for the fabled Yamashita Gold Treasure and Harry, with his new young wife, were cruising around the south Florida coast in their newly acquired boat, "DAWN."

Miss Jane, also known by her stage name, Calamity Jane, agreed to meet us at the IRS office to be interviewed. Present during the interview were Don, myself, Larry, his supervisor and the Assistant U.S. Attorney assigned to the case. As the five of us sat around the conference table, Jane openly described how she met Bert and how they became involved in an affair. According to her, Bert's nephew was the drummer in her band and Bert had travelled to Reno to see the band perform. After the gig in Reno was over, her band lined up a gig in Las Vegas. She said that she was living in her motorhome at the time. When she arrived in Las Vegas, Bert allowed her to park the motorhome on the back of his property. While living on the property, she came to feel sorry for Bert. Jane said that Bert's wife Martha was "always ragging on him." So, one morning, when Martha was out of town, she snuck over to Bert's house. She went into Bert's bedroom and "gave him a treat just to bolster his ego." Don and I were wondering the same thing then, and when I glanced over at Larry, I was sure he was too. Question was, should we ask what the treat was? No one asked.

Miss Jane claimed that because of the "treat," Bert became enamored with her and the affair between the two ensued. Bert invested large sums of money in helping her obtain her night-club and providing startup expenses to get the club open. Miss Jane even obtained a limited gaming license, which allowed her to operate 25 slot machines in her club. In the beginning, with Bert bankrolling her, she had headliner bands appearing at her club. She also admitted that she accompanied Bert and Harry to Mexico on some of their trips. The Mexican organization had told Harry and Bert that it would look better if women accompanied them on their visits. So, Jane set Harry up with her 23-year-old girlfriend Dawn. Harry became enamored with Dawn. Jane admitted that Bert had provided her with quantities of cocaine, some which she redistributed to others, even once to her ex-husband, David Sizemore, in Anchorage Alaska. Jane was now looking at money laundering charges as well as possession with intent to distribute cocaine. But we were after bigger fish, namely Bert and Harry, so she would cut a deal, as would many that were indicted.

George had told us that Jane regularly would do her Sharon Stone act from the *Basic Instinct* movie when unsuspecting men were around. According to George, Jane often did not wear underwear and had shaved her pubic area. When in the company of an unsuspecting male, she would subtly expose her shaved pubic area to him. Harry Ashley later told us that Jane had "flashed" him once when he visited her at her nightclub.

George also provided us with the name of a pilot in Reno, Nevada, who was to become the replacement pilot for Bert. Mike Edmonton would be a hard nut to crack. We would get him to confess, but he was not about to admit that some of his assets were derived from his illegal activities. Don and I tracked Mike down and, by a stroke of luck, we located his newly acquired older Queen Aire aircraft hidden in a hangar at the Chino, California, airport. We also discovered he owned a front business to create the appearance of being a legitimate businessman. When Don and I interviewed him, he initially requested an attorney, but he was soon to realize that Don and I would not go away. Eventually, he would cooperate in the investigation and admit that he "was trying to be a criminal." He would never admit that some of his assets were purchased with proceeds from his criminal activity. Someone had "schooled" Mike on the "cash hoard defense." Mike claimed that over the years, he acquired his money from real estate and business transactions. Mike further claimed that he did not trust banks, so, for many years, he kept his money in coffee cans buried in his back yard. Even Larry had to admit that a cash hoard defense is very hard to disprove. But Mike, too, would cut a deal with the government for leniency.

George also told us that old Will Hodges, five years from the day of the crash of his aircraft N911CF in Mexico, showed up in Las Vegas with his daughter to extort money from the organization. According to George, Will and his daughter purchased a cake at a local store. They then redecorated the cake, took it to Harry's house, and left it on the door step with a note that read "give me a piece of the cake." The cake had been redecorated with the words, "Requiem to a Queen" across the top, referring to the crash of Will's Queen Aire aircraft. Harry supposedly gave Will $3,000 to shut him up. Don and I were sure that this event furthered Will's participation in the conspiracy, but we could not convince the U.S. Attorney to see it our way.

Through an aircraft broker in Memphis, Tennessee, I was acquainted with, Sam Vires, I learned that Harry sold his King Aire aircraft and used the proceeds to purchase a boat in Alabama. We did locate the marine repair shop where Harry was having the vessel refurbished per his specifications. I monitored the repairs to the vessel. When the vessel was released, I placed the vessel "DAWN" on lookout with U.S. Customs and the U.S. Coast Guard.

Several months later, I received a call from the U.S. Customs office in Naples, Florida, advising that the Coast Guard encountered the Dawn motoring around the west coast of Florida. I was also advised that the Coast Guard was escorting the vessel back to their dock in Naples, Florida. Don and I travelled to Naples, Florida, arriving before the Coast Guard arrived at the dock. As the vessels docked, I learned from the officer of the Coast Guard vessel that Harry provided a driver's license as identification at the time his vessel was boarded. It turned out to be the driver's license belonging in to his brother.

As Harry stepped onto the dock, I approached him, saying, "Hi, Harry how are you?" Harry knew he was caught. Harry was placed under arrest for making a false statement to a federal officer, which carries a five-year prison sentence and a $10,000 fine. As we escorted Harry in handcuffs to the Coast Guard office with Dawn in tow, sobbing, she proclaimed her love to Harry: "Harry, I love you, I am sorry I have been such a bitch." The vessel was seized by U.S. Customs. Don and I tried to get Harry to cooperate against Bert and Lizarraga since Harry had withdrawn from the conspiracy during the marijuana phase of the operation. But Harry asked for an attorney. End of conversation.

After his trial and sentencing in Las Vegas, I had the opportunity to speak with Harry. I told him that had he cooperated with me in Florida, I could have saved him a 10-year prison sentence and the $100,000 in attorney's fees. Harry said that he knew that now. Dawn was not present at his trial. We never saw her again.

George informed us that Bert had gotten involved in the Yamashita Gold Treasure venture in the Philippines and had invested large sums of money in the venture. Supposedly, at the close of World War II, high-ranking Japanese imperial princes hid tons of looted gold bullion and other stolen treasure in caves and tunnels throughout the Philippines, to be recovered later. "This was the wealth of twelve Asian countries, accumulated over thousands of years. Some stories claim that the U.S. Government under President Harry Truman found a dozen of the vaults containing most of the treasure but decided to keep the discovery a state secret in order to create a secret global political action fund. The Black Eagle Trust would be used to bribe statesmen and military officers, and to buy elections for anti-communist political parties."[6]

However, through the years, many treasure seekers and scam artists solicited unsuspecting investors to the venture to locate caves rumored to still exist.

Bert attended one of the investment presentations in Las Vegas and was drawn into the hunt for the treasure in Manila. Bert sold his Merlin II aircraft, his Jaguar coupe, and some of his classic cars, and, using some of his remaining drug proceeds, became an investor in the operation. Bert also paid $75,000 to the Philippine government to become a resident of the Philippines so he could move to Manila and participate in the actual digging operations. Bert would not collect the proceeds from eleven of his classic cars. U. S. Customs would seize three of them, and I would seize the proceeds from the sale of the other eight.

One Friday, I drove by Bert's home and observed that a semi-tractor trailer was parked in the driveway with eight classic cars loaded on it. There was also a goose-neck trailer attached to a flatbed truck, which had three classic cars on it. The next day, Lucia and I were returning home in our personal vehicle when the two trucks passed us going in the opposite direction. Don lived nearby, so I had Lucia drop me off at Don's house. After I informed him of what I had observed, we jumped into Don's assigned government vehicle and gave chase. We caught up to the two vehicles as they were approaching Henderson, Nevada. Don did not have any red emergency lights in his vehicle so, as he was honking the vehicle's horn, I leaned out the vehicle window, flashing my badge at the semi-truck driver. Both trucks pulled to the side of the road. I approached the driver of the flatbed truck and learned that he was

Bert's brother. He was taking three of the classic cars to his classic car business in Oklahoma. The other eight were being taken to a classic car auction in Phoenix, Arizona. I contacted the Assistant U.S. Attorney assigned to the case, hoping he would authorize me to seize the eleven vehicles. The attorney would not authorize the seizure, instead opting for seizure of the proceeds from the sale. He did not want to burden the government with the expense of storing the vehicles. I documented the make, model, and vehicle numbers of the vehicles. At the time of the auction, I travelled to Phoenix to attend. Bert had not placed a reserve, a minimum sale price, on his vehicles, so they were sold to the highest bidder. I had arranged with the manager of the auction to seize the check from the sale. He did not want to hand the check to me. He wanted to hand the check to Martha. I could then take it from her. As Martha entered the manager's office, I was anxiously waiting. The manager handed her the check. I immediately presented Martha with a seizure warrant for the check. Martha broke down into tears and left the office. I later saw her outside on the street, still crying. Agents in Oklahoma City then seized the three other vehicles from Bert's brother.

After the 20 indictments were handed down in the Requiem to a Queen case, Bert and Rigoberto Lizarrago were the only two that had not surrendered or been taken into custody. Lizarrago was in Mexico and it was unlikely that he would be returned to the U.S. Bert was another story. It turned out that the DEA attaché in Manila had located where Bert was living with his young girlfriend. Through official DEA channels, we arranged to have Bert deported from the Philippines. Originally, we planned to travel to the Philippine to escort Bert back to the states. I thought it would be a good opportunity to get Bert talking on the long flight back. But Don was not of the same mind. He had never been to Hawaii before, so he saw an opportunity to get a trip to Hawaii at the government's expense. Originally, Don led me to believe that we would fly to Hawaii, then continue on to Manila. After we arrived in Hawaii, Don informed me that a Philippine Immigration Officer would escort Bert to Hawaii. We had to wait a day for the Pan Am 747 to arrive. Don was a happy camper. When Lucia found out I was in Hawaii while she was in El Paso unpacking our household goods from the move there, she was not a happy camper. I would hear about that for years. When the flight arrived in Hawaii, the airline personnel asked all passengers to remain seated as Don and I boarded the aircraft. We located the Immigration officer and Bert, then escorted them off the plane. Bert was placed in handcuffs and taken to a detention facility, where I provided him with a copy of the indictment. When he finished reading the indictment, his only comment was, "That George is one smart son-of-a bitch." Bert realized that George's name was not mentioned in the indictment, meaning he must have been cooperating with us.

Only four individuals out of the 20 went to trial: Harry, Bert, his wife Martha, and Friel. Martha was only charged with money laundering. She had squandered copious amounts of Bert's drug proceeds on $15,000 of carpeting, fashionable clothing, two Cadillac sedans and a trip around the world for her and a friend.

Bert and Friel were facing life in prison for the copious amounts of drugs they had distributed. Friel would not attend the trial, as the prosecuting attorney thought it would be too disruptive for him to attend while lying in a bed in the courtroom. A remote TV hook-up to his house was established so he could watch the proceedings from his waterbed at home. I did not like the idea of Friel being in the courtroom in the first place—I was afraid that one of the female jurors would feel sorry for him and deadlock the jury. George was the star witness, linking Bert to multiple 1500 kilos shipments of marijuana and cocaine. But John Bruce turned out to be the most entertaining witness. At trial time, John Bruce had been released from prison and was living in a halfway-house in Las Vegas. John Bruce recounted for the jury the night that he broke into the storage sheds and discovered all the cash. The entire court listened intensely. After the Assistant U.S. Attorney completed direct examination of Bruce, it was Bert's defense attorney's turn.

The defense attorney approached Bruce, saying, "Mr. Bruce, I have only one question to ask you. Mr. Bruce, you have testified that you found eight suitcases that night. Mr. Bruce, I just have to ask you, why did you not take all the suitcases?"

Bruce answered the million-dollar question, "Well I thought I had enough money already." There was a chuckle throughout the court room. Even Bert laughed and shook his head.

Harry was convicted on the marijuana charges and sentenced to 10 years in Federal prison. Bert and Friel were both convicted on the distribution of copious amounts of cocaine and sentenced to life in prison. Bert was incarcerated in Lompoc Prison in

Lompoc, California. Several years later, he died of a heart attack. Martha was convicted on money laundering and was sentenced to two years in prison. Friel's long-time attendant surrendered him in his wheelchair to the U.S Marshal's office in Las Vegas. He was transferred to a Federal medical facility in St. Louis, Missouri, where he would live out his days. The Federal Government was awarded the $11,500 monthly workman's compensation payment to pay for Friel's care.

Old Will Hodges was never charged with a crime. Don and I located his ex-wife in Flagstaff, Arizona, where she was living with her current husband. We informed her of her daughter's whereabouts and the two were soon reunited. That gave Don and I some satisfaction.

There was no time to bask in the glory of the successful prosecution of the case. It was time to move on to other cases. However, the Assistant U.S. Attorney, Don, Larry, and I did all go out to celebrate that night at the Olympic Gardens Gentleman's Club in Las Vegas. To show our appreciation for his excellent presentation of the case, Don, Larry and I all chipped in and bought the Assistant U.S. Attorney a "table dance" from one of the young ladies working that night.

Asshole from El Paso

Lucia and I reported to El Paso in February of 1991. On the first day there, we met with the agent in charge. He advised me that I would be working in Las Cruces, New Mexico 40 miles north of El Paso, not El Paso. I knew how to play that game, so I offered no objection. The next day, I reported to Las Cruces. I was told that since I had a background in working conspiracy drug cases, I would be working two existing semi-truck drug cases that needed a workup for their upcoming trial. I hit the ground running, getting convictions in those two cases and then developing them into a 32-person conspiracy, the "Thunder Road" case, three years later.

For the first 90 days of my assignment to El Paso, I was detailed back to Las Vegas to help prepare the "Requiem to a Queen" case for trial. The agency was paying for me to commute from El Paso to Las Vegas each Monday morning and then return each Friday. After about six months of being assigned to the Las Cruces office, I was asked when I wanted to start working in El Paso. My answer was, "How about tomorrow?" I was then reassigned to the El Paso office, but instead of being assigned to a narcotics investigations group, I was assigned to a white-collar fraud group. I could continue the development of the "Thunder Road" conspiracy. The retaliation seemed to cease when management realized that I was exhibiting a positive work ethic and I was putting the Las Vegas experience behind me.

I was assigned to an ongoing two-year fraud case that had stalled due to the company's attorneys "circling the wagons" around 22 of the current employees, all of whom were exerting their Fifth Amendment privilege. It would take me three years and hundreds of thousands of dollars of the company's money in Washington-based attorney's fees to wear the company down. I interviewed all 22 of the employees, with company attorneys present. All but two of the employees exerted their Fifth Amendment privilege. The company claimed that they were being cooperative in the investigation. It didn't seem that way to me. One employee gave me a portion of what I would need to break the case.

I had subpoenaed business documents from the company's twin plant operation in Juarez, MX. Washington-based attorneys travelled to Juarez and spent several days copying all the documents. In time, they notified me that they had finally accomplished making copies of the documents for the period in question. The attorneys asked to meet me at them at one of the El Paso Ports of entry so they could deliver the documents. Fortunately for me, on that day, I was driving an old Chevrolet Suburban, anticipating a document dump by the company attorneys. They did turn over 12 boxes of copied documents, which filled the back of the Suburban. I already had the "smoking gun" document, but I wanted the attorneys to think that I had discovered the document in those provided. The smoking gun document had been provided years before by the original informant. I never did review the 12 boxes of documents, but at least the company had to bear the expense of the attorneys travelling to Juarez and making the copies.

In time, I was contacted by the lead attorney for the company, Roger Zuckerman, requesting a meeting with myself and the Assistant U.S. Attorney assigned to the case. Roger travelled to El Paso, where he and I met with the government attorney. During the brief meeting, Roger was the consummate professional, maintaining a respectful demeanor throughout. However, the government attorney, in my opinion, was rude to Roger. I was embarrassed by the way he talked down to Roger. Instead of reconciling matters in the investigation, the government attorney decided afterwards that we would indict one of the current company officers on making a false statement due to his submission of Customs documents misdescribing the flat rolled steel as "air conditioning cabinet wrappers." The indictment and subsequent arrest would bring the company to the negotiating table. The company had a bank charter and could lose the charter if one of the company officials was convicted of a crime.

After the indictment, I obtained an arrest warrant for the company officer and forwarded it to my Oklahoma City co-case agent, Cynthia Gonyea, requesting that she execute the arrest warrant. Instead of serving the warrant, she called the official and had him surrender himself, which had a less dramatic effect than I had hoped for. The cowboy in me was not pleased.

On the day that the Oklahoma City Federal Building was bombed by Timothy McVey, Cynthia was running 15 minutes late for work, so she had not arrived at the office before the bomb exploded. However, two of her colleges, Claude Mideras and Paul Ice, had. Paul was standing at the secretary's desk talking to her. Claude was at his desk. Both died instantly. Miraculously, the secretary survived after she was recovered from the rubble hours later. Cynthia suffered from survivor's remorse, having survived by being 15 minutes late. In time, she was transferred to Washington D.C. to assist in her recovery.

In time, the company realized the expense of the investigation to the company and suggested to their attorneys that they seek a settlement in the case. I was approached by Roger Zuckerman, their Washington-based attorney, to consider a "global settlement" in the case. The company had been importing flat rolled steel, copper, and ball bearings through their twin-plant operation in Juarez, Mexico, without paying the appropriate duties. A settlement sounded great to me. The company attorneys requested a meeting with me and management in El Paso, so they could present a "genesis" of the investigation. The company suspected that we had a previous company employee as an informant in the investigation. They were right.

On the day that the attorneys presented the "genesis" of the case, I requested that I be allowed to tape record the presentation. The attorneys granted my request. That would be an expensive mistake. As the meeting was breaking up, the lead attorney, John Dowd, and I were discussing the case.

He said, "Frankly, god damn it, we were just trying to get the stuff up there to Oklahoma City the easiest way possible." Did he really just say that? I thought. Did he realize that the tape recorder was still recording? He did not, and that slip would break the case wide open.

When the Washington-based law firm learned that I had recorded the statement, I got a call from one of their irate attorneys demanding a copy of the tape. I was more than happy to oblige them. The company decided to settle. With duties and penalties, the settlement would cost them 1.6 million dollars. Their attorneys travelled to El Paso and presented me with a 1.6-million-dollar company check. One attorney asked me how much I was going to pay my informant. I would not acknowledge that there was an informant or how much I would pay him, but I did inform the attorney that the informant policy was that I could pay up to 25% of the amount recovered. I paid the informant another $240,000. He had already been paid $10,000.

I gave the 1.6-million-dollar check to my supervisor, Jay, so he could forward it to the National Finance Center (NFC) in Indianapolis, Indiana. A couple of weeks later, Jay approached me, requesting that I call the company attorneys and ask that they submit another check for 1.6 million dollars. Evidently, my supervisor had prepared a cover letter and sent the check and cover letter to NFC. But when a young clerk opened the envelope, she only retrieved the cover letter, leaving the check in the envelope, which was then shredded, along with the 1.6-million-dollar check. I told Jay that there was no way I was going to make that call, explaining that it made us, the federal government, look like a bunch of idiots and that was too embarrassing. I gave him the attorney's telephone number and he made the call, getting the check resubmitted. I was glad to be rid of the white-collar case.

One day at work, I got a call from an investigator with the Office of the Inspector General (OIG) in Washington, D.C., regarding my Merit System Protection Board case in Las Vegas. He wanted to know about the discrepancies between Adolph's and my supervisor's statements regarding who and when the decision was made to transfer me. The investigator was considering possible perjury charges against Adolph. Before the investigator ended the call, I asked him why all this old business was being revisited. He informed me that his office had received an anonymous letter regarding the charges and that he assumed I was the person that sent the letter. I told him I did not, but I think I know who did: Lucia. It would not be the last time she would do something behind my back. It would be one of many fractures in the trust in our relationship.

Lucia had mentioned the possibility of reporting Adolph's inconsistent statement to OIG (Office of the Inspector General), but I told her to forget about it, as it would only bring negative attention to me when I was trying to put all that behind me. When I confronted her about the anonymous letter, she admitted that she had written it, but she was "going to tell me about it." That was one of her regular excuses when I had discovered things done without my knowledge. The trust had been fractured and would never be repaired.

I later learned that my former supervisor in Las Vegas had also been contacted by OIG regarding the matter. He provided them with a 14-page affidavit documenting his recollection of the matter, supported by telephone records of Adolph's telephone calls to him. I also learned that OIG was investigating the accuracy of Adolph's application for employment to U.S. Customs back in 1987. There was the possibility that he had not accurately reported the reason for his forced transfer to the FBI New York City office.

After the investigation was completed, the matter was referred to a Customs Disciplinary Review Board for its recommendation. One of my current office managers was a member of that review board. He would never tell me what the board recommended, because the board's recommendations were kept secret to protect the privacy of the employee. However, he would imply that Adolph "was going to get his."

I later learned that Adolph was given a notice of termination. He would spend the next six months trying to get his job back. What goes around comes around after all.

In time, I would be transferred to a newly-formed narcotics conspiracy group. At first, I served as the supervisor for the group until another dethroned former manager, Oran Neck, was detailed in from Washington to head up the group. Oran was a former rising star from our days in Arizona. He had made some missteps along the way and now he was serving out his time until he could retire. I always liked the guy, but his last misstep cost him dearly. He was now serving out his penitence in a staff position in Washington D.C. His temporary assignment to El Paso was a gesture of compassion toward him and his wife. They were living separately, he in Washington, D.C. and she in Brownsville, Texas. He had hoped to finish out the rest of his career in El Paso, but someone in Washington would not allow that. After a brief time, he was summoned back to Washington. Instead of reporting back, he submitted his retirement papers and went home to Brownsville. There have been so many that have finished out their career in that manner. I would again assume the role as supervisor of the conspiracy group. I have always believed that at some point we outlive our usefulness to the service. In five years, I would find myself in that same situation.

Within the U.S. Customs Office of Investigation in El Paso, there were several Hispanic agents. Two of the Hispanic male agents were assigned to my group. Jose and Mateo were experienced journeymen agents. Jose was a very street-wise law enforcement officer, having spent several years as a Border Patrol Agent and U.S. Customs Inspector. Mateo was a very capable agent, but he seemed to harbor some animosities toward management. Jose, Mateo, and Lucia were all being considered for promotion to Senior Special Agent. The Hispanic Special Agent in Charge selected Jose and Lucia to be promoted. Naturally, Mateo felt slighted and felt that Lucia should have not been promoted over him. He felt that management only promoted Lucia because she was a Hispanic female. Thus, management had promoted one Hispanic male and one Hispanic female, preventing any successful EEO complaints. What Mateo did not know was that he and Jose were originally the two that were selected for the promotion, but fortunately for Lucia, a friend of hers, the office manager, Haydee, was present during the selection process. Before the selection was finalized, Haydee interjected, "What about Lucia?" The managers then rethought their decision and selected Lucia instead. In time, Mateo would also be promoted, but not until he had copped an attitude for being passed over. His resentment, agitated by Senior Special Agent Sanchez eventually lead to riff among the races in the office. There are those that are perpetual victims and thus they are perpetually offended when matters do not suit them. Being offended just re-enforces their victim mentality. Over the many years in the federal government, I have encountered many that have been conditioned to believe that the system is stacked against them, and when things do not go their way, it only re-enforces their beliefs.

What management did not know was that Sanchez would covertly agitate the younger Hispanic agents, all the while posing as a "company man" when in front of management. The riff between the Hispanics and Anglos developed to a point where someone in the office labeled the disgruntled Hispanics as the "Mexican Mafia." The whole situation spoke loudly of arrested adolescence. Sanchez would keep the younger agents agitated to the point that they started voicing their dissatisfaction over issues in the office. Sanchez would never step forward to voice his concerns. He could usually agitate Jose into doing it for him. Jose was a very good agent, but he wore his emotions on his sleeve. He was not afraid to speak out. Sanchez would covertly engage in "victim pimping," convincing the younger Hispanic agents that they were getting the short end of the stick. In time, Sanchez, Jose, and Mateo were transferred to the Internal Affairs Office in El Paso. One of their Hispanic buddies was Agent in Charge and hired several Hispanic agents from our office to staff the Internal Affairs office.

Within a very brief time, Sanchez had created a clique situation within the smaller Internal Affairs Office. Now their small office was divided, Hispanic vs Anglo. In time, a management review team was sent from Washington D.C. to review the matter. As Mateo and Jose's former supervisor, I was interviewed by the team regarding the situation. I shared with them my thoughts on Santillano. The review team eventually recommended that several agents in the Internal Affairs Office be force-transferred to other offices throughout the United States. Jose was transferred to Dallas, TX, Mateo was transferred to Denver, CO, and the ringleader, Sanchez, was transferred to Houston, TX, where he would eventually retire. A similar number of Anglos were transferred to other offices. Thus, the Hispanic employees could not claim discrimination. Jose could not handle life in Dallas and soon volunteered to take a downgrade to a position in the Customs Aviation Branch back in El Paso. In time, he worked his back up the ladder and retired from a management position. Jose had overcome the negative experience.

Another Hispanic agent, Arthur, also had created some issues within the office. Arthur was nicknamed "Foo-Foo" due to his spiffy work attire. He considered himself a lady's man and had commented that he had screwed half the women in town, and the other half wanted to screw him. Naturally, that comment did not sit well with the married agents in the office. One male agent confronted him about the comment. He asked Arthur if he was saying that he had screwed his wife, or she wanted to screw him. Of course, Arthur immediately clarified this comment.

Arthur was dating a manager in another division of U.S. Customs, Marci. That Christmas, Marci hosted a Christmas party at her house. As the evening wore on, Marci commented to another lady attending the party that Arthur was "not very romantic." Arthur took great offense at that comment. After all the party-goers left, Marci and Arthur got into a heated argument, which turned violent. Arthur beat Marci severely, causing her multiple injuries. Arthur immediately realized what he had done, but he would not allow Marci to get medical help. He knew if he was charged with domestic violence, he could not keep his law enforcement position. Arthur kept Marci prisoner in her own house for three days, hoping that her condition would improve. Finally, Marci's supervisor came to her house to check on her.

Arthur was charged with domestic violence and immediately transferred to another office north of El Paso pending the outcome of the investigation. Many months later, Arthur was placed on a pre-trial diversion program wherein he could avoid a conviction if he successfully completed the program. In time, Arthur was notified that he was being force-transferred to Puerto Rico. Initially, Arthur planned to fight the transfer. I shared with him my experience in Las Vegas and suggested that problem would go away sooner if he accepted the transfer. Arthur saw the wisdom in my advice and accepted the transfer. But he would not keep his mouth shut. He told a so-called friend that he had lied to Internal Affairs about the incident. When that came to the attention of Internal Affairs, he was served with a notice of termination. Arthur resigned in lieu of being terminated. He returned to El Paso and went to work as a manager in twin-plant operation in Juarez, Mexico.

In early 1992, I was detailed back to Las Vegas for another 90 days for the "Requiem of a Queen" trial. I rented an apartment on the Las Vegas Country Club. My former supervisor gave me the loan of a government undercover Mercedes sedan. I was living large, but by then, Lucia and I had been separated six months with the two separate details to Las Vegas. In retrospect, I should have paid more attention to the effects of so much time spent apart.

After a three-year investigation, we indicted 32 violators in the "Thunder Road" case. We executed 14 simultaneous arrests and search warrants, rounding up most of the violators. We seized several million dollars in assets, with the premier property being the Truck Center of El Paso, which had been built new, from the ground up, with drug proceeds. The case had blossomed from the two semi-truck cases that were handed to me in Las Cruces in 1991.

Many times, over the course of the three-year investigation, supervisors would sarcastically ask, "When are you going to indict that case." I just maintained my silent resolve until the morning that we executed the 14 arrest and search warrants. That morning, when most of our office, the FBI SWAT Team, and IRS agents filled our huge conference room to brief for the day long operation, those doubters were the ones being silent.

One of the defendants in the case who was not apprehended fled to Mexico. Ruben was one of the drivers who drove the loads across the border at the Fabens, Texas, port of entry. His daughter, Lilia, was also involved in smuggling narcotics with her com-mon-law husband, Jose Val Verde. I received information from the original "Thunder Road" informant that Lilia and Jose were using older model Dodge vans with 40-gallon gas tanks to smuggle nar-cotics in the modified gas tanks. The informant, Lilia's uncle by marriage, provided me with the license plate number of the vehicle she was currently using to smuggle the drugs. I entered the vehicle license plate in the U.S. Customs lookout data base.

After brief period, I received a call notifying me that Jose and Lilia had been apprehended in Laredo, Texas, while attempting to smuggle 80 pounds of meth secreted in the modified gas tank. Jose and Lilia, accompanied by their 18-month-old son, agreed to co-operate with the government and deliver the meth to its intended destination. Originally, Jose told agents that the intended destina-tion was El Paso.

After the drugs were discovered in the modified gas tank, it was cut open to remove the meth. The gas tank had been modi-fied in a similar manner as the diesel tanks that were modified by Lilia's father's organization. Lilia and Jose agreed to participate in a controlled delivery of the narcotics to El Paso to receive con-sideration in their case. Since the original 40-gallon gas tank had been destroyed when the meth was removed, another gas tank had to be installed in the vehicle. Another 40-gallon tank could not be located, so a 27-gallon tank was installed instead by a government contractor. Lilia, Jose, and their 18-month-old son were escorted by five Laredo agents to El Paso in anticipation of doing the con-trolled delivery operation. The family was housed in a motel under

24-hour guard to ensure that they did not contact anyone. All telephones were removed from the motel room.

Since I provided the original lookout informant on the van, and I was familiar with the family and their current residence, I was assigned as lead agent for the El Paso operation. The next morning, the family was brought to our office in El Paso for an operational debriefing. The first thing I told Jose was that if I caught him in any lies, all deals were off, and he and his wife would both be prosecuted. Jose then changed his story and informed us that the real destination was Los Angeles, California, where the van was to be dropped off at a strip mall. After weighing all the operational considerations, the Laredo agents decided to continue the operation to Los Angeles. At first, it was decided that Lilia and her 18-month-old son would remain in El Paso under 24-hour guard, but Jose convinced the Laredo agents that it would look more convincing if Lilia and his son accompanied him to Los Angeles. The Laredo agents agreed to allow the family to travel to Los Angeles together. It would be a very costly decision.

Thankfully, my participation in the operation ended when the family and the agents crossed over the state line into New Mexico. The operation was handed off to each Customs offices that had operational jurisdiction for that area. When the agents and family arrived in Phoenix, Arizona, the family was again housed in a motel under 24-hour guard. Again, the telephones were removed from the motel room. The next morning, the family was fed, and their vehicle's gas tank was filled with gasoline. The convoy of vehicles then entered Interstate 10 from Phoenix, travelling westbound to Los Angeles. No one will ever know why the family's van left the interstate at a high rate of speed, travelled into the medium, then crashed into a cement piling supporting an overpass. Only Jose and Lilia knew, but they took that information to their graves.

Approximately 2.8 seconds after the family van left the interstate and crashed into the cement piling, the vehicle burst into flames. The agents rushed to assist the family trapped inside, but the flames were too intense to allow a rescue of any of the family members. All three family members were burned alive. A lengthy and impartial accident investigation was conducted by the Arizona Department of Public safety, but it could not determine why the accident happened. It identified the cause of the fire as the installation of the smaller 27-gallon gas tank on the vehicle. According to the report, when the van impacted with the cement piling, the smaller tank broke loose from the metal straps holding it in place, spilling the gas throughout the undercarriage of the vehicle and onto the heated engine.

When the parents of Lilia and Jose learned that they were involved in a law enforcement operation when the van crashed, they sued U.S. Customs, the five agents, and the contract facility that installed the gas tank for five million dollars. After lengthy litigation with the families, Customs settled the suit for 3.2 million dollars. Lilia's father, Ruben, who was still a fugitive from federal prosecution, would share in the settlement.

The accident investigation report suggested probable causes of the crash. It was suggested that Jose might have intended to crash the vehicle to disable it so he would not have to continue cooperating in the operation but had not anticipated the gas tank breaking loose. It was also suggested that Lilia and Jose possibly may have been involved in an argument, causing Jose to lose control of the vehicle. Jose and Lilia may have even entered into a suicide pact, so they would not have to go to prison. Personally, I do not give any credence to the last theory. I could not believe that Lilia and Jose would sacrifice their infant son's life to stay out of prison. I always believed that Jose was simply attempting to disable the vehicle.

Ironically, Adolph, from my Las Vegas days, somehow interjected himself into the follow-up investigation of the crash. He suggested that I not be informed of the crash or the results of the investigation because I was "a whistle blower." That always smelled of a cover-up to me.

During the development of the Thunder Road case, I visited over 20 federal penitentiaries to solicit the cooperation of inmates who were serving time for their involvement in the international and multi-state conspiracy. On two occasions, I visited Leavenworth Federal Prison, one of the oldest federal penitentiaries. It was considered one of the country's worst places to be incarcerated. Even as a Federal Agent, entering the rotunda of the main entrance was intimidating. I did recruit many of those I approached as witnesses in exchange for having their sentences reduced. Three were serving 15-year prison sentences, and their sentences were reduced to half. Before the trial began, we had enlisted the cooperation of more than half of those facing charges. We went to trial with 17 defendants out of the 32 that were indicted. Some defendants were not apprehended and fled the U.S. The courtroom was not large enough to accommodate all the defendants and their 17 attorneys at the defense table, so some graciously agreed to sit in the front rows of the visitor seating. They hoped that by doing so, the jury focus would be on the other defendants.

The Reverend Umberto Garcia and his former stripper wife, along with their new baby, sat in the very first row. Umberto had a Bible in his hand the whole time. His wife was wearing a very proper looking dress with a high-necked lace collar, cradling her new baby girl. Ah, such jury appeal, I thought. Umberto looked much different in court than he did on that Saturday I arrested him outside his church, when he was dressed in those pink shorts and pink T-shirt. When my female IRS co-agent and I arrived at the church to arrest Umberto, he was not there, but as we were leaving, we saw a guy hurrying down the street towards us. Not knowing that it was Umberto, we waited. When he approached, I asked if he was Umberto and he acknowledged that he was. I told him I had a warrant for his arrest. He then responded, "Darn, I thought you two might be new parishioners." Sorry Umberto. We are from different flock.

Umberto's case was the first time I used a female cooperating undercover informant and the first and only time I used a sister against her brother. Learning my lesson back in Yuma, I insisted that I have a female agent with me when dealing with Gloria. Gloria and her husband, Felipe, had been arrested with 500 pounds of cocaine. Gloria was working off her charges. Her husband was serving 15 years in a federal prison in Florence, Colorado, on his charges. I already approached Felipe to solicit his cooperation in the case, but Felipe wanted to play hardball with me. That was never my preference, but I can play hardball when I have to. When I first visited Felipe in prison, I offered him a business deal: his cooperation in exchange for a sentence reduction. I showed him eighteen photos of those I had identified as members of the organization. I wanted to convince him that I had done my homework and was not blowing smoke up the lower part of his anatomy. Felipe figured he could outsmart the old gringo, because he had a plan to get out of prison. What he didn't know that by then his wife was cooperating in the case in exchange for staying out of jail. He would find out the hard way he should have accepted my deal. Maybe his mother, too, had warned him about that. Felipe wanted to be a standup guy with the organization. So, I would have to break him.

Felipe's plan was to claim that he was a Mexican citizen, and then apply for the U.S.-Mexico prison exchange program. After he was shipped to the Mexican prison, he would buy his way out of prison by paying off Mexican authorities with the $60,000 that the organization owed him. For him to do that, he would have to have the assistance of his wife to collect the $60,000 from Umberto, her brother. That sounds great to me, Felipe, I thought. I was more than glad to help. After I had visited Felipe, he wrote a letter to his wife requesting that she collect the $60,000 and warn his "buds at the Truck Center that the Feds were here asking questions."

"We will do that for you also, Felipe, but your wife will be wired when she does," I said to myself. The prison officials intercepted the letter and advised me about its contents. Gloria also brought me her original letter, which was seized as evidence. It implicated the "buds at the Truck Center."

We wired up Gloria with a body transmitter and sent her in to see the manager of the Truck Center. The transmission was not very audible, but at least the manager did not say, "I don't know what the hell you are talking about." Now it was time to go collect Felipe's $60,000 for him, but I would keep it. Gloria would not wear a wire when she visited Umberto because she said that he was too "huggy" when greeting a person and he might find the wire. We searched her before she went into the church so Umberto could not claim that she had the money on her when she got there. When she came out, she had the $60,000, which I seized. Now it was time to play hardball with Felipe.

I had him transferred from the nice new prison in Colorado to that old prison in La Tuna, Texas, just outside El Paso. I also convinced the U.S. Attorney to grant Felipe forced immunity for his testimony in the case. By doing so, we could not use anything he said in court against him, thereby preventing him from exerting his Fifth Amendment privilege. If he refused to testify, he was looking at another eighteen months added to his sentence. He was about to learn a hard lesson: don't play hardball with this old gringo.

The morning before he was scheduled to testify, I visited him at the La Tuna prison. He had already been moved to an interview room where he sat by himself, wondering what his transfer was about. When I entered the interview room, he looked up and said "Damn, I should have known it was you." I then proceeded to explain Felipe's situation to him. I reminded him about our meeting six months earlier and the deal I had offered then. I told him I was still willing to honor that deal even though he had tried to rat me out to his buds. I also told him that I knew about his plan to get out of prison and I had put the nix on that. But it broke his spirit when I told him his wife was cooperating and she had collected the $60,000 from Umberto, which I seized. I offered him some consolation by telling him that I had awarded Gloria 25% of the money to help her with support of his children. I thought that was a nice gesture on my part, but Felipe failed to see it that way. Then I told Felipe about the forced immunity and the possibility of additional time to serve.

His response was, "Damn, I had better talk to an attorney." I told him that I had arranged for a federal public defender to talk to him the following morning before court convened. I left him to think about it overnight. I had already had one defendant refuse the same offer and I made sure Richard, one of the gringo defendants, got another eighteen months added to his current sentence, so it was no idle threat.

The next morning, Felipe took the witness stand. He testified about his knowledge and involvement in the organization. Ironically, he knew the defendant who had been involved in the "Boston case," a totally unrelated case, as well and had a couple of nicknames for him: Los Indios and Tons! I loved that Tons nickname. The nickname "Los Indios" came about because he wore his hair in a ponytail. The ponytail was cut off by trial time. He was giving the nickname "Tons" because had bragged to others that he had distributed tons of narcotics. Felipe would also testify that the load he was caught with was a load that he and others were doing behind the back of the main violator. That revelation would cost three members their lives. They were summoned to Mexico and never seen again.

Tons had been providing copious quantities of marijuana to a dealer in Ft. Lauderdale, Florida. Steve Alexander had retired from the marijuana business and was living a legitimate lifestyle. However, a former associate of his was not. When the associate got busted for distribution of marijuana, he cut a deal to set Steve up. Initially Steve declined to participate but finally agreed to arrange for the associate to receive a load of marijuana from his El Paso source. To me, the case was borderline entrapment. After his arrest, Steve pled guilty to conspiracy to distribute marijuana. He was sentenced to 15 years, and he forfeited all the assets he had acquired. Steve was very glad to see me when I visited him in the Federal Prison in Tucson, Arizona. He agreed to cooperate in exchange for his sentence being reduced by 50%.

Technically, a defendant's sentence is not supposed to be reduced unless the defendant provides new information that was not known to him at the time of his original sentencing. However, many judges do not like the mandatory minimum sentencing passed by Congress. The policy allows the judges very little leeway in sentencing defendants. The judges are usually receptive to U.S. Attorney sentencing reduction requests. After the trial was over, the Assistant U.S. Attorney asked me if I wanted to proceed with the request to have Steve's sentence reduced. My response was that we are only as good as our word. If we get the reputation of reneging on our deals, our word will not be credible in the future. The request was filed, and the Assistant U.S. Attorney and I travelled to Ft. Lauderdale to testify at Steve's hearing. His 15-year sentence was reduced by half, and with time served, he would be out of prison in a couple years.

I always made it a policy to contact the responsible case agent before I would agree to a sentence reduction. It did not seem right to me go behind the back of the case agent that may have put in many long hours on the case. I had had attorneys do that to me on some state cases. I had had judges issue a verdict of not guilty on some of my defendants and other judges overturn a guilty verdict for defendants I had spent 3-4 years trying to convict.

Due to the number of exhibits and witnesses in the Thunder Road case, the U.S. Attorney Office should have assigned a second attorney to the case, but for some reason, they did not. We started the case with over 700 exhibits and more than 25 witnesses. Presentation of the case by one prosecutor would be a herculean task. When the trial started, the prosecuting attorney had not sufficiently prepared himself for the task. It would soon show in court. In the first week of the trial, the prosecutor was stumbling so much that the presiding judge, the Honorable Harry Lee Hudspeth, asked the prosecutor how long he anticipated that the trial would last. The prosecutor responded, "I think I can finish the trial in three weeks, Your Honor." Judge Hudspeth then told the prosecutor, "This trial is dragging on, and anytime a trial drags on, it is the fault of the prosecutor. If you do not finish it in three weeks, I will finish it for you." Oh shit, we are in big trouble, I thought. After court that night, my co-case agent and I went back to the evidence room and cut the exhibits to less than 300. Even after doing that, we would not get most of the exhibits in evidence.

"Tons" had a prior arrest many years before for a narcotic charge in Boston, Massachusetts. But as hard as I searched, I could not find a deposition on the DEA case. DEA was not receptive to my requests for the deposition of the case. I was aware that there had been a drug case years before involving some people from El Paso bringing in a boatload of marijuana into the Gloucester, Massachusetts, area. The boat crashed onto rocks during a storm and marijuana bales were found up and down the beach. One of the infamous Chagra brothers of El Paso was allegedly involved in the venture. The book *Dirty Dealing* by Gary Cartwright,[7] details the downfall of the Charga brothers of El Paso, Lee, Jimmy, and Joe. Lee was murdered during a robbery. Jimmy and Joe received long prison terms for their participation in smuggling large shipments of narcotics. Jimmy was actually charged with hiring Charles Harrelson, father of actor Woody Harrelson, to kill Federal Judge John Wood. Jimmy was acquitted of the charge, but Charles Harrelson was convicted and sentenced to two life terms.

Tons made the mistake of taking the witness stand in his own behalf. During questioning by the prosecutor, the defendant tried to minimize his involvement in the organization. While the prosecutor was questioning the witness, I slipped him a note suggesting that he ask the witness how much marijuana was involved in the Boston case. The defendant had already acknowledged his involvement in that case. I did not know the answer regarding the amount of marijuana. I did not think the prosecutor would ask the question, because attorneys do not like to ask questions that they do not know the answer to. He did ask it and got the answer I suspected. The defendant said the case involved 29 "tons" of marijuana. That is what I wanted the jury to hear.

Randy was our premier witness in the case and the only "gringo" in the smuggling operation. He was serving 15 years for transporting 480 pounds of cocaine in his semi-tractor. Ironically, he was arrested at the same border patrol check point as the first two semi-tractors in 1991. It would take me six months to connect the three loads that were all owned by the organization. Randy would serve out the remainder of his sentence in a witness protection facility after his sentence was reduced by half. Randy spent six years in an organization that normally does not trust "gringos" enough to allow them to be held in confidence. He had pulled off the recovery of a loaded vehicle from law enforcement custody. That showed the organization that he had "big balls" and could be trusted.

In the beginning, the organization was using older Ford F-150 pickups with false beds to transport their narcotics throughout the U.S. even as far as Indianapolis, Indiana. The organization had regular customers in San Diego, San Francisco, northern New Mexico, Dallas, Indianapolis, and Florida. Two of their F-150 pickups attracted the attention of the sheriff's department in Deming, New Mexico. One of the pickups got away, but the second one was impounded when the driver could not produce proper documentation proving ownership. The organization was inclined to just let the sheriff's office keep the vehicle, but Randy convinced them that he could get the vehicle back. He convinced the organization to provide him with a phony bill of sale that he could present to the sheriff's department. Bill of sale in hand, Randy walked in to the sheriff's and demanded his pickup back. The bluff worked, and Randy drove off with the pickup with 280 pounds of marijuana concealed in the false bed. Randy was a hero for the next few years until he was arrested. Then he became toxic because "gringos" roll. That would work to my benefit.

In time, the organization started using horse and stock trailers with false beds. But, after an incident where they lost a loaded trailer in Northern Arizona, they soon rethought that mode of operation. Randy and his boss were transporting a loaded trailer westbound on I-40 to their operation in Escondido, California. They were driving along, wrapped up in their conversation, when they suddenly noticed that the trailer was no longer behind them. Randy's boss wanted to get the hell out of there, thinking the loose trailer may have killed some motorist. Randy again persuaded him to go back and look for the trailer. Just about 5 miles back, they found the trailer sitting in the medium of the interstate with only a bent trailer tongue. They towed the trailer to a shop, where a worker straightened out the tongue, and then continued their trip.

When I finally located Randy after his arrest, he was housed in a contract temporary holding facility awaiting assignment to a federal prison. Initially, our meeting did not go well, but after he realized that the organization had abandoned him and his attorney would no longer take his calls, his attitude changed. He was willing to listen to my sales pitch about possibly reducing his 15-year sentence after I got a telephonic guarantee from the U.S. Attorney's office for the sentence reduction. During the debriefing, he told me about his ranch in Perris, California, where he had an underground bunker, which had $100,000 in cash stashed in it. He described how the bunker was hidden under the goat pen at the ranch. He also provided me with the location of the ranch on "Thunder Road" in El Paso, TX, that the organization transshipped their loads out of after they were smuggled in from Mexico. Randy described how two brothers-in-law, posing as daily workers, would cross into the U.S. at the Fabens, Texas, port of entry several times a week with narcotics in the false beds of their Ford F-150 pickups. The loads would be stockpiled at the ranch on Thunder Road until there was enough for a large shipment. He also informed me that the local narcs had raided the ranch at Thunder Road a couple years before. Tracking down that information would become critical to the case.

I requested the agents in Riverside, California, conduct a search of the ranch in Perris. The agents were successful at finding the bunker under the goat pen, but there was no $100,000 there, nor was Randy's cherished Eddie Bauer Ford Bronco to be found. The ranch had been cleaned out and so had Randy, but that betrayal by the organization cemented our relationship for the next few years. I did track down the information pertaining to the raid on the Thunder Road ranch and, unbelievably, the assistant district attorney that handled that case for the sheriff's office narcotics squad was now an Assistant U.S. Attorney in El Paso. I contacted that attorney. He remembered the case, informing me that when the sheriff's narcotics squad raided the ranch, they videotaped the whole raid. According to the attorney, the tape should still have been over in the district attorney's office. After several attempts, we finally located the original tape. The video showed how the organization was now modifying 100-gallon semi-tractor diesel saddle tanks to conceal narcotics within them. The 100-gallon tanks were fitted with smaller "pony tanks" within them under the fill spout. The bulk of the tank capacity was filled with either marijuana or cocaine and the pony tank contained enough diesel fuel to get the past the Border Patrol check points. The 100-gallon tank was accessed through a trap door on the inner side of the tank. Each time the tank was loaded with narcotics the trap door was secured in place with sheet metal screws, "bondo" was applied and painted. The modification was very hard to detect, but they did not realize that running a semi-tractor without a loaded trailer over the interstate highway soon raised law enforcement attention.

I had committed Randy's entire first debriefing to writing, but before I finalized the report, I wanted to revisit him to confirm my facts. It was a damn good thing I did—Randy had given me the facts about the organization alright, but he had changed the names of some of the members, intending to protect the members of his immediate organization. After he learned of his missing money and Ford Bronco, he was willing to give up the members of his immediate organization. Had I finalized that report for the case file, I would have had it stuck up the lower part of my anatomy come trial time, and it would have damaged Randy's credibility. During multiple interviews with Randy, he complained that he felt had his 15-year sentence was too harsh. I reminded Randy that he admitted that he had been a member of the organization for six years and had been distributing copious amounts of narcotics for all those years without consequences. I informed him that had he been sentenced based on all the drugs he had distributed, he would be serving a life sentence. That seem to provide some consolation to him.

After I had submitted the paperwork to the U.S. Marshalls Service requesting that Randy be placed in the Witness Protection Program, I also requested that Randy be released from prison for one week into my custody. Both applications were granted but the release had strict conditions. The strict conditions were that U.S. Customs Service had to provide four armed guards to guard Randy at all times, he had to be housed in a federally approved detention facility each night, and I had to deliver him to his new facility in Arizona. It seems that there had been some issues with housing released prisoners in the past, and a released inmate had been provided with booze and a prostitute in his hotel room.

I got approval to utilize a U.S. Customs aircraft, two pilots, and four agents for the release so I could transport Randy throughout the U.S. to show me where he had delivered loads of narcotics. We picked Randy up at a Federal Detention Facility near Jessup, Georgia. All went well for the first four days. The first four nights, I housed Randy in federally-approved county detention facilities.

On the fifth night, we were in San Diego, California, which had a Federal Detentions Center downtown.

Late on the fifth night, we took Randy to be housed overnight in the San Diego Federal Detention Center. Randy waited in the car with the other federal agents while I contacted the shift lieutenant on duty at the center. When I gave him Randy's prisoner number, he entered it into their computer system. I do not know what he saw on that computer screen, but his expression was that of a frightened man.

Then he said, "You can't bring that guy in here, don't you bring him in here." I tried to explain that I was required to per the release agreement. He said, "I don't care. You are not bringing him in my facility." I wasn't sure what was going on, so I called the Witness Security Coordinator in Washington D.C., waking her up at three a.m. She then informed me that when I picked up Randy in Jessup, Georgia, he was then placed in the Witness Protection Program. I wish they had told me. That would explain the strict release conditions and all those armed prison guards with assault rifles at the Jessup airport when we picked Randy up.

The witness coordinator said that she would call the shift lieutenant and arrange for Randy to be housed overnight. I was then allowed to bring Randy into the center, but you would have thought Randy had a contagious disease. The officers wanted no part of him. The lieutenant informed me that the only place he had to segregate Randy was in the women's unit, which was fine with Randy and me. Randy had requested that he be allowed to shower that night since he had not showered in the previous four days.

The shift lieutenant on duty that night said that he would do what he could.

The next morning, I picked Randy up and he informed me that they would not allow him to shower. I asked the different shift lieutenant about why Randy could not shower. The lieutenant advised me that there was no way in hell he would be allowed to shower on his shift, because "if he falls and breaks his arm, it is my ass." He said he just wanted Randy out of his facility. Randy was delivered to one of the several federal witness security units that day.

Another highlight in an otherwise lowlight trial came when one of the Customs agents took the stand. The agent was to testify that he was the agent who originally handled the first two semi-tractor cases in Las Cruces in 1990 and then turned the cases over to me. I had given the agent the two original case files for review. Ole Kent is one of the most likeable guys you will ever meet. We are still friends to this day. Well, that day, of all days, Kent had an attitude. Seems he had drawn an elk tag for an elk hunt, but the trial had prevented him from going elk hunting. He had also had copped an attitude for having to stay after court several days, waiting for the prosecutor to pre-trial interview him, but he was never interviewed. That was a costly mistake with Kent.

The first two semi-trucks were seized, one late on the evening of Nov 30, 1990, and the other early in the morning on Dec 1, 1990, at the same border patrol check point. They both were carrying over 400 pounds of marijuana. When the prosecutor asked Kent what he was doing on Nov 30, 1990, he said he did not remember. The prosecutor then asked Kent what he was doing on the morning of Dec 1, 1990. Kent again responded, "I don't know. I don't even know what I am doing here." The prosecutor realized his mistake and ended the questioning. The judge then asked the defense if they had any question for the witness. The lead defense attorney stood up and said, "Your Honor, I have no questions for this witness. I could not top that." Kent was excused without testifying.

At one point in the Thunder Road trial, the judge summoned the prosecutor and me to his chambers. He let us know, in no uncertain terms, that he did not like one of our witnesses. He did not like the way he was dressed or the fact that he was wearing sun glasses in his court when he testified. I did not like it either. The judge said our witness looked like someone from the mafia. I had to agree. I explained to the judge that I had placed the witness in the Witness Protection Program. He was under the control of the U.S. Marshall Service. I had not seen him since he went into the program. The witness was the brother-in-law of one of the main defendants. He was wearing the sun glasses because he could not bear to look his brother-in- law in the eye during his testimony. He was dressed in black pants, black shirt, and a black tie, with Elvis style sunglasses. The witness was eventually kicked out of the Witness Protection Program when he hired an attorney to complain to the Marshall Service about them not continuing the support of his family.

During one of the recesses in the trial, one of the defense attorneys approached me outside the courtroom. He said, "You know

Gil, you clean up pretty good for a federal agent." I thought, You arrogant bastard, at least I do not show up in federal court with a western cut suit and cowboy boots, and your hair transplant looks like shit. Then he said, "I know what you are trying to do. You figure if you throw enough shit on the wall, some of it will stick." I told him that his client was lucky that the judge was not letting me throw all the shit I had, or his client would be in trouble. That shut him up.

A few weeks after the trial, I was contacted by Umberto's soon-to-be ex-wife. She wanted to rat Umberto out. I would have never recognized the former schoolmarm-attired Mrs. Garcia. I could see now how she had supported herself for eleven years as a topless dancer. She was a very well put together woman; she had a perfect hourglass figure. Not only was Umberto a money launderer for the organization, but he was also a wife beater. The Reverend also was a regular drug user, and as well as a regular customer at the strip club where he met his wife. Mrs. Garcia claimed that Umberto was laundering drug money through his church. Maybe he was just doing the lord's work and tending to his flock, but I doubted it.

Only two defendants did not see the wisdom in accepting the sentenced reduction deals I offered them. Old Roberto suffered a mild heart attack and had to be taken to the medical unit during my last visit to him in prison. It was not me he afraid of. He was worried about being labeled as a snitch while serving his time in prison. He made a point of telling me not to come visit him again. He would see me again in court. Richard wanted to play hardball like Felipe had. He would not even testify when granted forced immunity. Seems he did not want to testify against his brother-in-law, but I only wanted him to testify against the defendant that was involved in the Boston case. So, I played hardball and got eighteen months added to his existing sentence. A man has gotta do what a man has gotta do, so said John Wayne.

Despite all the problems with the trial, we convicted 12 of the 17 defendants. The judge ordered a directed verdict of not guilty on the other five when the prosecutor rested his case. The judge cited that the prosecution had not presented sufficient evidence to prove their guilt. He was telling the prosecutor that he did not like the case as he had presented it. For several years afterwards, I would still be dealing with issues from the case in the form of appeals, asset seizures, etc. The prosecutor did apologize to me for his ineptness in presenting the case.

Some years later, after I retired, Dave, the prosecutor, volunteered to go to Iraq to assist in the prosecution of Saddam Hussein. Dave was a Major in the Marine Corp Reserves. He had recently divorced his wife of many years. He was not handling the divorce very well. As a Catholic, he did not believe in divorce, so he sought to have the marriage annulled, claiming that theirs was never really a marriage even though they had three children. According to Dave, his wife was frigid and would only begrudgingly allow him to have sex with her. He had even asked me to testify at his annulment, but I declined. He had told me that his wife was virgin on their wedding night and the wedding night was a disaster.

Dave eventually began dating another woman, but after returning from Iraq, their relationship was struggling. The lady wanted to break off the relationship, which did not please Dave. After an argument, the lady left their apartment to go for a walk. Dave went into the shower, put a 357 revolver in his mouth and pulled the trigger. When the lady returned, she found Dave's body in the shower. Presumably, Dave had the decency to end his life in the shower so as not to create a bloody mess throughout the apartment.

It was about this time that I first saw the cracks appearing in my relationship with Lucia. She was also working long hours on cases. The oldest daughter had graduated from high school and left to college in Austin, Texas. For Lucia, there seemed to be a sense of relief not having to worry about her headstrong daughter as much. I got the sense that I was starting to outlive my usefulness in our relationship as well. She was now making over $120,000 per year. Maybe she did not need the old gringo anymore. I began to withdraw and build a barrier around myself. Marriage tends to build fences around relationships. If one spouse wants to venture outside the boundaries, the other spouse cannot become the "gate keeper." I have always refused to be the "gate keeper," even though I suspected that Lucia was getting restless within the relationship. During that year, she was gone for approximately six months. Some of the assignments that required her to travel were assigned to her. Others, like Peru and Honduras, were ones she had volunteered for. I told her that, for a married man, I sure spent a lot of time alone. She seemed unaffected by that. If the woman is earning her own money, I also refused to be her "banker," allowing her to spend her money as she pleased. That was the year that she bought the first of three BMWs sedans—only one I had any input on. The 325i and the Z4 roaster BMWs she bought against my advice. I was out of town when she bought the Z4 roaster.

Soon after the "Thunder Road" case was over, I found myself back doing "rookie" "bagem and tagem" port of entry cases. I was just another asshole from El Paso. The El Paso office was responsible for prosecuting the drug cases that were interdicted at the five ports of entry in the El Paso area: Fort Hancock, Fabens, Isleta, Bridge of the Americas, and Paso del Norte. These cases were normally handled by new trainees as they reported in from the academy, but as the work load increased, all hands were going to have to start working the cases. When I first arrived in El Paso, it was said that we would burn our people out within the first five years. As time wore on, and especially during the marijuana harvest season, the burnout rate was down to three years. With the agent and informant developed cases, you could be away from home for extended periods of time, assigned to surveillance. The work load demanded that everyone carry their weight, so I found myself, at 50 years old, again doing "rookie" cases. There is little satisfaction in doing the port of entry cases, as many of those arrested are just poor Mexican people who had been offered an opportunity to earn $200 to drive a loaded vehicle into the U.S. When busted, they were usually looking at 4-6 years in federal prison, depending on the weight of the load. I always felt some empathy for these poor people. They were just gettin' by. I found no joy in that work.

The straw that broke the camel's back was when I got called

out at two a.m. one morning to handle two port cases. One of the defendants was a 72-year-old man who got around with a walker. His story was that he had been down to Juarez, Mexico, visiting one of the "whore houses." After his visit was over, he did not have a ride to his home in El Paso, so "someone" offered to lend him the use of their old, beat-up pickup truck. As he was coming through the port of entry, he was stopped. There was a burlap bag of marijuana under the hood of the vehicle. The old timer claimed he did not know the marijuana was there, that he was duped into driving the vehicle. He would not change his story, so I hauled him and the other defendant off to the county jail.

At eight o'clock that morning, I had to pick the two defendants up to take them to the federal building for their initial appearance. When I got to the jail, the jailers had the 72-year-old man in a wheelchair and had my other defendant all ready to go. Jesus, this is going to be embarrassing for a 50-year-old man wheeling this 72-year-old man in handcuffs down the street in broad daylight to the federal building. I handcuffed the second defendant to the wheelchair and made him push the old man down the street while I walked a few feet back. I anticipated the jokes I would encounter when my colleagues saw me in court with the old man in a wheelchair. "Hey Gil, are you that desperate for cases?" "Hey, did you have to run him down?" "Hey did he put up a fight?" "Did you have trouble getting the cuffs on him?"

Later, I met with the old man and his attorney. He stuck to his story; I could not break him. I ran down every lead he gave me, but I could not disprove his story. There was no way in hell I was taking that old man in a wheelchair to trial. I would be wasting the government's money and my time. No jury would convict him. His case was the only case I ever agreed to dismiss.

It was after that case I realized that doing law enforcement work, most of the time you are dealing with society's underbelly. I knew it was time for me to move on, and the opportunity soon came via a phone call. Those that can, do, and those that can't, or those have grown tired of doing, teach or go into management.

Ain't That a Beach

In late summer 1996, Lucia was in Houston, teaching assets forfeiture to a financial group. After her presentation, she was approached by the Director of the U.S. Customs Service Academy in Brunswick, Georgia, asking her if she was interested in being an instructor at the Federal Law Enforcement Training Center in Glynco, Georgia. The director told Lucia that he had no female instructors and was looking for capable women. Lucia said she was interested but she was married to an old Customs Agent. The director told her to call me. I was in the right frame of mind, so I said, "Let's do it!" We faxed our applications, and the next day, we were selected. My current boss took offense at my departure, but I had had enough, especially if I was going to be working those "rookie" cases. My current boss and I would reconcile a year and a half later. He would need me again, and not for any "rookie" cases.

Once in the Brunswick area, we rented a condo not far off the beach on St. Simons Island for the first sixty days. Then we bought a small three-bedroom cottage on St. Simon's Island about a mile from the beach. There was a causeway to cross to get to the island. After moving in, I had the master bedroom and bath expanded to make it was roomier. The house already had a beautiful sunroom with a fireplace attached to the back side of the house. I also had a large gazebo built over the hot tub in the back yard. St. Simon's Island is a beautiful little island, with the highest point, at the airport, 13 feet above sea level. I regularly rented an aircraft from an aircraft rental service at the airport and flew up and down the beach and around the area. St. Simon's Island had an abundance of wonderful places to eat, and we tried them all.

In the evenings, after a jog around the parts of the island, I could kick back in the sunroom, feet up in my recliner, a glass of Merlot in one hand and a Nicaraguan cigar in the other, with no worries about being called out for a case. This seemed like the good life to me, but I still remembered what the poor folks were doing: gettin' by. I regularly visited the fish shops to purchase fresh fish, which I would grill on the barbecue, often grilling grouper for grouper sandwiches. I was getting into this island lifestyle.

At the academy, Lucia was assigned to the advanced field training group and I was assigned to the basic academy-based training. She often would travel throughout the U.S. with her colleagues, presenting training to agents in the field. I taught different blocks of instruction to new-hire students going through the academy. Rarely did I find myself in a classroom teaching for more than six hours. The rest of the time was dedicated to class preparation or physical fitness. Lucia was gone a large portion of the first year on field training. We did travel together for a week-long training presentation to Customs Officials in Columbia, South America. I also travelled to Budapest, Hungary, for a week to present training to a group of Russians, Czech, and Polish law enforcement officials. This beat the hell out of being called out at 2-3 o'clock in the morning. This must be the good life. I was no longer just gettin' by.

I owned two classic Ford Mustangs, one a fully restored 1965 coupe and the other a 1973 metallic gold white top convertible, which I often showed in classic car shows in the area on weekends. Several times, I won first place in my category with both cars. There was so much to do in that coastal area. We were only one hour's drive from Jacksonville, Florida and Savannah, Georgia. Charleston, South Carolina was only a two hours' drive away. The area offered deep sea fishing, kayaking, hunting, and many other types of fishing. In all, it was a whole different life than how I had lived before. It seemed like a good place to retire.

As a 50-year-old instructor, I could not relate to the young students as they attended the four-month academy. Many were right out of college and had never held jobs. Many were not prepared for the rigors of attending a four-month academy. They were not prepared to put their personal lives on hold during the four months. One young lady from the New York area called me before she even arrived at the academy, inquiring about rescheduling her arrival to a later date due to recent knee surgery, even though she had recovered from the surgery. I assured her that the physical requirements of the training were not that critical, and we had not failed anyone due to not passing the mile and a half run. I did persuade her to report as scheduled. Shortly after reporting, her grandmother died, causing her to request leave to attend the funeral. The leave was granted. Students could miss three days of classes without having to be recycled. Before she returned home, she approached me, suggesting that since she would be missing class, it might be better for her if she dropped out and recycled to another class. Again, I persuaded her to return to her class. Academically, she was at the top of her class, but she was struggling with the physical training associated with it. It was obvious that the young lady had never exercised in her adult life. Running with the class in the evenings was torture to her. I usually ran with the class during their physical training, hoping to motivate the young students. The night before the young lady dropped out of the academy, I ran with her and another student at the back of the class, hoping that I could encourage the two to finish the run. However, the young lady dropped out of the run and could barely finish the course walking. From the waist down, she was overweight, carrying most of her weight in her thighs and legs. The next morning, the young lady came to my office wanting to drop out of the training until a later date. I tried to persuade her to stay, but she was determined to throw in the towel due to the physical training.

Sometime later I received a call from a supervisor at the New York Port Authority inquiring about recommending the young lady for employment. I was not about to recommend the young lady for employment. I bluntly told the caller that if he were to hire her, she would become a supervisor's worst nightmare. In my opinion, she would be creating issues when asked to endure any hardships associated with her job.

A young man that was hired from the Immigration Service in San Diego attended the same class. The young man accepted the training dates, knowing that his young wife was due to deliver their first child during the period he was in training. He moved his wife from San Diego to Seattle, WA, to stay with her parents while he attended the academy. As the arrival date approached, the young man requested three days' leave to be home when the child arrived. The leave was granted. When he returned to the academy, he approached me, asking to take another day of leave in conjunction with a long weekend so he could travel to Seattle again and attended a "family photo shoot" his wife had arranged. I informed him I would have to check with the Assistant Director before granting the leave. He was not pleased with the Assistant Director's response. I informed him that the Assistant Director stated that he had already take three days leave, and that he knew his wife was pregnant when he accepted the training dates. Further, the Assistant Director, who had had a long military career, stated he was not even in the country when his three children were born. The young man became highly upset hearing that. I then referred him to the Assistant Director, who evidently granted the young man the day of leave.

While in Georgia, I learned that my former supervisor of the white-collar crime group in El Paso, Jay, had been called to active duty with the Army National Guard and deployed to Bosnia. As time passed, management began to wonder why Jay had not returned to El Paso after more than a year of deployment. In time, management would learn that Jay was under military house arrest in Bosnia. Apparently, the military had intercepted some classified documents that Jay had sent home to his wife in El Paso. Jay reportedly claimed that the documents were "research for a book he was writing." In time, Jay pled guilty to the charges and was sent back to the States. On the day he reported back to work, he was served with a proposed termination notice due to his felony conviction. However, Jay had enough time in service to retire at a reduced annuity before he was terminated. Jay went back to school. He obtained a graduate degree and began a teaching career.

Twice during the first year, I was telephonically interviewed for two supervisory positions, one in El Paso and one Calexico, California, a real hellhole. Others were selected for those positions, but Lucia's and my applications were still being considered. Toward the end of 1997, approximately one year after arriving in Georgia, we got word that El Paso had two supervisory openings and the positions were to be filled by the end of that work week. Friday came and at about 4 p.m. EST time, 2 p.m. El Paso time, I walked down the hall to Lucia's office to ask her if she had heard anything. She said that Don, her former supervisor, had called, leaving a message. I asked her what he wanted. She said she didn't know, as she had not called him back. I told her she should call him back to find out what he wanted. Lucia asked what would happen if she was selected and I was not. I told her if that is the case, I would just go back to El Paso in the senior investigator position I was in before. She then picked up the phone and called Don. I stood there for 10 minutes, listening to her end of the conversation. After she hung up, I asked her what he said, and she said that we both had been selected for supervisory positions in El Paso. Damn, it would be nice if someone had called me. The way the selection process works is that the selection is not official until Washington signs off on it. The selectee is not supposed to be notified until after the selection is official, but it is always leaked out to the selectee. When we were still in El Paso, Lucia had been selected for a Customs Attaché position in Monterey, Mexico, but her selection was rejected by the assistant commissioner in Washington. She was very disappointed, but it was a relief to me, as I did not want to live in Mexico.

Later that evening, while we were out celebrating our unofficial selection, I got a phone call from my former boss in El Paso. He informed me that I had unofficially been selected for a supervisory position, making a point of telling me that this phone call never happened. After it was official, Don finally called me asking me if I could come back earlier than Lucia because they wanted me to take the place of a current supervisor whom they intended to fire from his supervisory position. It seems the supervisor, Francisco, was running roughshod over his subordinates. His investigative group had mutinied, led by the office "golden boy." Francisco was being sent to the 'elephant bone yard,' better known as the El Paso Intelligence Center (EPIC). Not only had Francisco been running roughshod over his subordinates, but he was also creating much discontent among the other agencies at the Paso del Norte port of entry. It was also rumored that he had more than a professional interest in one of the boss's female staff members. The boss was worried that there might be some sexual harassment issues. They wanted me to come back early so I could smooth things over with the employees and other agencies. Damn, what a position to be put in, I thought. I agreed to report back 30 days earlier than Lucia.

What was I thinking? Oh, I remember now. It was the pay increase and that my annuity was calculated on my last three years' salary. I could retire in three years at age 53. With Lucia and me both being promoted, we would be earning a combine income of approximately $280,000 a year. That would be more than just gettin' by.

Years later, after I retired, I learned from my former boss that he and Joe Bob did not want to hire Lucia as a supervisor. Joe Bob did not think that Lucia exhibited the maturity to be a manager. But Don had influenced their decision to promote Lucia. My former boss stated that he only agreed to hire Lucia because he thought I might not take the position if I was promoted and she was not.

Throughout the period that Don supervised Lucia, she openly exhibited a flirtatious interest in him. Don was married to an El Paso school principle. He had two sons and a young daughter. According to Kent, Don had served three tours in Vietnam and was wounded twice. Kent had become close with Don through their mutual interest in horses. Kent had discovered that Don had a dark side, which he hid from most people. Don had confided in Kent that when he was in Vietnam, he had reported other soldiers for misconduct, even testifying against them. Don's younger son had died because of a gunshot wound. The newspaper version described the incident as an accident. But Kent had learned that the son committed suicide. Kent described Don as very controlling with his wife and children. The older son had run away from home and the daughter could not wait to get out of the house when the time came. Colleagues of his wife regularly advised her to dump Don due to his controlling ways

After Lucia and I arrived back in El Paso, she and Don were sent to attend a three-day financial conference in Ruidoso, NM. I had sent one of the agents assigned to my group to attend the conference also. About noon on the third day, the agent assigned to my group arrived back at my office, informing me that the conference was only a half day on the last day. When I arrived home that evening, Lucia was not home. She soon arrived and announced that "I got a wild hair up my ass to go horseback riding," so she and Don rented horses and went off on a ride. Over the years, I would hear from Kent, who was at the conference also, that Lucia had pressured Don into going horseback riding with her.

The Old Gringo

I arrived back in El Paso after only a year in Georgia. I was told that a management review team from Washington looked into the employees' complaints about Francisco. The team found that Francisco needed to be removed from his supervisory role. Seems Francisco had a habit of patting his side arm and telling people, "There is a new sheriff in town." The first Tuesday after I arrived in El Paso, Don called Francisco and me into his office. Francisco looked like he had just gone a couple rounds with Mike Tyson after coming from the boss's office, where he was informed of his immediate transfer. Don calmly told Francisco to give me his pager, his cellphone, the cell phone charger, his government credit card, and the keys to his government car. Francisco seemed like someone who had no idea where he was or what he was doing. Shortly after that, Francisco left the building and was not seen around our office for three years.

I knew I would have to tread lightly while supervising a narcotic investigative group led by the office golden boy that had just gotten their previous supervisor fired. The golden boy had done some good cases in the past and had a direct line to upper management. He was a good agent, but he would soon create an unpleasant situation in our office, resulting in him being transferred to another of our offices. My secretary, a cute, little married mother of two, took a shine to the golden boy. The married golden boy took a shine to her to. It would not be long before the rumors started circulating about the two being involved in an affair. The young lady's husband also seemed to be aware of the rumors. I was forced to call them both in to make sure that the situation no longer impacted the work place. It is a very delicate situation when you call a married woman into your office and suggest that she is having an affair with a married male coworker.

I called the golden boy in first. He admitted to an impropriety with the young lady, saying, "Gil, I broke it off when I found out my wife was pregnant with triplets." He unconvincingly acted as though he was remorseful. The young lady would only say, "We are just friends." So, I left it at that. Evidently, the golden boy led the young lady to believe that there was a possibility that he might leave his wife to be with the young lady. She was distraught when she found out that she had been misled and that the golden boy's wife was pregnant with triplets. The golden boy was transferred to another investigative group, but he would regularly sneak back to our office to visit the young lady. I finally had to ban him from my office. As it would turn out, the golden boy had a history of liaisons with female employees in the past. He was also suspected of having inappropriate physical contact with a female agent in the workplace in the past. When questioned about the incident by internal affairs, he answered, "I may have, but I don't recall." Great answer. He was not lying, nor was he admitting anything. When interviewed by internal affairs, lying will cost you your job. This would be the first of many times that I would ask myself why I hadn't I just stayed in Georgia.

Soon after I arrived back in El Paso, the agent in charge who hired me for the supervisory position retired and went to work for a private company. His assistant, Joe Bob, was soon promoted to agent in charge, which left the assistant job vacant. The dynamics of the entire office would be changed by the person who would fill the assistant vacancy. The new assistant agent in charge was transferring in from another office in Texas. His nickname, "Speed Bump," preceded him. We would soon learn that his nickname was well- deserved. "Speed Bump" was hardly a facilitator in the office. On the contrary, he made things as difficult as possible with his micro-management. When the retiring Special Agent in Charge learned of "Speed Bump's" tentative selection, he traveled to Washington D.C. to try and persuade the Assistant Commissioner to hire someone else. The Assistant Commissioner would not be persuaded otherwise; she insisted on hiring a Hispanic for the position. Once I met him, I tagged him with another nickname, "Jabba the Hutt," due to his 350-pound girth and the way he looked sitting behind his desk. He was so round at the girth that he had to sit with his arms fully extended to write. I had no respect for the man. In a brief time, I would soon tag him with another nickname: "Dr. Evil." He would always talk in a condescending manner to his management staff. He was never interested in hearing what the first line supervisors had to say. He just wanted to hear what he had to say. "Dr. Evil" just wanted us to "zip it." We soon learned to keep our thoughts to ourselves at supervisory meetings. Lucia was the only one who would regularly interject her thoughts into the meeting. She was routinely dissed. Things would only go from bad to worse for me with Dr. Evil. I did my best to avoid him, but he routinely liked to hold "court" with his first line supervisors. Court usually lasted a couple hours while he went through his dissertation on management matters.

As first line supervisors, one of our responsibilities was the preparation and submission of award requests for our subordinates. I was very generous when requesting dollar amounts to be awarded to agents in my group. They were subjected to working long hours. At times, they put their jobs, lives, and marriages on the line. I thought nothing of requesting a $1500 award for an agent who had worked long and hard at putting a good case together. Dr. Evil did not appreciate my generosity. He would routinely reject my awards requests because of the amount requested. Dr. Evil would not have any contact with the agents assigned to me for months at a time and knew little, if anything, about the effort they had put forth. Dr. Evil had never walked the walk. He had never done the job he was supervising. Dr. Evil directed me to prepare future award requests but when doing so, I was to "pencil in" the dollar amount requested, allowing him to erase my amount and replace it with his own amount. That did not sit well with me. I refused to pencil in the amount. I continued to type it in. I told him he could cross out the amount I requested and replace it with his own, but I wanted a record of what I was requesting. Many times, he would award a secretary the same amount for assisting in the annual Combined Federal Campaign as he would an agent that had spent weeks or months working on a case. He and I would never see eye-to-eye on this issue. It would be the first of many head-buttings he and I would have.

I was assigned a new agent who had just graduated from the academy in Georgia. J.R. was a very like- able and conscientious young man who already had several years of experience in law enforcement. I took a liking to the young man from the beginning. I learned that he was engaged to be married soon to his longtime girlfriend. J.R. would soon be treated to a rude introduction to federal law enforcement. "If not by the grace of god there I go, as many had gone before him."

One of the many duties agents were assigned was to serve as armed escort for the movement of copious amounts of narcotics to a contract burn facility in Tucson, Arizona. The destruction of the narcotics was the responsibility of the uniformed Customs Inspection Division. Whenever a large shipment of narcotics was readied to be transported to Tucson, we were required to assign two armed agents to accompany the narcotics and the Customs Officers transporting the shipment. Unfortunately for J.R., I assigned him to the detail. A senior agent from another group was also assigned the task. All went well until 5 p.m. that day.

Throughout the entire day, 14,000 pounds of marijuana was transferred into the burn incinerator. Shortly before 5 p.m. the last of the marijuana was loaded into the incinerator. The contract facility employee advised the Customs officers that he was not paid overtime, so he was going home. All the marijuana was in the incinerator burning, so the employee secured the facility and the

Customs Officers signed the destruction declaration. However, the facility employee turned off the gas to the incinerator, leaving the tightly packed marijuana to burn on its own. As was the practice for many years, the Customs officers and agents left the facility also. J.R. suggested to the senior agent that they stay since the marijuana was still burning, but he was dissed by the senior agent. That simple suggestion saved J.R.'s job.

When the burn facility opened the next morning, all hell broke loose. It was later learned that that two former employees of the facility had broken into the facility during the night and, using the facility's front loader, removed approximately 400 pounds of unburned marijuana from the incinerator. The theft was reported back to El Paso and then to Washington D.C. You would have thought that someone had stolen the crown jewels. All employees involved in the burn operation were summoned before upper management and placed on administrative leave with pay until further notice. Each employee could not leave El Paso and they had to report to their managers every morning by 10 a.m. Dr. Evil completely circumvented me by having J.R. and the other agent report directly to him. Throughout the next several weeks, while an investigation was completed, J.R. and I met at the gym every day to work out. As Thanksgiving approached that year, I asked Dr. Evil if J.R. could travel back to his hometown and celebrate Thanksgiving with his fiancée but Dr. Evil would not allow it, saying "someone will have to take him in, because he can't leave town." From that point forward, I had nothing but distain for Dr. Evil. J.R. and his fiancée spent Thanksgiving at my house.

Through a source I had in Washington D.C., I was informed that all the employees except J.R. were to be fired. J.R. was to be force-transferred to Chicago. If he showed any resistance to the transfer, he would be fired. Seven uniformed employees and the other agent were given notices of termination. The other agent's supervisor was out of town that day, so I got the unpleasant task of being with him in Joe Bob's office when he was given the termination notice. I was asked by Joe Bob to escort the agent out of the building. It seems that the then Commissioner, Ray Kelly, was showing no mercy to any of the employees.

Before J.R. and I were summoned to Joe Bob's office that afternoon, I had J.R. meet me at the gym. I prefaced my conversation with, "We never had this conversation." I told him about the pending transfer and that if he showed any signs of defiance, he would be fired. I told him that when he and I were called to Joe Bob's office, he was to act like he was hearing about the transfer for the first time and not to show any disrespect to Joe Bob in any manner. It all went as well as could be expected, but least J.R. kept his job and was permitted to return to work. I had arrived at Joe Bob's office before J.R. arrived. As Joe Bob and I stood looking out his office window, silently contemplating what we were being forced to do to the Senior Agent and J.R., I expressed my amazement at all the hoopla over the whole Tucson incident.

I told him, "What's the big deal over another 400 pounds of marijuana on the street when at best we were interdicting 10% of what's being crossed into the United States."

Joe Bob replied, "You had better not let Commissioner Kelly

hear you say that, or you will be out of a job." Before J.R. was transferred, he and I found ourselves answering to a management review team for a lost load of marijuana. Georgia was on my mind.

Joe Bob was a 6"4" laid-back guy who was liked by all, but as a manager, he tended to be lazy when it came to attending to the administrative paperwork aspect of his job. As if I could talk. For a big guy, Joe Bob could get emotional especially during a farewell presentation for an employee. Like House Speaker John Boehner, he would choke up at times. The Tucson burn detail debacle would result in even a worse fate for Job Bob than for J.R. Commissioner Kelly effectively placed Joe Bob on probation for approximately the next year before he got "kicked in the balls" hard enough that he landed in New York City. Commissioner Kelly upgraded the agent in charge positions in El Paso and New York from General Service grades to Senior Executive grades and announced the positions on the internet, forcing Joe Bob to reapply for his job. The tactic had been used before when Washington wanted to get rid of a manager. Joe Bob was unaware that his position had been upgraded and announced on the internet. I found out the morning after it was announced and called Joe Bob. Joe Bob sounded disheartened, saying, "I just found out about it myself." The upgrade would only result in a $3000 a year increase in pay for Joe Bob if he was selected for his job. Joe Bob applied for the position, not realizing that he was applying for both positions, El Paso and New York.

Things went smoothly for Joe Bob for the next few months, but another incident on a Tucson burn detail would be the last nail in Joe Bob's coffin. The evening after the burn detail was completed, another agent assigned to that burn detail got intoxicated, creating an incident in the hotel parking lot. The incident was reported back to El Paso and then to Washington. Things did not look good for Joe Bob. A short time later, Joe Bob was summoned by the Commissioner to meet him at Tucson International Airport, a five-hour drive for Joe Bob. He must have thought during that drive that he was to be informed that he had been re-selected for his position, but it was not the case. Joe Bob met the Commissioner on the tarmac at the airport as his plane landed and walked with him to the terminal. During that short walk, the Commissioner informed Joe Bob, "I am not ready to give you that job yet," end of conversation. It was a long drive back to El Paso for Joe Bob. After his stop in Tucson, the Commission then traveled to Yuma, Arizona, where it just so happened his son was stationed at the Marine Corps Air Station.

Several weeks after, J.R. was permitted return to work pending his transfer. Our group was conducting a controlled delivery of marijuana to some individuals in El Paso. An informant had been authorized to cross the marijuana into the U.S. under our direction and drop off the vehicle at a predetermined location. The marijuana was then to be picked up by a second party and driven to a second location. We maintained surveillance on the loaded vehicle all night and most of the next day, when it was moved to the second location. As the loaded vehicle was being moved to the destination, the driver of the vehicle spotted the surveillance team and successfully eluded them. As J.R.'s luck would have it, he was point man on the surveillance when the vehicle got away. We could not locate the vehicle again, so now we had to report a "lost load" to our management. For three days afterwards, we were questioned by a management review team lead by an agent from Washington, assisted by Dr. Evil's protégée, "Mini-Me." Mini-Me was not happy with me because I would not allow the inference that J.R.'s inexperience led to the load vehicle getting away. It was too soon after the Tucson debacle, and I thought I might be used against him. We were all cleared of any responsibility but Mini-Me and I were on a collision course. After that three-day management review, I filled out all my retirement papers, sealed them in a large envelope and labeled the envelope "emergency retirement package," which I carried with me daily in my briefcase until the bitter end. I would not be subjected to another management review team inquiry.

We were delivering another load of marijuana to a residence on the east side of El Paso. When the vehicle was parked at the residence by an informant, Tom, the case agent, would give the signal to hit the house. As the informant parked in front of the house, two individuals exited the house to meet him. On Tom's command, we approached the house, jumping out of our cars to arrest the recipients of the load. One of the individuals from the house made a dash for the back of the house to avoid arrest. Tom and I chased the young man. Tom, being the younger and faster, caught him as he tried to get through the back gate. Seeing that Tom had the guy handcuffed, I returned to the front of the house. As I approached the front, a neighbor from across the street came up to me shouting, "You can't do this without a permit," (meaning warrant). I told him I don't need no stinking permit, and I aggressively straight-armed him to the chest, telling him to "get the fuck out of here" before I arrested him for interfering with a law enforcement officer. He immediately returned to across the street.

Another agent, Alexis, was the controlling agent for an informant that would not take guidance, no matter how sternly he was instructed to do so. He had been told not to bring a load of narcotics across the border unless we had received authorization to do so. As I walked out of my office one day into the vehicle inspection area, I observed the young man getting out of a stalled car and attempting to push it into the U.S. I approached the young man at the back of the car and assisted him in pushing the car out of the traffic lane. As we did, he whispered, "The trunk is loaded." Soon as we got the vehicle clear of the traffic lane, I hauled the young man into our office and turned him over to Alexis. Alexis proceeded to chew his ass for not notifying us prior to crossing the load. He claimed that he did not have time to do so. As Alexis chewed him out, the young man began to cry, which irritated Alexis, causing him to throw a rubber eraser at the young man, hitting him in the head, thus tagging him with the nickname of ERASERHEAD. I entered the office as the young man continued to cry, which irritated me. I kicked the leg of the chair he was sitting in and told him to knock off the bullshit. The crying seemed fake to me. After we cleaned up the mess, I instructed Alexis to deactivate the informant, fearing that he would cause someone to lose their job.

I few days later, I was at the central office and encountered Joe Bob stepping outside his office. He summoned me into his office for a talk. As I closed the door, Joe Bob said, "I am wondering if you are not a Jekyll and Hyde." I had no idea where this ass chewing was going. He then proceeded to relate what he had heard about me throwing the neighbor off the property in east El Paso. I reminded him that the same scenario was a training scenario presented at the academy when a neighbor tried to interfere during the execution of a search warrant. I admitted that I was very aggressive in that situation due to the adrenalin flowing after the foot chase and the neighbor pissing me off. I then explained what had happened with ERASERHEAD and him crossing the load without authorization. He was satisfied with my explanation, but he said he had never seen the aggressive side of me. I later learned that he had gotten the version of incidents thirdhand from a female friend of his.

Our group was conducting another controlled delivery of marijuana to a residence on the east side of El Paso. We had briefed that morning and all the agents assigned to my group were on surveillance at the residence, watching the loaded vehicle that was parked there. I would need a relief surveillance team later that night to relieve the agents who were there all day and evening. Dr. Evil was out of the office that day, which left Mini-Me acting assistant agent in charge. So, I called Mini-Me and asked that he arrange a relief crew for the midnight shift. He informed me that he wanted me to send half my surveillance crew home now, and he would arrange for other agents to take their place, so my agents could come back at midnight to resume surveillance. I tried to explain to Mini-Me that I only had eight agents in the field working the surveillance and if I sent half home, I would only have four units. He also would have to arrange for a relief crew at midnight anyway for the other four agents that were to remain. He would not be swayed, saying that he wanted me to send half of my agent's home, because it would be easier for him to get someone to work the afternoon shift than the midnight shift. Mini-Me also had never walked the walk when it came to working narcotics cases. I told him I would not do that, he was not going to run my group, and he could forget about my request. My group worked the case all the way through till the next morning, when we busted the house and discovered a seconded loaded vehicle in the garage. Be careful whose toes you step on today, because they may be connected to the ass you must kiss tomorrow; however, I may have stepped on his toes, but I would not kiss his ass. A man of character does not ingratiate himself to another man for favor. However, he may occasionally have to ingratiate himself to a woman for her favor.

As my luck would have it, and as you may have guessed, Monday morning, it was announced that Mini-Me was promoted to Dr. Evil's assistant. But Mini-Me was not through with me yet. In his new position, Mini-Me did not have any direct line authority over me, but he would fix that. Mini-Me had been removed from four previous first line supervisory positions after he created such a hostile work environment. Mini- Me would always single out at least one person in his group and use his position of authority to avenge a perceived challenge to his authority, all under the guise of making the employee do his job. Only after the situation escalated to an intolerable point would upper management step in and reassign Mini-Me to another position. At one-point, upper management created a detail for Mini-Me that would require him to travel away from the office for several weeks, "making contacts" with other law enforcement agencies throughout the area. The previous agent in charge had tried to transfer Mini-Me to Washington D.C. but his reputation had preceded him, and no one would accept him.

In the summer of 1999, at the suggestion of Levi and the encouragement of Lucia, I bought my first Touring motorcycle, a 1996 Yamaha Venture Royal, which I bought from the proceeds of the sale of my 1965 Ford Mustang Coupe. I did not really want to spend a lot of money on the motorcycle because I was not sure I wanted to pursue that lifestyle. I had never envisioned myself in that life; I had always thought of myself as the husband in "Married with Children." The Yamaha was inexpensive, but I never did get comfortable with it. I felt that it was top-heavy, and my long legs were always cramped when riding it for extended periods of time. After I purchased the bike, Levi and I decided that we would ride up to Jerome, Arizona, then back down into Prescott, then over into Wenden, Arizona. It is a beautiful ride till you get down into the desolate area around Wenden. Wenden is nothing but a run-down agricultural town inhabited by many Hispanic laborers. The Wenden area is a large cotton producer. As we were coming down from Prescott into Wenden, we passed a late model red Chrysler Sebring convertible with California license plates occupied by two younger males. They had the top down on the convertible, and I noticed that the passenger had a silk scarf around his neck that was flapping in the breeze. They were chilling as they drove along with the wind in their hair.

As Levi and I pulled into Wenden, we turned into the only gas station in town, an old-style station that still had the pumps that had to be cranked to recycle the meters on the pumps. Levi pulled to one side of the pump island and I pulled to the other side. After Levi filled his tank, he moved his bike away from the pumps just as the red Sebring pulled up to the pumps. I was still filling my tank as I watched the two guys in the vehicle. I noticed that they appeared to be "light in the loafers," or of an alternative lifestyle, especially the passenger. The driver got out and started to fill the vehicle tank. The passenger briefly got out to stretch his legs. I noticed that, as he walked around the passenger side of the vehicle, he was manipulating large steel Chinese therapy balls in his right hand. Levi noticed as well. The passenger then got back into the vehicle, continuing to manipulate the balls with his left hand while the driver continued to fill the tank.

For some unexplained reason, Levi walked over to the driver's side of the vehicle. He told the passenger, "You do that well." The passenger seemed elated by the simple compliment, stepping out of the vehicle again while switching the steel balls to his right hand and pacing back and forth, demonstrating his dexterity to Levi. It was a good thing that the old gas pump had an automatic cutoff on the filler handle, or the driver would have spewed gas all over his loafers. He had his jaw locked in anger and the blood vessel in his left temple noticeably protruded while he glared at Levi and his partner. Just as unexpectedly as he began the conversation,

Levi turned and walked away. I could not believe what I had just witnessed.

It was a Sunday afternoon, and in Wenden, there is nothing for the Hispanic laborers to do but sit in the shade and drink beer. Wenden accordingly has one of the highest beer sales on Sunday afternoon as any place in the state of Arizona at that little convenience store. There were a large group of Hispanic laborers sitting in the shaded side of the buildings, watching the exchange between these two old crusty bikers and the two young males in the red convertible. At Levi's retirement party, I retold that story and presented him with some therapy balls and a silk scarf.

On another of our motorcycle trips, Levi and I had gone to Big Bear, California. After visiting Big Bear, we headed down Hwy 18 to Los Angeles, California to visit of friend of Levi's. Highway 18 is a narrow mountainous road dropping down into the Los Angeles basin. Levi was leading the way as we followed the narrow, serpentine road down out of the Big Bear area. As we travelled down the road, I remembered thinking to myself that Levi was hot dogging as he was negotiating the turns. Levi was feeling "groovy," laying that large Harley Davidson Ultra Classic into those sharp turns. It was almost like watching a waltz as he swayed back and forth into the turns. About halfway down the road, Levi came upon a "switchback" turn to the left. He quickly realized that he was going too fast and would not make the turn unless he leaned the Harley more to the left to tighten up his turn. He leaned it as far as he could, but in doing so, his left foot board scraped the pavement of the road, causing his tires to break traction with the road.

I was breaking to avoid running over him as he and his Harley
went into a slide off the roadway into a gravel turnout. I got my
bike stopped in the turnout without running into Levi. I watched
as his bike and he both slid about 20 feet through the gravel. Levi
was in a picture perfect slide into home plate on the left cheek
of his ass, right behind his sliding Harley. The Harley still had
enough momentum as it slid into the embankment that it uprighted itself, smacking the right side of the motorcycle against
the embankment. Just then, Levi slid into the embankment as his
Harley came down on his right leg. The windshield of the motorcycle came down across Levi's helmet. It was clear Levi was in pain
as he got out from under the bike.

We uprighted the bike and assessed the damage. Most of the
damage was cosmetic to the right side of the bike. The impact
knocked the headlight out of its mounting. Levi quickly grabbed
the headlight and bungee-corded it to the back of his bike. He
tried the starter. It started, so Levi said, "Let's get the hell out of
here before someone calls the cops." At that point, I was sure Levi
must have had severe "road rash" on the left cheek of his ass.

We travelled down the mountain a few miles until we came to
a wide turnout. There, we reassessed the damage to Levi's bike. I
then noticed that the left rear pocket of Levi's pants was gone, and
his bulky wallet was exposed where the pocket once was. Only the
double stitched border of the pocket was still intact. Levi had slid
20 feet in the gravel on his leather wallet with no road rash to his
ass. We headed down to Levi's friend's house, where we spent the
night. Levi's right leg was giving him a lot of pain and he needed

the rest. The next day, we headed back to Yuma, where Levi lived. I continued to El Paso. Levi repaired the damage to his Harley, it eventually being in almost as good a condition as it was before the accident. Levi removed the remaining portion of the pocket from those pants and placed the pocket in a picture frame. He says he still has it in his workshop to remind him of how "stupid" he was that day.

Levi learned one of life's lessons that day. That pushing the envelope, a term used in aviation when loading an aircraft, will sooner or later bite you in the ass. You may get away with pushing your luck, living on the edge, taking risks for a while, but it only takes one mistake and you'll pay the consequences.

Once back in El Paso, one of the first things Mini-Me did in his new position of authority was to orchestrate my transfer from the narcotics group to the white collar group, which would place me under his line of authority. He falsely purported to Dr. Evil that I was the only supervisor that had any experience in white collar crime. It was a ruse to get me under his authority. In late July 1999, a memo was faxed to my office notifying all employees of the pending reassignments, which would be effective August 13th. The transfer was never discussed with me, nor was it ever communicated to me in person by Dr. Evil or Mini-Me. They did call my secretary and confirm receipt of the fax. I was away from the office when the memo was faxed, but I was tipped off before I returned to the office. I would again assume Tom Horn's attitude: "You are going to say what you are going to say, you are going to do what you are going to do, but I am not going to give you the satisfaction." I never acknowledged the faxed memo, nor showed any signs of displeasure with the reassignment.

On August 13th, I reported as assigned to the main office for my new job. I was never told by Mini-Me which supervisory office I would occupy, but I had a good idea—right between his and Lucia's offices. All that first day, I had no contact with Mini-Me while I wandered throughout the main building, visiting with the agents assigned to my new group. I never did occupy my new office that day. At 8:45 the next morning, I got a call from Mini-Me, asking where I was. I informed him I was in route to the office and I would be there in about 3-5 minutes. His response was, "You come and see me when you get here." I had been waiting for this moment for years. I was 53 years old and had 35 years of service, 36 years with the year of sick leave I had on the books. I was already eligible for 82% of my salary for my annuity, so I was coming to work each day for 18% of my paycheck. Had I been able to stick out the next four years, I would have qualified for 90% of my salary as my annuity.

Mini-Me and I were the same pay grades, but he had the title of Assistant Agent in Charge, where as I was only a first line supervisor. Mini-Me started the conversation with, "Where were you yesterday?" to which I responded, "I was here all day." He then said, "Well, I didn't see you." Then he said the phrase I had been waiting for: "Let me tell you what my expectations are of you." I interrupted and told him I was glad he used that phrase. Now it was my turn. I told him he should not have any expectations of me since he had orchestrated my reassignment as a punishment reassignment. I told him he should not have any expectations of someone who is placed in a punishment assignment in their last year before they retire. I told him that I was already eligible for 82% of my salary for retirement and was coming to work for 18% of my paycheck. I was not going to give him 100% percent, but I would obey orders so he could not bring me up on insubordination charges. I told him I would like to get along with him for the next several months until I retired, but that was up to him. He was taken aback by my bluntness, but Mini-Me would not let me ride out the next several months, as it was not in his vengeful makeup. Your relationship with your immediate supervisor influences your attitude toward your job. If your immediate supervisor is going to ride you and micro-manage you every day, you will dread going to work every day. Such was the case with me, but I would not let Mini-Me break me like he had done to several of his employees over the years. Like the great white father told the American Indians in the movie The Outlaw Josey Whales, I would have to endeavor to persevere again.

A few months before my transfer to the white-collar crime group, I completed my commercial, multi-engine instrument flight training and passed my written exam. I had already obtained a seaplane rating, having pipe dreams of working as a commercial pilot after I retired. I would realize that dream, but when I learned of the risks I would be taking and how little low time pilots are paid, I found myself looking for another new adventure. I did not relish the idea of living the "milk toast" life one of my uncles had lived. He had worked for the post office all his life and when he retired, he sat on the couch watching TV for the next eighteen years until his death. I must have something new going on in my life or I feel like I am stagnating.

A couple months later, I bought my first Harley Davidson motorcycle, planning on hitting the road after I retired. It was suggested to me by Ol' Levi from Yuma. He had just bought a Harley in anticipation of his retirement. A short time after I bought mine and got familiar with riding that 850-pound machine, I decided I would go on my first ride. My plan was to ride Highway 1 up the west coast from southern California to Olympia, Washington. I scheduled my departure for a Friday after work to maximize travel time on the first two days, allowing me to make it to southern California early Saturday afternoon. The planned Friday arrived, and in hopes of avoiding a confrontation with Mini-Me, I prepared a short memo to him advising him of my departure plans. I placed the memo in his inbox. I had planned to go home at lunch time, change clothes, and drop off my assigned government vehicle, then return to work on my Harley. By doing so, I could save myself the 1-2 hours of delay, as I could leave directly from work. Well, that plan backfired.

After I returned from home, Mini-Me stepped into my office. Upon seeing me in Levi's and a t-shirt, he asked, "Who gave you the authority to change the agent in charge's dress policy?" He could barely contain his anger. He was literally shaking from holding it in. I explained my intentions and plans, which calmed him a bit. Then he said, as he stabbed his right index finger in the air like an anxious proctologist, "That memo was a zinger to me, it was a zinger!" Mini-Me had more issues than I realized. He finally calmed down, but it would not be the last confrontation he and I would have. The Harley trip went off as planned, or almost.

The Highway 1 trip started off as planned. I made it all the way from El Paso to Eloy, Arizona, on the first evening. The next morning, I was on the road westbound by 6:30 a.m., arriving in the Los Angeles area by early afternoon. I headed up to Lompoc, where I would pick up Highway 1. As I entered the town of Lompoc, travelling through the main part of town, I did not see the right-hand turn to Highway 1 till I was almost up on it. I quickly changed lanes into the right-hand turn lane, but I was going too fast. Just as I started my right-hand turn, I noticed that the two center lanes were under repair and had been excavated out at least a foot lower than the other lanes. I knew I was not going to be able to make the turn going at the speed I was going, so as I rounded the corner, I decided I would have to ride the bike over the one foot drop off into the excavated area. Thankfully, it was a Saturday and there were no workers in the area. I went straight off the drop off into the lower excavated area. Somehow, I managed to not drop the bike, though I did bounce a couple times. I got it straightened out and rode it about a block out of the work area.

Once I got out of the area, I stopped in a parking area to assess the damage to the bike. As soon as I got off the bike, I noticed that I was leaving an oil trail. It did not look good. It was a good thing I stopped. As I checked, I realized that I had only cut the oil line from the oil cooler back into the engine. That would be easy enough to fix once the bike cooled down, but I would have to find a hose and figure out a way to remove the hose clamp on the hose where it was connected to the engine. I found a hose and bought a long flex shaft screwdriver that would allow me to get the hose clamp off in the confined space near the engine. I got it all back together, but I was not sure if I had tightened the hose clamp tight enough on the hose as it went back into the engine. The clamp was holding at idle speed, but would it hold at 32 psi at highway speed? I would have to highway test it to find out. I originally planned to stay in Lompoc and start out the next morning, which is what I should have done.

As I got out on the highway, it appeared that the oil pressure was holding at 32 psi, so it looked like I had the hose clamp tight enough. By then I was several miles north of Lompoc, so I decided that I would continue on to the next town along the coast and stop there. It was the wrong decision. Starting at Pismo Beach California, every small town I stopped in along the highway had no hotel vacancies. Then it dawned on me as it was getting dark that it was a three-day weekend. I continued northbound during the night, checking each small town for hotel vacancies. No luck. I stopped at a truck stop, thinking I could sleep on the grassy area, but the noise was so loud, I could not sleep. So, I continued northbound. At about 12:30 a.m. the next morning, I found myself in in the Bay Area. I thought I should detour over to the east bay, where I might have better luck finding a hotel. Finally, at 1:15 a.m., I found a La Quinta Inn that had vacancies. I had been travelling approximately 20 hours. I hurriedly checked in. I asked the desk clerk where the nearest convenience store was, so I could buy some beer. When I got to the room, I had a couple beers and crashed till later that morning. By travelling during the night, I missed a large portion of Scenic Highway One. I kept that on my bucket list.

After returning to work, rumors started circulating throughout the office that the supervisor and members of his undercover narcotics group were being investigated by the internal affairs office. The "red flags" that something was not right were there, but they were ignored due to the number of arrests and narcotics seizures, "the stats" the group was generating. The stats could lead to a bigger budget, more personnel for the office, and Washington recognition. But where there is smoke, there is fire. As will often happen in an undercover operation, officers step across the line onto the "dark side." It was suspected that the group supervisor, Raymond, and some of his subordinates had crossed onto the "dark side."

At times, the workload of agents at a border station like El Paso was overwhelming. The narcotics seizures that were generated at the ports of entry taxed the agents and the U.S. Attorney's office. During the marijuana harvest season, narcotics seizures could be as high as 11-14 cases in a 24-hour period. New agents were usually burned out in three years. In Raymond's group, they were worked such long hours that they were burned out in only one year. Many would start looking for a transfer out of the group or out of the office to a less intense work environment. When you are dealing with that kind of work load, you start finding ways to cut corners, which can lead to mistakes. If you have done that job, you realize the mistakes that are made by cutting corners and tend to be more forgiving but crossing over to the dark side is not to be forgiven.

Raymond would always ask management to staff his group with the agents fresh out of the academy. The new, inexperienced agents were more likely to do as they are told by a supervisor and work the long hours he demanded of his agents. After arriving back in El Paso, I was told I had to transfer three of the agents assigned from my group to Raymond's group. I volunteered one of the senior agents in my group as one of the three, but Raymond would not have it. He pressed upper management for three newer agents. One of the three would not forgive me for years for that transfer. His promotion was held up for years as a result. The Internal Affairs office was convinced that he had gone to the "dark side." He was eventually cleared and allowed to transfer to Washington D.C., where he is now serving out the remainder of his career.

To me the most glaring red flag was the consistency with which the group successfully used the same informants repeatedly in operations without "burning them"—exposing them as informants. To continue to use informants in an undercover capacity without exposing them usually indicates that the informants are working "both sides." As it turned out, the informants in Raymond's group were working both sides, unbeknownst to some agents but with the knowledge of some controlling agents. The informants realized that they could do "one deal for the cops and three for themselves." It cemented their credibility with the cops as well as with their organization, but it is a thin line to walk. Some of the agents were even suspected of taking bribes to allow criminal conduct by the informants. This was later proven to be the case.

Another glaring red flag was that Raymond himself was the controlling agent of some of the group's informants, which was not the policy of the agency. Supervisors were not to document or control the informants. That is done by the working agents. Raymond would receive the information from the informant, then send one of his agents out to work the information. The poor, unsuspecting new agent would blindly follow orders. On more than one occasion, Raymond's informants had smuggled the narcotics then staged them at a location in the El Paso area for Raymond's group to seize. The informant then would be paid a cash award for the information. Once the narcotics were seized, it was policy that the narcotics and any other property be turned over to the Fines, Penalties, and Forfeiture Division of U.S. Customs for custodial keeping. It was later learned that Raymond had not been turning in all of the narcotics, property, vehicles, etc. for custodial keeping. They were being stored at the undercover location and used for future cases. This type of activity is not only unethical and illegal but also compromises the prosecution of the case and other cases presented to the U.S. Attorney's office. Any agent who knowingly presents false testimony under oath can never present a case in in court again. His credibility is damaged forever. Once a liar, always a liar, as the defense attorneys would say.

One thing informants learn, and agents should recognize, is that the first time an agent takes a bribe from an informant or smuggler, the agent is effectively handing the criminal informant a "get out of jail free" card. The informant can continue his criminal activities. He will carry that "card" in his wallet, knowing it can be a ticket to avoiding prosecution, excepting murder. The first time the informant is arrested, he will utter the words, "I can give you a federal agent if I am granted immunity from prosecution." Any Assistant U.S. Attorney hearing that statement will jump at the chance to prosecute a federal agent. I have seen it several times.

As the Internal Affairs investigation developed, it was discovered that Raymond and some of his subordinates in his group were taking bribes and knowingly allowing informants to smuggle un-interdicted loads of narcotics into the United States. Crossing the line to the dark side will cost an agent his job and maybe prison time if he does not cooperate in the ongoing investigation. Crossing the line to the dark side when you are in a management position will ensure you a lengthy prison sentence for betraying the public trust.

The collateral damage done to Raymond's undercover group was widespread and long lasting. Some agents were resigned or were terminated when their involvement was discovered. The special prosecutor out of Washington was convinced that the whole undercover group was dirty. The investigation continued for years and the agents under suspicion were effectively guilty without due process. Once Internal Affairs opens a "red book" on an employee, the person cannot be promoted or transferred, effectively punishing the employee for the duration of the investigation. The Internal Affairs office is supposed to finalize the investigation and notify the employee as soon as possible of the results. That does not always happen. They can keep the investigation open for years. Such was the case with some of the employees in Raymond's group.

The special prosecutor's office in Washington D.C., in an effort to elicit the cooperation of other employees, indicted two members of the undercover group. The prosecutor was convinced that David and Frank knew more than they were telling. The prosecutor was going to play hardball with them if they did not cooperate and give up other members of the group. David and Frank were two standup guys. They were not in a position to give up anyone else. I was David's instructor when he went through the academy. Frank was a local police officer assigned to the undercover group. They did not deserve what was being done to them. Their trial was the only time I would volunteer to testify for the defense on their behalf. Thankfully, I had retired before their case went to trial.

I took the witness stand at their trial, testifying to David's and Frank's character. The special prosecutor was not pleased with me. The prosecutor tried to shake my belief in David's character by asking me "what if" questions. "Agent Andrews, what if you knew David had been driving around in a government vehicle drinking beer with an informant? Would that change your belief in him?" She did not like my answer: "If not by the grace of god there I go." She was stunned, as I was effectively admitting that I had done the same thing. I had, but that was years before, and she couldn't do anything about it now. The magistrate judge ended my testimony and I was excused. Thankfully, David and Frank were acquitted of all charges. It was a great day.

Raymond was relieved of duty and subsequently pled guilty to charges, receiving a 10-year prison sentence. He deserved all of it and more for the lives he ruined. Two of his subordinates also were terminated. Raymond had a beautiful wife and daughter who had to pay the price for his actions. His wife was in a management position with Customs also, so together they earned over $200,000 per year. Anyone that takes a bribe when you make that kind of money is just plain stupid. It was also discovered during the investigation that Raymond was living a double life ("money for nothing and the chicks are free"). He had a secret bachelor pad and girls on the side, one of whom was Lucia's niece.

In time, it was announced that Joe Bob was selected for Senior Executive Service position in New York City, not in El Paso. As Joe Bob walked passed my office the morning of the announcement, I congratulated him on the promotion. Joe Bob said, "What are you talking about? That is a kick in the balls. It only amounts to a $3000 a year raise, and it will cost me more than that to live there." Joe Bob would appeal his transfer, but the Commissioner had wisely prevented an effective challenge to the transfer by making it a promotion. Joe Bob did challenge the transfer based on protection from the Whistle Blower Protection Act. His argument was that his complaints about the local internal affairs office's unethical practices were really the basis for his transfer. At the merit system protection board hearing, the Commissioner testified that he was not punishing Joe Bob but, in fact, he was promoting him to Custom's most prestigious office, New York City. Joe Bob was in number 7 World Trade Center when the planes crashed in to the twin towers. It would have a lasting emotional effect on him.

Thankfully, Commissioner Kelly resigned as commissioner on the last day of the Clinton Administration.

Mini-Me did not like that I would allow agents assigned to the white-collar group to continue narcotics cases they had prior to being assigned to my group. One of the newly assigned agents was working information from an informant about a loaded vehicle parked at a residence in El Paso. When he approached the house, it was also discovered that a van containing a large amount of marijuana was parked in the residence's garage. The agent called me at home and reported the arrest and marijuana seizure to me. I, in turn, reported it to Mini-Me. Mini-Me posed a question to me about one of the vehicles that was at the residence. I told him I did not have that information, but when the agent called me again, I would obtain that information. That did not please him, so he yelled over the phone, "That is not good enough. Joe Bob wants an answer to that question now." I just hung up the phone, so he called back, but I would not take his call. I wasn't putting up with Mini-Me any longer. I would maintain my quiet resolve.

The next day, I assumed Tom Horn's attitude again and the day ended without incident. I had submitted my retirement package directly to Washington D.C. I had also visited my doctor, informing her of my retirement plans and the excessive amount of sick leave I had on the books. I asked her if she would sign an excuse from work due to her treating me for stress. I wanted to burn up some of the excessive sick leave. I told her about Mini-Me and how I wanted to choke the little shit, so she signed the excuse. I also told her that "I would just as soon kick his ass as look at him." The next day, I went to work as usual but, toward the end of the day, I contacted one of the senior agents in the group, asking him to meet me at the office so he could give me a ride home. I informed him that he would be in charge of the group for the next few weeks while I was on leave. I did not tell him I was retiring. I never returned to work after that. Eventually, Dr. Evil and Mini-Me would learn that I had submitted my retirement papers. Mini-Me made a point of calling at my home, leaving a message on the answering machine that I had to turn in my issued weapon. I would do that on my own time and in my own way. To process out, I would have to turn in my badge also, but I had arranged to have it retired and sent to the property specialist at the academy in Georgia to have it encased in Lucite with my other three badges. I was not about to turn in my badge to the local office, allowing someone to switch badges for my lower number badge. That had happened to me once before.

Only a little over two years before, Customs management asked that I come back to El Paso to fix a problem they had created by promoting Francisco to a supervisory position. But now, I had outlived my usefulness to them. In three short years, I would out live my usefulness to Lucia as well. Customs already had my replacement waiting in the wings. So, did Lucia. Customs found a younger agent in San Francisco and Lucia would find a younger replacement in El Paso. Ironically, the younger agent would turn out to be one of the five agents who were sued over Jose and Lilia's death. Management in El Paso would rue the day they hired him. He would only last a little over a year as a supervisor before he would seek and be awarded a full medical retirement because of the emotional trauma associated with witnessing Jose, Lilia, and their baby son being burned alive. The real story was he had been caught lying to management about a case. They were planning to discipline him over the matter, so he bailed out before they could. Lucia would also rue the day her younger silver-tongued truck driver came into her life, changing her lifestyle dramatically. She would not be driving BMW motor vehicles in her senior years. But she would soon be seven months behind on her mortgage.

By now, Lucia and I were drifting toward different, separate lives. We were just getting by in the marriage. She, being the more social creature, wanted to hang out with her family and friends. I preferred to keep to myself. I had gotten the impression that she was anxious for me to retire so she would not have her husband in the same work place as her. I also got the impression that she thought the old gringo cramped her style at work. Things were about to take a dramatic turn for us. At her encouragement, I frequently accompanied Ol' Levi on motorcycle trips throughout the U.S., including Alaska. She seemed to want me out of her hair.

Ironically, after I retired, Mini-Me made Lucia the focus of his harassing management style. Within a few months, Lucia filed a Hostile Work Environment and EEO complaint against him. A three-member management review team from Washington D.C. was sent to look into her complaints. Again, management had to rein in Mini-Me, marginalizing him temporarily. The review team also found that Lucia had acted unprofessionally by using the "f" bomb in a heated exchange between her and Mini-Me. She withdrew the EEO portion of the complaint, but the review team determined that she lied to the team about that portion. In order to avoid it looking like retaliation, the agent in charge waited a year and then issued Lucia a formal Letter of Reprimand for lying to the review team.

A few weeks after my retirement, Joe Bob called me to meet so he could present me with my "retirement watch" and award for my lengthy service. I agreed to meet him at a restaurant for lunch. I did not want to return to the Customs office. Initially, I hoped that I might get to explain my side of the events preceding my retirement. As it turned out, he did not want to hear it. He said that I was burned out. I told him I was not burned out, I was pissed off, but he did not want to hear that either. For the next three hours, he used me as a sounding board for his argument to be used before the Merit System Protection Board in appealing his transfer. He was claiming protection under the Whistle Blower Protection Act. Based on what he told me, I did not think he had a case. He did lose the case before the board and was transferred to New York City. I haven't seen Joe Bob since that day. One thing you learn when retiring from an organization is that, "when you are out, you are out." As in the movie About Schmidt with Jack Nicholson, you quickly learn that someone is always standing in the wings waiting to replace you. When Schmidt leaves the building he once worked in, he sees the contents and files of his office, the sum of his entire career, set out for the garbage collectors.

Mean Woman Blues

Shortly after I retired, in March 2000, I was hired as a contract co-pilot in a Cessna Citation aircraft owned by three individuals on a time share basis. I was not type-rated in that aircraft, but the pilot had single pilot wavier, which allowed me to serve as an un-rated co-pilot. It was an excellent job while it lasted. Ironically, the pilot, Teddy, also retired from U. S. Customs. He spent most of his life in the army and government as a pilot. Teddy had an almost unlimited cash expense account, so when we traveled, we always had a rental car and stayed at nicer lodgings. At meal time, the bar tab always was a part of the meal service. It was a good life for the brief time it lasted.

One of the three owners of the aircraft, Ed, operated a prof-itable construction company in El Paso. However, Ed had been forced to sign over 51% of his company to his wife. His wife had discovered that Ed was having an affair with his married secretary. His wife had learned that Ed had rented an apartment so he and his secretary could meet during the day to carry on their affair. Ed's wife boldly knocked on the door one day and was greeted by Ed in his underwear. Ed did not even try to deny the affair, openly admitting, "Ya, I was banging that pussy." To keep his wife from divorcing him and taking him to the cleaners, Ed agreed to giving his wife controlling interest in the company. Additionally, he had to pay his secretary $80,000 to settle a sexual harassment suit.

Teddy was married to a young woman 25 years his junior named Precious. She had had a daughter out of wedlock when she was a teenager. During much of the time in the cockpit, Teddy would talk about how great a relationship he and Precious had and how wonderful their marriage was. He would jump at any opportunity to break out his wallet and show anyone the picture of "his girls," Precious and her 16-year-old daughter, Cheryl Ann.

After several months, the owners of the aircraft decided that the Citation aircraft's cabin was too small. They decided to sell it and get a larger aircraft that had a "standup cabin" and a lavatory. We delivered the Citation to the buyers in Toledo, Ohio on April 20th, 2001 and returned to El Paso via commercial carrier. Lucia and Precious met us at the airport. As we exited the arrival area, I noticed that Precious seemed awkwardly uncomfortable. She and Teddy exchanged kisses and held hands as they walked from the terminal, but it did not seem natural. In a several months, I would discover why. Lucia would soon exhibit the same behaviors.

The partners then bought an older Hawker 400, which would require them to hire a type rated copilot for the aircraft. So, I found myself out of a job. I then started piloting an aircraft that was used to drop skydivers at the Santa Teresa, New Mexico, airport. There was no pay involved. I just logged the hours to increase my total flight hours, as many low time pilots will do. I did that job for almost a year until I was hired by an on-demand freight and passenger charter operation at El Paso airport. We were paid 14 cents a mile based on established mileage. Because it was an on-demand operation, there was no schedule. The chief pilot told me when I was hired that I would be burnt out in a year, and he was right. I did not like flying those light twin engine aircraft in the severe weather, especially coming out of Albuquerque at 6 a.m. in ice and snow.

On July 21st, 2001, just a few short months after I stopped flying with Teddy and listening to how wonderful his relationship was with Precious, I got a call from him telling me that he had just gotten out of jail. Precious had had him arrested for domestic violence. My response was, "Oh, you are bullshitting me." Teddy said that it was true, and he had spent the night in jail. He gave me a brief version of what had happened the night before, so I asked him where he was. He said he was at the aircraft hangar, where he would live for the next year or so.

I immediately drove out to the hangar to hear his story. For the next two years, I would get daily updates of what had happened and was going to happen leading up to their divorce. Then he would hear me echoing some of the stories he told me. It seems it all started in late 2000, when Precious got hired by U. S. Customs, thanks to Lucia's and Teddy's efforts. Originally, she was working for the Border Patrol in El Paso, thanks to Teddy's contacts within that agency. Precious was hired as an investigative assistant, which is a glorified secretarial position. For the right person, it could be a stepping stone to a criminal investigator position. Funnily enough, it is the same position that Lucia held when I met her. According to Teddy, Precious started showing signs of wanting to venture outside the bonds of the marriage soon after she was hired by U.S Customs Office of Investigation. She no longer liked the 58-year-old gatekeeper's constraints. After eight years of marriage, Precious decided that she wanted Teddy to adopt her now 16-year-old daughter, something that she had resisted for the previous eight years. They started the adoption proceedings in October of 2000. They were subsequently visited by an officer of the court to do a family survey to determine if the adoption should be approved.

During the visit, Precious, Teddy and the daughter all stated that theirs was a happy household. But, unbeknownst to all, Precious had a plan. On June 12th, 2001, the judge signed the adoption order. On June 13th, Precious called Teddy to meet her for lunch, but he would not enjoy that meal. Precious bluntly told him that the adoption order had been signed and she wanted a divorce. Teddy was blindsided. Teddy has a "gift" of seeing things the way he wants to see things. I wish I had that gift. Sometimes men are so short sighted, they can't see any further than the head of their penis.

After leaving the restaurant, he drove straight to the county court clerk's office to see what his options were. The clerk, who was niece of the Judge who signed the order, advised Teddy that once an adoption is signed, it is almost like it is written in stone unless he can prove the adoption was fraudulent. He would be paying Precious $1500 a month spousal support and $1000 a month child support for more than a year. Precious had done her homework, but she had a co-conspirator. Teddy could not figure out what had happened to his marriage, but he would not like what he and I were about to discover.

Teddy moved out of the house and into the hangar office at the airport. For many months, he slept in the recliner in the office. When I visited him that day at the hangar, I spent the rest of the day listening to what had transpired over the last few months. All the money he had in his travel expense account as well as 3-4 hundred thousand dollars they had in joint accounts was missing. After living in the hangar for a couple weeks, Precious called, wanting to meet Teddy. Naturally, he went running back to their house, and in no time at all, they ended up in bed. Teddy was a wounded man and he needed comforting, but Precious needed to play him for just a while longer. She convinced Teddy to move back into the house for a two-week trial reconciliation. She would soon reveal that she had made an offer on a small condominium, but she could not close the deal by herself because she was still married. Teddy would have to sign a quit claim deed for her to close the deal. Teddy was not so wounded that he would fall for that. He wanted answers first. Teddy would be listening to the sad songs for the next couple of years.

Teddy had started to suspect that there was another man involved with his wife right after she was hired by U.S. Customs. In time, he would learn there were two. Evidently, shortly after Precious was hired by Customs, she and a male coworker named Monk began a close working relationship. Monk was a player who could not be trusted. He spent more time chasing skirts than he did doing his job. One evening, Precious came home unusually late from work, passing quickly through the living room, straight to the shower. Teddy said he noticed that she had a sweaty sheen about her complexion. Teddy got up from his chair. He followed Precious to the shower, where he noticed her panties lying on the floor. They had a wet stain in the crotch. He then opened the shower door and inserted his two fingers into her vagina. As he withdrew his fingers, he raised them up in the air, saying, "I have another man's cum dripping off my fingers." Amazingly, Precious offered no resistance or denial. Teddy went back to the living room and seated himself in his recliner.

Soon, freshly showered, Precious entered the living room wearing only a towel and, while standing in front of Teddy seated in the recliner, she dropped the towel and began massaging her own augmented breasts saying, "My boobies hurt. I need someone to massage them." As you might have guessed, wounded Teddy needed comforting again, so he gladly obliged Precious by massaging her perfectly symmetrical enhanced boobies, which led to the couple ending up in the bedroom. What is a man supposed to do? Precious had once again soothed the old gringo, but not for much longer.

On the evening that Teddy was arrested, he had been pressing Precious for answers about "what happened to our marriage?" Teddy does not have Tom Horn's demeanor. He insisted that she log onto her email account and produce her cell phone records, which she was resisting. Precious made an excuse to go to the garage to avoid complying with Teddy's demands. Teddy made the mistake of following her, demanding that she go back in the house, log onto her email account, and provide her cell phone bill. Precious brushed by Teddy, knocking his extended arm out of the way as he pointed toward the door to the house. When he entered the house, he assumed that Precious had gone to the bedroom to avoid him again. He went back to his recliner to watch the movie King Kong. Shortly thereafter, the 16-year-old daughter arrived home, asking where her mom was. When Teddy informed her that she was in the bedroom, the daughter went to check but could not find her mother. When she came out of the bedroom and informed Teddy that her mother was not in the bedroom, Teddy said that she must have gone out to walk the dogs. The daughter then retrieved her kickboxing gloves and left for her class.

A brief time later, Teddy began to wonder where Precious was himself and got up to go look in front of the house. As he walked out the front door, he noticed a police cruiser pull up in front of the house. As the officers got out of their car, Teddy asked what was going on, to which the officers replied, "We have a call of domestic disturbance."

Teddy replied, "Oh ya, on this street?"

The officers said, "Yes, at this house." Precious had gone next door to call 911 to report domestic violence at the hands of her husband. The officers took a statement from Precious, in which she said that while the two of them were in the garage, Teddy had pushed her and thrown beer on her. Teddy was drinking vodka and Fresca that night. Precious would tell others that Teddy had tried to choke her and kill her. The officers could find no evidence of domestic violence, but they informed Teddy that, as a result of the widely-publicized abuse in the O.J. Simpson case, the El Paso District Attorney had a zero-tolerance policy on domestic violence cases. Since Precious had made the 911 call, guess who is going to jail? Teddy was taken into custody and booked into the country jail. It would not be his last arrest on charges by Precious. His next arrest would lead to charges against Precious for making a false statement and a false 911 call. It would take weeks of work on our part to find the parking lot video that cleared him.

As I listened to his version of the story, naturally I thought there two versions to it. But as time wore on and his story remained consistent, I began to believe his version of that night. I also concluded, based on the story about the "shower scene," that Precious was having an affair and had been intimate with another man on that night. As I told Teddy, any woman who was violated in the manner he violated Precious in the shower that night would not come out of the shower and initiate sex with the man who had just violated her unless she was guilty. It would be a long time, if ever, before she would allow him to touch her again. As I also told him, I believed him because I don't think any man would make up a disgusting, degrading story like the shower scene and repeat it to a close friend. I also told him that because of the legal situation he now found himself in, he had to be careful about measures he took to prove his innocence, but I did not. I had a new case to work. One thing Precious did not know was that Teddy had secretly installed an automatic audio recording device on their home phone. Teddy played for me a portion of the recordings he had retrieved from his house. Monk could clearly be heard on the recording describing how he liked to bend Precious over and enter her anally. He also bragged that anytime someone gave him any trouble, he would cock his eyebrow like the actor Dwayne Johnson and give the person that "pinche Rock look," causing the person to back off. I told Teddy that the recording device was illegal since neither party in the conversation was aware of the device. He said he knew that and had removed the device. I was no longer in law enforcement, so I was no longer obligated to report him. The tape could never be used in the upcoming divorce proceedings

The other thing Teddy learned during the two-week phony reconciliation was that Precious had another suitor, one of her new managers who had shown more than a professional interest in Precious. During the two-week reconciliation, Precious bragged that the assistant Special Agent in Charge, Brian Player, was visiting her regularly at her satellite office, telling her that he would help her in her quest to become a special agent with U.S. Customs. In fact, he would hand-carry her application to Washington for her. Precious bragged that she was told by Player that she would be a special agent within a year. I could not let that happen. I was not motivated by revenge; someone as unethical as Precious should never be allowed to provide testimony in a criminal case. According to Precious, she knew how to handle Player. She was going to "play" him; he was sniffing around her like a little puppy. Teddy warned her about her attempts to "play" him, but she responded, "I know what I am doing, you old fuck. It is called Sexual Harassment, and I am going to play him like a banjo." She was setting up Player for blackmail. Even though Player deserved it, I could not let that happen to my old agency. I could not let a woman like Precious become a Federal Law Enforcement Officer. As I left the aircraft hangar on July 21, 2001, I had a new mission in life, but it would have lasting effects on my own marriage. I told Teddy that what I was about to do I would not be able to share with him because of his legal situation. All I could tell him was that I intended to preempt Precious's plans through the time proven method of "divide and conquer."

A question that has always remained in my mind was how Precious, at the early age of 25, had learned to use her sexuality to play grown men so well. I have always suspected and will always believe that Precious exhibited signs of a woman who had at an early age been repeatedly molested by an older relative, possibly her stepfather. I suspect also that her child is possibly the result of that molestation, as in the case of my younger sister.

Monk had worked for me a brief time before I retired. Player and I also had a brief history in Yuma, Arizona. It was time to rectify some unsettled issues. After Monk left my group, he was assigned to Mini-Me's group, where he intentionally and falsely reported his involvement in a narcotics case, which caused the case to be dismissed. It was the first of many disagreements between Mini-Me and myself. Monk was a "snake in the grass," playing both Precious and his ex-wife, who Monk had played while she was married to her previous husband. I would have to let them both know that they were both being played. Player had a younger wife with two young daughters who deserved to know that he was up to his old tricks. The story was that the current Mrs. Player had been played by her husband when he was married to his first wife. What the players all needed to realize was that if they will do it for you, they will do it to you. In other words, a married person playing around with you while they are married to another will play around when they are married to you also.

The difference in personalities between Monk and Player were 180 degrees. Monk was a raw, streetwise player, but Player was a mild-mannered, soft-spoken, kind gentleman. Their goals, however, were the same—the seduction of any available females. Even Lucia, when she first met Player, came home and told me how nice he was. I informed her I had known him and his reputation since 1977, and he was wolf in sheep's clothing. Player was the classic example of a suit, a bootlicker. He literally had held staff positions since he was hired by U.S. Customs in 1977. He drew law enforcement overtime pay and received a law enforcement retirement, but he never performed law enforcement duties. Soon after he was hired by Customs, he attached himself to another bootlicker, who pulled him all the way to the top. At one time, he held a position of "liaison to the Pentagon" before he was assigned to the "bone yard," the El Paso Intelligence Center (EPIC). When Customs abolished their positions at EPIC, Player was reassigned to the assistant Special Agent in Charge position at Customs Office of Investigations. He was supervising a job he had never performed. Player epitomized the term "puss of a man." He used that orifice on his face to utter words that would get him what he wanted in life, be it promotions, reassignments, or women. That was the extent of the effort that he had put into his career.

Monk, on the other hand, had been a street cop in Las Cruces, New Mexico, where he served as a motor officer. That role suited his needs for high visibility. He met his ex-wife while he was a police officer. But Teresa was married to another officer in the same department. After her husband divorced her, Teresa married Monk, and they soon had a child. Rumor had it that Teresa had already had a child, which Monk supposedly adopted. Was he the one that schooled Precious on adoption and domestic violence? Monk and Teresa's marriage did not last long. Monk found himself paying child support for two children. Monk was eventually hired by U.S. Customs uniformed Inspection Division and subsequently selected as a special agent in our office. Monk now found himself living with his parents in El Paso. In time, Teresa would file to have her child support payments increased due to Monk's increase in salary. Monk figured that he could keep Teresa out of court by convincing her that they might reconcile and get remarried. Initially, Teresa fell for the ploy, but she soon found out about Precious. And Precious would find out about Monk spending weekends at Teresa's apartment in Las Cruces. Precious confronted Monk about Teresa. Monk just told Precious, "You are just my little piece of jealous pie."

Precious and Teddy's story was even more colorful. According to Teddy, he met Precious when he was 50 years old, and she was 25 years old. Precious was married to a coworker of Teddy's, a fellow pilot. The coworkers would often get together for office social events. Teddy was recently divorced from his attorney wife and was self-appointed leader of the office social events. There was an

obvious attraction between Precious and Teddy that even her husband was aware of, once saying Teddy could have his wife anytime he wanted. Teddy has always had a "come hither" look in his
eyes, which women picked up on. One day, Teddy received a call
from Precious telling Teddy that she and her husband were getting divorced and that she wanted to talk to Teddy about it. Teddy
allowed her to visit his house, but within five minutes, they were
having sex. Precious became a regular visitor at Teddy's house,
even sometimes accompanied by her 8-year-old daughter. Soon
after they started seeing each other, Precious would often be sick
during her visits. She finally revealed that she was pregnant by her
husband and that they were still living together. But she said that
they only had sex one time. If you believe that, I have a bridge in
Lake Havasu, Arizona, I will sell you.

Teddy reluctantly broke off the relationship, telling Precious
that he would not continue to see her as long as she was married.
There was also the matter of the pregnancy, which she aborted. She
was soon divorced. She and Teddy resumed their lustful relationship. They were going at it like minxes, even though Teddy was 50
years old. Teddy was in lust and he had fallen into it hard. Within
no time, they flew off to Vegas and got married. Soon after they
were married, Teddy paid for breast augmentations for Precious's
25-year-old sagging breasts. He often praised the job the doctor
did on Precious's now perfectly formed breasts. He loved those tit-
ties. Teddy needed a reality check. He was not factoring in the age
difference. When she turned 35 and would be going through her
midlife crisis, he would be 60. He was already going through his

own midlife crises. I have often heard that sometimes men do not think with the head on their shoulders. At 50 years old, Teddy too was acting stupidly.

It was now time for a reality check for the threesome before the situation got out of hand. It was time to expose the office romances. It was time to divide and conquer. I could not report any unproven allegations to those who had the need to know, but I could pose pointed inquiring questions that needed answers. The place to start was the threesome's agency, the U.S. Customs Service Office of Investigation. I chose to make the initial notification to a female manager, one of Player's colleagues, in the hopes that a female manager would not sweep the matter under the carpet, as had so often happened in the good ole boy network of the past. I also hoped that the agency would handle the matter internally rather than airing their dirty laundry in public. I would soon learn that the manager decided to ignore the notification because the letter was anonymous. The female manager had also been soothed by Player's smooth ways. That was a mistake on her part. Allegations of sexual harassment cannot be ignored—they must be reported for investigation. If the agency chooses to ignore the allegations, they will have to be reported directly to Internal Affairs. Precious could not be allowed to blackmail her way into a Criminal Investigators position. The anonymous letter to Internal Affairs had the desired effect. They opened an investigation into the matter.

To expose Monk and drive a wedge between him and Precious, it was time to let Teresa and Precious know that they were being played by Monk and were, in reality, rivals for his affection. Each lady received a letter letting them know of the other lady's involvement, along with their respective addresses and phone numbers. Teresa also received a copy of Monk's current pay scale, which would help her in her petition to have her child support increased.

Mrs. Player would be a delicate matter. I could not report any unfounded allegations about her husband, but she would need to know that the matter was being considered. Initially she chose to believe her husband's soft-spoken denial, but when he announced his untimely retirement and she learned that he was a respondent in an upcoming divorce proceeding as well as a sexual harassment law suit, she became more than suspicious. She would need to attend Teddy's divorce proceeding to hear firsthand what her husband was up to.

On July 31, 2001, at 7:00 a.m., eleven days after Teddy's arrest, we were on our respective computers, arranging a meeting time for our daily morning coffee at the Starbucks in the Albertson's grocery store area on the west side of El Paso. We agreed to meet at 9:00 a.m. but we were both running a little late. He arrived at 9:07 a.m. and I arrived at 9:10 a.m., as the time check on the store video would show. After about 30 minutes, I got up to go use the restroom near the entrance of the store. As I approached the east entrance, I encountered two uniformed El Paso Police officers and noticed two more officers entering the west entrance to the store.

As I passed by the two officers near me, one asked, "What's your name?" I told the officer my name then continued to the restroom. I watched as they continued into the store. As I left the restroom, the two officers were escorting Teddy out of the store.

He was under arrest again. I followed them outside and watched from a distance as they placed Teddy up against the wall to pat him down for weapons. Damn, they had just done a felony arrest on Teddy, but for what? After I bailed him out of jail that afternoon, I would learn what had happened. But before Teddy was released on bond, he learned that Precious was in the process of having felony "making terroristic threats" charges filed against him.

Precious was up to her old tricks but, thanks to video surveillance cameras, this time, it would all backfire and turn her world upside down. She would be labeled criminally as a liar. She just ended her quest to become a criminal investigator. At 9:22 that morning, Precious had placed a 911 call to El Paso Police claiming that Teddy was stalking her that morning and had been making threatening phone calls to her, both misdemeanor charges. She also advised police that Teddy carried a weapon and was armed. That explained why four officers were dispatched for misdemeanor charges, affecting a felony arrest on Teddy. But he could not have stalked Precious that morning, because he and I were on our respective computers all morning, and his desktop computer was located 15 miles away in the hangar at the Santa Teresa, New Mexico airport. I could not prove that he was at the airport on his desktop computer, but I would in time realize that proof of his innocence existed elsewhere. It would take me two weeks to realize that the Albertson's store had video surveillance inside and out.

I notified Teddy of my revelation that, maybe, just maybe, there was proof on the video tapes. His divorce attorney provided us with a subpoena for the videos on the date in question. We were provided with copies of the tapes for that date by the store manager. We weren't prepared for what we were provided. The videos recorded 16 different frames from different angles at once. The video had to be taken to a professional to have sequential frames arranged in order. It was worth all the effort, because the video showed Precious conducting her false 911 call and making a false report to law enforcement.

The video from inside the store showed Teddy arriving at 9:07 a.m. and me arriving at 9:10 a.m. The parking lot video showed Precious arriving in her vehicle at 9:22, pulling into a parking place facing west but never exiting her vehicle. After a couple minutes remaining in the car, she backed her vehicle out of the parking space and re-positioned her vehicle facing east, with direct line-of-sight to Teddy's vehicle. At 9:31, the police officers arrived at the Albertson's store parking area. Precious then stepped out of her vehicle and met with the officers. She then made her false statement to law enforcement officers. It could not have played out any better if I had directed it myself.

Now Teddy needed to take that video to the Detective Division of the El Paso Police Department to clear his name. When he arrived at the police station, he contacted the detective's sergeant, requesting that he view the video. The detective who took Precious's complaint also watched as the video was played. As the detective viewed the video, realizing he had been played, he commented, "But she seemed so credible." That revelation would preempt the felony charges that were being considered by the police department. Precious would subsequently be facing charges of her own, one for making a false 911 call and another for making a false statement to a police officer. The charges were also reported to her agency.

To further expose Precious, it was time for Internal Affairs to consider the sexual harassment claims that I had reported. When Precious was approached by Internal Affairs, she acknowledged the sexual harassment but claimed it was unsolicited. She also provided her "blackmail ammunition" to Internal Affairs—33 interoffice emails between Player and her, which she just happened to have saved. She also provided an audio tape recording from her home answering machine, which contained a message left by Player. What a dumbass. How stupid was this guy? Was he that emboldened?

The message did not sound like a professional contact: "Hello, beautiful, I was just driving by and I thought I would give you a call and see how you were doing." I had preempted Precious. She could no longer claim she had reported the sexual harassment. I had. But she would argue that in her 1.2-million-dollar law suit against the agency.

Within six weeks of my reporting the sexual harassment and Precious's plans to set up Player, he announced his untimely retirement. I would later learn that the agency had issued a Cease and Desist order against Player, something that is rarely done. Player told his female colleague that he was retiring because there were rumors that he was having an affair and he loved his wife dearly. I would like to sell his colleagues that same bridge in Arizona. But the fix was in for Player. The new Special Agent in Charge who replaced Joe Bob created a golden parachute for Player, a lucrative government contract job which would start the Monday after he retired. The new Special Agent in Charge recruited Player's career-long, now retired mentor to staff the director's position over the contract job, thus ensuring Player the position. The director told one interested candidate that he was not even going to advertise the job because he was hiring Player. The new Special Agent in Charge would also create the same golden parachute in the same office for Mini-Me to induce him to retire. The good ole boy network strikes again.

What the Special Agent in Charge had just done was a contradiction of the government's Sexual Harassment Policy. You cannot say out of one corner of your mouth that as a manager you support the Sexual Harassment Policy and then tell your assistant manager you are going to create a lucrative job for the offender when he is caught red-handed. That conduct would have to be reported to the Inspector General's Office in Washington, D.C. The new Special Agent in Charge had also just made another misstep, which, combined with the handling of the Player situation, would cost him a job he had been promised. After the Internal Affairs investigation of the "golden boy" alleged sexual misconduct with at least two female employees, they provided the results to the Special Agent in Charge, but to their surprise, he responded, "I don't care what your investigation has revealed, I am not going to punish him." That answer was not in keeping management goals when it comes to Sexual Harassment. Internal Affairs did not like that answer.

Shortly thereafter, the Special Agent in Charge learned that he had not been selected for the job he had been promised in San Diego, CA. He retired shortly thereafter. As he would say at his retirement party, "That job had my name all over it, but it was not to be." After his retirement, he stepped into a very lucrative government contract job on the west coast himself.

Precious requested and received a transfer to office 40 miles from El Paso, thus separating her and Monk. Precious had been separated from Player and Monk—now it was time concentrate on Precious and her deceitful ways. After she had Teddy arrested the first time, she would only surrender enough of his personal items to him to allow him a couple changes of clothes. She disposed of everything else, even some of Teddy's memorabilia from his Army, Border Patrol, and Customs careers. I learned that a Border Patrol officer purchased Teddy's retired Border Patrol badge from a junk shop, so I located him and purchased the badge back. I then visited the junk shop and learned that he had purchased several of Teddy's items from a Goodwill store. I purchased some more of his items from the junk shop. I located some more of his items at the Goodwill, along with a copy of the receipt Precious was given when she dropped the items off. Seems she intended to use it as a deduction on her taxes.

The domestic violence charge and the stalking charges were dismissed against Teddy, but he had to hire a separate attorney to have the record expunged. He would also have to hire a separate family attorney to handle trying to get the fraudulent adoption overturned. In total, he would spend close to $200,000 in attorney's fees for the three attorneys. He lost their brand-new house when Precious refused to sign a short sale contract on the house. She lost her vehicle, which I purchased as a repo. She had cleaned him out of his life savings. The money was never recovered, but I did learn on reviewing his bank records that much of the money was wire-transferred to other banks. I believed that she transferred the money to her mother's account, who apparently was in on the scheme. Teddy did not seem to be interested in tracing the money. It was apparently Precious's intent not only to get rid of her old husband, but to also ruin his credit rating and his reputation.

Teddy tried to get a financial judgment against Precious for $68,000, but just before the court hearing on the matter, Precious filed a fraudulent bankruptcy, staying all other court proceedings. In time, he was awarded $1800, which Precious did pay.

Precious was charged with making a false 911 call and making a false statement to a law enforcement officer, but she was given the courtesy of surrendering herself. She cut a deal and was placed on a pretrial diversion program, wherein she could stay the charges pending successful completion of the program. The charges would then be dismissed, thus avoiding a guilty plea. But she had an arrest record and she would never be a Criminal Investigator with the U.S. Customs Service Office of Investigation. Once a liar, always a liar, and with that label, she could never testify in a criminal case as a credible witness. She would eventually lose her $1.2 million Sexual Harassment law suit against U.S. Customs. She claimed in her suit that she had committed professional suicide when she reported Player's harassment of her. She had committed professional suicide, but it was her wicked, conniving ways that did her in. I reported the sexual harassment and her scheme. I was at the sexual harassment hearing so Precious could see me. The jury decided that her suit had no merit. She eventually transferred to another agency in her home town of Albuquerque.

At the divorce trial, before the same judge who had signed the adoption order, Monk and Player were subpoenaed to testify. Player was accompanied by his wife, who sat in the courtroom during the entire day and a half proceeding, thanks to a timely letter to her notifying her of the upcoming proceeding in which her husband was a respondent. Her husband could not keep her away. Player never did admit to any sexual contact but would admit to "maybe meeting Precious two times after hours to discuss her personal problems." He explained all the phone calls from him on Precious's phone records as just business.

In the beginning, when Teddy began having suspicions about Precious, he had her followed by friends on the nights she attended the University of Phoenix just two miles down the street from Player's house. During the first semester, she attended classes on Thursday nights, but after the semester ended, her classes were on Tuesday nights. The surveillance team could never determine where she went when she left school on her break halfway through the class. It was later learned that she drove directly across the street to the parking lot of the Billy Crews restaurant. Coincidentally, Player had boys' night out on Thursday nights at Billy Crews restaurant, which later was switched to Tuesday nights. Nothing was proven, but Player's wife heard it all.

When Monk took the witness stand, he admitted having sex "just one time" with Precious in his truck. A Customs Internal Affairs agent attended all of the proceedings. Monk would only say that he and Precious were just friends. He was caught off guard when he was presented with a photograph in which he and Precious posed for the photo with Air Force One in the background when President Bush visited El Paso. I had learned of the photo and was able to obtain of copy of it from the person that took it with his digital camera. There was also a photo of Monk, Precious, and Precious's daughter with the same background. The daughter was aware of her mother's association with Monk. During the phony reconciliation with Teddy, Precious admitted that she had access to two different apartments, one on the west side of El Paso and one on the east side. It was always suspected that Monk and Precious met regularly at these apartments during work hours.

During the hearing, Precious took the witness stand but never admitted to any intimate contact with Player. When she was asked about the quality of her marriage over the years, she stated "it was never any good. He was not good at anything, but he was a good provider." She turned toward Teddy when she said he was never good at anything and glared at him. The judge noted that statement. It was in direct contradiction to her statements to the court officer during the family survey for the adoption. The judge immediately issued a bench decree, stating, "As of this moment, you two are no longer married." He told Teddy's attorney, "You have shown cause, now move onto the property division."

I voluntarily took the witness stand, testifying to the recovery of Teddy's personal property from the junk shop and Goodwill store. The proceedings were pretty much over at that point.

At the end of the proceedings, Player's wife approached Teddy with tears in her eyes, saying, "You have been screwed." She then knew the kind of person her husband had been associating with.

In the matter of the fraudulent adoption, a hearing was scheduled before the same judge who had signed the order and had presided over the divorce proceedings. Before the hearing, Precious's daughter asked to meet with Teddy. It was the only time in two years she had any contact with Teddy. Teddy agreed to the informal meeting, in which the daughter asked to keep Teddy's last name. Teddy agreed. I suspected that Precious had put her up to it. The adoption was let stand but Teddy would not be financially responsible for the daughter. It would be the last time he would ever see his adopted daughter. As she told Teddy during their meeting, her loyalty was to her mother. I never understood Teddy agreeing to the meeting and allowing the daughter to keep his last name. It never made any sense for the 17-year-old girl to want to keep Teddy's name. In a few years, she would probably marry and change her name anyway. I think Teddy needed it as some consolation to his shattered ego.

Teddy walked away from his lucrative corporate pilot position and is now living in Colombia, South America, on his reduced annual income with his 24-year-old girlfriend, more than 40 years his junior. He lives in an apartment in a little fishing village near a bay. Teddy seems to have that need to have a sweet young thing on his arm, a trophy chick. I think it is his way of denying that he is getting old, his way of saying hey, look at me, I still got it. His own grown children will have nothing to do with him. He broke off contact with me three years ago. I believe it was because I was never impressed with his choice of women. He thought they were great looking, but I thought they were average.

Teddy received an expensive reality check. A sweet young thing can turn into a vicious, conniving bitch when she is denied her wants, but he did not learn from it. As the saying goes, you never truly know a woman until you meet her in divorce court. I guess there is something in his makeup, his vanity, his ego, that has a need for younger women. I understand that he spends most of his time reading paperback books and watching videos. I would soon find myself being treated to a similar reality check, but I was ready to move on as well. I had spent the last few years of my marriage just getting by in the relationship.

Woman On Top

In December of 2000, ten months after I retired, I secretly planned a cruise to the Mexican Rivera for Lucia and me as an anniversary present to her. The difficulties started immediately on the drive to board the ship. She was on her cell phone to a younger male subordinate for the first hour of the drive to San Diego until she lost cell phone reception near Deming, New Mexico. She was almost giddily flirtatious during the phone call. I would later learn others were aware that she had an interest in this young black subordinate. I was told that she had made "overtures" toward the young black agent during a Tucson burn detail they both attended. Supposedly, she had spent the evening drinking and dancing, and after they returned to the hotel, she called the subordinate's room at 2 a.m. At breakfast that morning, Lucia tried to justify making the call to the young black agent, stating, "Oh Dennis, did I call you last night? I was so drunk." After returning to El Paso, some of her subordinates jokingly stated, "Dennis is going to do her for the group." There were ripples throughout the trip, but we got through it. It did not turn out the way I had hoped. Lucia did not seem to be interested in any togetherness. I thought we might rekindle something we once had. Admittedly, I had invested much of myself in my job over the last two years and I thought we needed more time together. All things considered, the entire trip was a bust.

I regularly rode with a group of motorcycle riders who were retired and active duty law enforcement officers. The organization is called the Blue Knights. One of the wives rode her own Harley with the group. Lucia was so impressed that she decided that she would buy her own motorcycle and ride with the group. One day, she called me at home, asking me to come to her office so I could ride her motorcycle home. I had no idea that she had made such a purchase. Initially, I was supportive of her attempts to learn to ride, but I soon realized that her riding created much anxiety in me. It was like watching your eight-year-old daughter trying to learn to ride a bicycle in a busy city street. She took the motorcycle rider safety course three times, but she failed. Finally, on the fourth attempt, she barely passed the course. The instructor suggested that riding may not be a wise thing for her to pursue. It was obvious that she was too childlike in her pursuit of riding. She literally was an accident looking for a place to happen. She just wanted to be seen riding the bike. I encouraged her to continue practicing riding her motorcycle in un-congested areas. Once, I did to convince her to practice at the high school parking lot after hours, but she dropped the bike and wanted to quit and go home.

A riding instructor told her that her motorcycle was too high off the ground and that she might feel more confident if she had a motorcycle that was lower. Again, unbeknownst to me, she purchased another motorcycle, a Harley Sportster. But that was too high for her short legs also. This time, the seller of the Sportster delivered the motorcycle to our house. She then was convinced to have a lowering kit installed on the bike, so her legs could more easily touch the ground. She decided to have a friend of ours install the kit, but he lived approximately 40 miles east of El Paso. On the day that she had arranged to have the lowering kit installed, I signed up for a motorcycle poker run throughout El Paso. I suggested to Lucia that she wait until I had completed the poker run. Then I would ride with her to the mechanic's shop. But she insisted that she wanted to take the bike to the shop on her own.

About three quarters of the way through the Poker run, I received a call on my cell phone. It was from Lucia's cell phone. When I answered, a strange female voice asked, "Is this Gil Andrews." She then informed me that Lucia had been in a motorcycle accident approximately 10 miles east of El Paso. The only other thing she said was that Lucia had regained consciousness and was being taken by ambulance to the hospital. I rushed to the accident location, blowing all the red lights along the 10-mile route. When I arrived at the location, the ambulance had already departed. To my surprise, the motorcycle mechanic was already there. Lucia had had the woman motorist call the mechanic before she called me. I was told which hospital Lucia was taken to, but before I left, I told the mechanic to fix up the motorcycle the best he could and sell it. I did not want to see it again.

When I got to the hospital, Lucia was still in the emergency room, waiting to be attended to. Her right knee was cut all the way to the knee cap. She had cuts and scratches to her face, which was caked in dried blood. Fortunately, she was wearing her helmet. I eventually learned that she had drifted off the interstate highway into a soft, sandy shoulder, causing her to flip the motorcycle. It was a long recovery for Lucia after the deep gash to the knee got infected. To my surprise, her motorcycle was repaired and delivered back to our house. She never did ride it again, so it just sat in the garage taking up space. But Lucia was a Harley owner. I was always suspicious as to why she insisted on going to the out-of-the-way mechanic's shop by herself, but I knew that Lucia was not one to pass up a chance to flirt with a male.

One of the traditions of Harley riders is that when a rider is injured in a motorcycle mishap, the person is given a "broken wing" embroidered patch to affix to their riding jacket. I bought one for Lucia and gave it to her. Later that year, Levi and I were going to ride to Key West, Florida. Lucia wanted to go, but she wanted to travel via air carrier to Ft. Lauderdale, where I would pick her up. She would then travel with us to Key West on my motorcycle. On trips to Skagway, AL, and Glacier National Park, she found she liked meeting us somewhere along our route. After she arrived in Ft. Lauderdale, we met up with a friend of Levi's, and the four of us all went out to dinner. During dinner, Lucia announced, "I have a surprise for Gil." I was totally caught off guard, not knowing what the surprise could be. To my surprise, she announced that she had gotten a tattoo of the "broken wing" patch tattooed on her right breast. Then she exposed the top part of her breast to show us the tattoo just above the nipple area. I was pissed that she had gotten a tattoo behind my back and that I was being informed in a public setting. Again, Tom Horn intervened, preventing me from showing my disdain. But it was obvious that I was not pleased with her surprise.

In May of 2003, I received an email from a former coworker informing me of openings for instructors at the Federal Law Enforcement Training Center (FLETC) in Artesia, New Mexico. The positions were government contract positions for one year that could be extended. I resigned with the flying service in anticipation of being hired by FLETC. I was notified of my selection as a firearms instructor in October of 2003, with a reporting date of November 3, 2003. At that time, we taught the use of firearms to new Border Patrol Agents, Bureau of Indian Affairs Police Officers, Transportation Security Administration Air Marshals, and Commercial Airline Pilots. After a weeklong training course, the airline pilots would be authorized to carry a handgun in the cockpit of their aircraft subsequent to the September 11, 2001 attacks.

A few years after resigning from my flying job, my decision to end my flying career was reinforced when I learned that my former boss at the flying service, Matt Juneau, was killed along with three of his passengers. Matt flew his twin engine Cessna 421 into the side of a mountain. A couple years later, Gene Dawson, the check pilot that gave me my check ride for my commercial, multi-engine instrument rating, crashed on takeoff in his twin engine aircraft. Initially, Gene and his three passengers survived the crash. Gene was hospitalized with the most serious injuries. After a several days in the hospital, he was released to rehab. A couple days later, rehab sent him back to the hospital where Gene died two days later.

We owned a small weekend cabin in Ruidoso, New Mexico. My plan was to sell the cabin and buy another weekend place closer to FLETC, so I could reside at the new weekend residence during the week and return to El Paso on the weekends. During the first two months, I lived in a small efficiency apartment in Artesia, New Mexico. Then I purchased a small place about halfway between Artesia and El Paso, which would allow me to commute to work every day. In late November, Lucia was notified that she was selected as an assistant Special Agent in Charge in El Paso. It did not mean an increase in pay, just a title change. She would now be Mini-Me's counterpart. She would be one of six assistances. She was managing the administrative staff.

All seem to be going as planned at first, but by February 1, 2004, things would start to unravel. Apparently, Lucia had different plans. The events are ingrained in my memory. Lucia visited me at the cabin on the weekend then returned to El Paso on Sunday, February 1. At midday, I lay down to take a nap before Lucia was to leave for El Paso. Lucia joined me in the bedroom and initiated sex in the woman on top position, something she had never done before. The other thing that was strange was that we were having a water well drilled right outside the bedroom window, and Lucia was not one to engage in sex if there was someone else around that might discover our activity. Soon after she was finished with me, she departed for El Paso. I thought the whole incident strange and cold.

I soon learned that I had failed the sex test, the love test Lucia was administering on me. In her mind, if she had sex with her husband and she did not feel that emotional glow afterwards, that meant she did not love me anymore and emotionally she was free to find someone else to love. She already had a candidate picked out, whom she met in late 2003 at a girlfriend's birthday party. Sometime between February 1st and the 7th, Lucia consummated her relationship with her new love. When I arrived home on February 8th, she was a different and cold woman who had difficulty making conversation or even eye contact with me. I will be the first to admit that my mother did not raise a brain surgeon, but Lucia seemed to think I was an idiot. I sensed something was amiss. She exhibited all the classic signs of a woman who was having an affair. That evening, she came into the TV room carrying a pillow. She lay down on the couch, embracing the pillow with her back to me, faking sleep the whole evening.

The following Saturday was February 14th, Valentine's Day, I was scheduled to work half a day that day. I worked that week, but on February 12th and 13th, one of the worst ice storms to hit the area in many years arrived, with black ice covering the entire area. I made it to work on the 12th in my little front wheel drive Daewoo sedan. That car is another story. On Friday the 13th, I decided I might be safer driving my 1973 four-wheel drive Scout International, but that would turn out to be a mistake. I made it 20 miles from the house, where I lost control and rolled the vehicle, totaling it. The only thing that saved me from severe injury was the roll bar installed in the vehicle. I did hyper extend my lower back, which would require treatment for six months. I called my supervisor and advised him that I would not be in to work that day, or for the half-day assignment on Saturday. I got a ride back home with the tow truck driver. I went back to bed because my back was causing me much pain. Later that day, I drove the 125 miles to El Paso, which Lucia was not expecting me to do.

At 4:15 p.m., when I got in cell phone range, I called Lucia's cell phone, leaving a message that I was headed home. I got home at a few minutes before 5:00 p.m., only to find Lucia already home, freshening up her makeup. It was so unusual for her to be home right at quitting time. She anxiously told me that she had a prior commitment. Her supervisor asked her to fill in for her at a meeting at Jaxon's restaurant. She said she figured I would not want to go, so she asked her brother Alex to go with her. Well, I can take a hint and realized I was not invited, so I went to dinner by myself. I did not even have time to tell her about the wreck. I am not going to be the gatekeeper for a woman that is already showing signs of having stepped outside the fence. Again, I would maintain my silent resolve.

When I got home from dinner, Lucia was already home. She said that she had "gotten the dates mixed up" so she and Alex stayed and had a couple drinks. According to her, the meeting was not till the following week. I also noticed that evening that there was a single red rose in a vase on the kitchen table, but I chose to ignore that, too. She didn't seem to realize I spent 29 years in law enforcement acquiring a built-in bullshit meter that had been constantly activated since I got home. Tom Horn's attitude surfaced again (you are going to say what you are going to say, you are going to do what you are going to do, but I will not give you the satisfaction). I did not call her on the bullshit. You can learn so much more by playing along with the ruse.

The next day, Valentine's Day, we had plans to go to dinner with some other couples. Lucia is a social butterfly, but at dinner, she was unusually quiet, acted very uncomfortable, and again was unable to make eye contact with me. After a very long awkward silence on Lucia's part, she looked up from her plate and, addressing me, blurted, "Oh, I have great news. I now have nine employees." I thought that such an unusual thing to say. It was though she was searching for just anything to lessen the tension. I was glad when it was time for me to return to the cabin the next day. I asked Lucia to drive to the cabin the following weekend, because I wanted to ride with her back to El Paso after the visit, so I could ride my Harley back to the cabin and keep it there.

After her visit that weekend, I rode with her the two-hour drive back to El Paso. During the entire trip, very little was said. The whole time, she looked off to her left, avoiding eye contact with me. Her guilt would have shown if she were to look me in the eyes. That evening, I returned to the cabin on the Harley. After that weekend and on each successive weekend, I would experience the same coldness during each of my visits. But the worst was yet to come, on March 28, 2004. On one of the weekends in El Paso, Lucia took me to see a condominium she had made an offer on. Does this sound familiar? I would not be signing any quit claim deed so she could buy that. Tom Horn's attitude surfaced again. On March 28,, Lucia and I went to dinner at Jaxson's restaurant. As we got in her 2003 BMW Z-4 roadster, the radio was playing

Country music. She had never listened to country music in her life. She only listened to passionate Mexican music. Even she was conscious of the strange music, saying, "Oh, I have been listening to the words, I like the words in the songs." It was obvious to me that another man who liked country music had been in the car. But the Tom Horn attitude in me would not let me call her on that either. During the whole dinner, she could not look me in the eye, instead looking off to her right, out the window. She obviously was trying to get through the next 20 hours. It was going to be a long, strange night for us.

After we arrived back I home, I decided to go for a walk to walk off my dinner. When I got back from the walk and entered the darkened living room, passing into the TV room at the back of the house, I did not see Lucia anywhere, so I figured that she went for a walk, too. After a long while, I began to wonder where she was at, so I walked throughout the house looking for her. There she was, in the darkened living room, lying on the couch with the cordless phone pressed to her chest. I thought that strange. I got myself a bottle of Merlot out of the wine rack and went back to TV room. After finishing off the Merlot, I went to bed. At 1:30 a.m. I woke up to use the restroom. I noticed that Lucia was still not in bed, so I checked the darkened living room. She was still on the couch with the phone pressed to her chest. After using the restroom, I put on my clothes and went to the garage to ready myself for an immediate departure. The Tom Horn in me decided I would leave without saying a thing.

I realized that her refusal to share a bed with her husband

meant that she thought doing so would be betraying her newly beloved.

I was loading my two dogs in the car when Lucia came to the garage and asked, "What's going on?" I responded that we both knew what was going on. I would not be staying where I was not welcome. She began to get emotional, knowing it was all out in the open. At least the part about my time having passed with her was, not that she had a lover.

I went back into the house to retrieve some more personal items. She followed me. I had one thing on my mind—getting out of there before things went from bad to worse and she ended up calling 911 to report a false domestic disturbance. I made sure that I kept the breakfast bar between us. All she could bring herself to say was that the last time we had sex, she realized she did not love me anymore and she wanted to live in the condo by herself. Sounded like bullshit to me, but I was out of there anyway. She insisted that she planned on informing me of all this just before I was to leave for the cabin later that afternoon. I was ready to move on. I would never regret the loss of the relationship. I left my wedding ring on the TV tray next to my recliner. I left and drove back to the cabin, where I would live alone for the next 10 years. I would rather live alone in the corner of a darkened room than live with a shrew. In total, I had been married for 33 years. As I drove back to the cabin that morning, I felt emancipated. I found myself embracing my new adventure.

Lucia had acquired the "rock star" mentality. With my help, she had climbed the professional ladder, acquiring a "title." She was making almost $150,000 per year, she had a beautiful home with a pool, she was driving a new BMW Z4 sports car, and her credit rating had risen to 825. She had completed her undergraduate and graduate degrees while we were married. But now she did not need the "old gringo" anymore. Both daughters had graduated from college. The married with children life was not for her anymore. It was time for her to party again. But within a couple years, like many who have achieved success, she would squander her success on her new manipulative spouse.

The following weekend, I returned to the El Paso house to retrieve some more of my things. Lucia was in Austin, Texas, at a function for her daughter. While at the house, I reviewed the caller identification on all the phones. One incoming call was more frequent than the others. It would not take long to identify "Mr. Bill" after I purchased 30 days of his cell phone records over the internet. He had over 1800 calls on his phone bill during that month, many to Lucia. One call was to her office phone, which lasted 59 minutes. I also had a private detective agency run a criminal and credit check on Mr. Bill. His credit rating was unbelievably low for someone who supposedly had a successful trucking operation. He had some non-payments listed on his credit record. He also had two minor incidents on his criminal record. One was for a bar fight, in which he got his front teeth knocked out. The other was for not having the proper paperwork for one of his trucks, which he continued to operate. He would soon be arrested for indebtedness while Lucia was in his company. Lucia certainly had picked herself a winner. She had to bail him out of jail that night.

The next weekend, I again returned to El Paso to retrieve more of my things. That weekend, Lucia was flying to Las Vegas to attend her mother's birthday party. During that visit, I noticed that the file cabinets containing our financial records and our safe had been removed from the house. Mr. Bill would accompany her on that trip to Las Vegas. Her family was already aware that she was divorcing me and had a new beloved. The oldest daughter was also aware, but the youngest daughter was heartbroken when she found out about her mother's affair with another married man. Lucia sent the oldest daughter to our house to have me sign a contract for an offer on our house. Lucia would cancel the contract before it closed when she realized that the proceeds would go into an escrow account until the divorce had been settled

One glaring item jumped out at me on Mr. Bill's phone bill. He regularly phoned his residence while he was away during the day. Damn, was Mr. Bill married? I had to find out. One Saturday, I was in El Paso. I located Mr. Bill's residence in a lower working-class neighborhood on the east side of town. I parked a block down the street from his residence and dialed his number. A lady answered.

"Is this Mrs. Bill?"

"Yes, it is."

"Are you and Mr. Bill still married?"

"Yes, who is asking?"

"This is Gil Andrews, and I think your husband is screwing my wife."

Mrs. Bill said, "I know. I have been trying to figure out how to get a hold of you to let you know."

Seems she found a picture of Lucia in Mr. Bill's coat pocket months before. She too had noticed Lucia's phone number on Mr. Bill's phone bill.

The Divorce Saddle

Mrs. Bill and I struck up a lengthy conversation, in which she told me that Mr. Bill moved out, taking most of his possessions, as well as some of hers. She said that Mr. Bill left behind a custom-made Billy Cook saddle with Silver Conchos, tooled leather, and silver latigo lacing, and his gun cabinet. I told Mrs. Bill that I had been looking for a good saddle and a gun cabinet. I suggested that she call her attorney and I would call mine to see if it would be legal for her to sell me the two items. After checking with our respective attorneys, we were told that the items were community property and she could dispose of them as she wished. I told her I would give her $1000 for the two items. She agreed. I told her I would be at her house in five minutes, to have the saddle on the front porch and the gun cabinet as close to the front door as she could get it, as I would only be there two minutes. We made the exchange and I was out there headed back to the cabin. When I got home, I placed the saddle on a saddle tree in my living room on display. I made up a little sign that hangs on the saddle horn, which reads: "I GOT A SADDLE FOR MY WIFE, IT WAS A GOOD TRADE." The saddle and sign decorate my living room to this day. Mr. Bill did not know for over a year what his wife had done with his prized saddle.

I noticed the red flags indicating that the marriage was fractured as far back as 1995, after the oldest daughter left for college. That was when Lucia worked up the nerve to tell me that she was not as interested in sex as I was and that she has never enjoyed oral sex, even though it had been a part of our marriage for seven years. That revelation was like a light switch being turned off in my head. From that point forward, that was eliminated from our marriage. I would never be comfortable engaging in that with her again. I found that I became reluctant to initiate sex at all.

In the fall of 1998, a few months after the oldest daughter graduated from the University of Texas at Austin and entered law school, we began getting a credit card statement in the mail. At first, I assumed it was just a credit card solicitation addressed to Lucia. I was not in the habit of opening mail that was addressed solely to Lucia, so I ignored the statement for several months. One month, I noticed that the statement or solicitation was addressed to Lucia and me, so I opened the envelope. I was pissed. It was a statement showing that we owed $6000 on a credit card I did not know we had. The original balance was over $7000. The Tom Horn attitude in me could not stop me this time. I wrote across the statement "WHAT IN THE HELL IS THIS" and left the statement on the breakfast bar. I have never carried a balance on a credit card in my life, and I wasn't going to start. When Lucia arrived home, she found my note.

"Oh, I was going to tell you about that." Her usual defense. I did not ask how she got the credit card in my name or what the charges were for. I just told her that when our tax return check came that she would take the tax return and pay off the balance owed on the credit card, which she did. I was not so lax about ignoring credit card statements after that. I was never told what the charges were for, but I always suspected that Lucia, "Mrs. Got Rocks," had picked up the entire expense tab for her family attending the daughter's graduation ceremony in Austin. I learned that she had purchased 43 graduation gifts for the daughter, though I never knew what they were.

I would soon learn that Lucia had paid for her mother's divorce from her sixth husband, Chava. Lucia did not like the 50-something-year-old Chava marrying her 70-something-year-old mother, so she talked her mother into divorcing him. It was strictly a marriage of convenience. Chava had a common-law wife in Mexico but he wanted a quick way to get a "green card." I could not believe that silver-haired, reasonably attractive Chava could bring himself to have sex with Lucia's mother. That woman gave new definition to the word "ugly." She had diabetes, weighed over 300 pounds at times, and had a chalky grey complexion that reminded me of a zombie from The Walking Dead. Lucia's mother wanted a chauffeur to drive her on her errands after she had had several minor accidents driving herself around town. Once they were married, Chava moved into Lucia's mother's house. Her mother bought Chava a Jeep Cherokee to drive her on her errands. They both had a need to use the other.

Several months after Lucia paid for her mother's divorce from Chava, that silver-haired, silver-tongued Latin lover talked Lucia's mother into remarrying him. He moved back into her house, un-

beknownst to Lucia. They stayed married and lived together until Lucia's mother moved to Las Vegas. She did not need sickly
Chava any longer because she had her youngest son to drive her on
her errands in Las Vegas. When Chava died, Lucia's mother did
not even attend her husband's funeral. His adult daughter had to
make all the arrangements

In the 16 years that Lucia and I were married, I never had one
conversation with her mother. We did exchange greetings and fare-
wells, but she did not speak English and I did not speak Spanish
well enough to carry on a conversation. I was not well thought of in
the family anyway. The family thought I was a "strange old gringo."
As it was explained to me, I was expected to be the dutiful son-in-
law to the matriarch of the family. As I explained to Lucia, I lived
my own life and I would not be controlled by an ancient traditional woman who never attended a day of school in her life. At age
five, Lucia's grandparents tried to send Lucia's mother to school,
but her mother threw a fit, refusing to go to school. The grandparents then had her work at home doing house work instead. Lucia's
mother never learned to read or write, even in Spanish.

In July of 2002, I purchased a 100-year anniversary model
Harley Davidson Electra-Glide Ultra Classic motorcycle. When
I contacted the AAA insurance agent to insure the motorcycle, he
and I were discussed the insurance policy. As he reviewed our policies, he informed me that one of the vehicles on the policy was a
2002 Daewoo. I asked, "What in the hell is a Daewoo?"

The agent said it was a vehicle. I told him we did not have a
Daewoo. He insisted that we did, and it was registered to Lucia

Andrews. That was news to me. The Tom Horn trait in me could not stop me. When she got home from work, I asked her about the Daewoo. She said, as usual, "Oh, I was going to tell you about that. I bought that repossessed car from the credit union for $7000 for my mother six months ago." I was neither her gatekeeper nor her banker since she earned her own money, so there was little I could say. Lucia also revealed to me that she had previously given her mother $1000 to buy a car, but her mother had spent it on something else, possibly buying a small rental house across the street from hers. Her mother was a compulsive gambler, often taking junkets to casinos to gamble. When I first met Lucia, her mother was literally a "numbers runner" for the book makers in Juarez, Mexico.

Shortly after Lucia bought her mother the car, her mother decided that she would move to Las Vegas, Nevada, where her oldest daughter and youngest son lived. Lucia wisely told her 84-year-old mother that she could not take the car with her to Las Vegas. Her mother and family called Lucia an "Indian giver." After her mother moved, I asked Lucia where the vehicle was. She replied that it was parked in the garage at her mother's old house in central El Paso. I told her that we were going to get the vehicle and bring it to our house. She was making monthly payments and insurance premiums on the vehicle while it sat in her mother's garage. After retrieving the vehicle, we parked it outside our house. Now we had three vehicles—Lucia's 2002 BMW 540 sedan, my 1973 restored International Scout, and the Daewoo, which would sit in front of the house for months. In time, I would occasionally drive the Daewoo to keep the battery charged, since my Scout was a gas hog around town. In September of 2003, Lucia informed me that she and the daughters thought I should pay the insurance premium on the Daewoo since I was driving it. I did not ask her, "Why in the hell are you discussing our financial situation with our 20-something-year-old daughters?" I did ask if she was having trouble meeting her monthly financial obligations. She replied that she was not, but in a couple months, she would be. I did not ask where in the hell her $143,000 a year salary was going. But I would solve some of her problems. I told her that the Daewoo would become mine as of that day. I would pay the vehicle off and pay the insurance premiums. She still owed $5000 on the vehicle, but since Daewoo Motors of America had filed for bankruptcy in 2003, the vehicle may have been worth as little as $1000. I drove that vehicle till it had 143,000 miles on it. I sold it for a $1000 even after I had killed two deer with it and replaced the timing belt.

Shortly after I moved to the cabin for good, I emailed Lucia an offer for our divorce settlement. I would give her the $200,000 house in El Paso with furniture and $23,000 from my stock account. I would keep the $145,000 cabin I was living in. She could keep her full retirement and I would keep mine. We would both retain our respective vehicles, hers being a 2003 $32,000 BMW Z-4 roadster, mine being the Daewoo and the Harley. Her response was, "My attorney will contact you." A year and a half later, after mediation, and $14,000 in attorney's fees, she accepted my original offer. I never did cite adultery as the reason for the divorce filing, but that would come out in the interrogatories. It never was revealed about the suspected "threesome," which I would soon learn about from the ex "Mrs. Bill." I just wanted to move on, but she wanted to feather her new nest for her newly beloved, "the man of her dreams," who would soon turn out to be a nightmare.

On May 23, 2004, I was riding the Harley to Yuma, Arizona, to hook up with Ol' Levi. We had plans to ride up Death Valley, California, and over into Bishop, California, to attend Mules Days in Bishop. I stopped in Lordsburg, New Mexico, for gas. I was stretching my legs when my cell phone rang. It was the soon-to-be-ex Mrs. Bill.

She started the conversation with, "You will probably be getting a call from Lucia."

I could only ask, "What in the hell are you talking about?" She then related to me a conversation that she had just had with Mr. Bill's three grandchildren. According to her, Lucia had thrown a birthday party at our house for the youngest grandson the night before. Mrs. Bill had pressed the grandchildren for more details. She learned that Mr. Bill's former secretary, Diane, had attended the party also. The grand children also said that "Papa" made Lucia cry that morning when he told Lucia that he did not want to be with her anymore because he wanted to be with Diane. Mrs. Bill asked the grandchildren if Diane had spent the night at Lucia's. They answered that she had. Mrs. Bill asked where Diane slept. They answered that she slept with Papa and Lucia. I then asked Mrs. Bill if she was suggesting that Mr. Bill talked Lucia into a threesome and then dumped her out of the threesome for the younger woman. Mrs. Bill said that is what it sounded like to her.

Lucia had suggested a threesome to me twice in the year before we split up, but I would not go for it.

The Tom Horn attitude in me could not stop me from making that phone call to Lucia. I immediately dialed Lucia's cell phone number and she answered. I immediately said, "I understand that Mr. Bill just dumped you for Diane."

Her hurt, venomous response was, "Do you have my telephone tapped? How do you know what I just said?" I told her that I would never do anything like that because it is illegal. I asked how it felt to be dumped. Her response was, "Well, we are even." I knew better than to ask her if she engaged in a threesome, so I asked if they all slept together last night. Her response was, 'I don't know what you are talking about." She was a broken woman, but somehow, she and Mr. Bill reconnected. I think Mr. Bill realized the error of his ways in choosing the younger but financially struggling woman over an older—seven years his senior—but financially secure woman. The custom-made house, BMW, and Harley Sportster in the garage lifestyle would not last long, not the way Mr. Bill would spend Lucia's money.

Being a private person, I never informed my friends and coworkers that Lucia and I had split. When they asked, I would just act like things were the same. I worked with three of her former coworkers in Artesia. Through Mrs. Bill, I learned that Lucia and Mr. Bill were openly dating in El Paso, so I thought it was time to end the charade. I did not want to have to repeat the story several times, so I sent out shotgun email to all those that might have had an interest:

FOR THOSE OF YOU THAT DO NOT ALREADY KNOW, AND SO I DID NOT HAVE TO REPEAT THIS 50 TIMES.
ME ESPOSA TIENE SANCHOS! ENGLISH TRANSLATION:
MY WIFE HAS A LOVER, YES LUCIA, A 44-YEAR-OLD MARRIED GEORGIA CRACKER TRUCK DRIVER.

I knew it would be viewed as airing our dirty laundry over the internet, but my dirty laundry was already being aired in El Paso.

In October of 2004, the youngest daughter married her long-time boyfriend in El Paso. I was honored when she asked me to give her away, even though her real father would be in attendance. She also wrote me a letter after she found out about her mother and Mr. Bill, in which she wrote, "When I have children, I will bring them to meet you and introduce them to you as the person that raised me, made me who I am; the person that made me responsible, punctual, and dependable." I could have never asked for a better tribute from a daughter. I still stay in touch with both daughters and their children.

In late 2004, almost one year after Lucia was promoted to assistant Special Agent in Charge, the agency upgraded the six assistant Special Agents in Charge's positions from GS-14 to GS-15, but the six assistants and others would have to compete for the five positions. The five senior male assistants were selected for the positions. Lucia immediately filed an Employee Equal Opportunity suit against the agency for sexual and racial discrimination. Her case went before a hearing in El Paso, but the presiding official decided against her, citing lack of merit.

After I moved to the mountains to live in the cabin full time, I got the idea that I would buy a horse to go with my saddle, so I could take up riding again. I mentioned my intentions to Levi on one of his visits. In late 2004, I got a call from Levi asking me if I was still thinking about getting a horse. I told him I still was, so he said he had one I could have. He told me he had won the horse, a one-year old registered Kiger Mustang stud named Cody, in a drawing for Hospice of Yuma. I agreed to pay all the upkeep on the horse until I could ready my place for his arrival. I fenced off the lower portion of my property and had a two-stall horse barn built. In early 2005, a friend of mine and I headed to Yuma to pick up the horse.

When we got there, the person who donated Cody to Hospice agreed to give me Cody's mother, Star, as well. Star was adopted out of the BLM managed Kiger wild herd in Oregon. She has the BLM brand on her neck. I was not too sure I wanted Star. She was hard to load into the trailer and I thought she was more than I could handle. Well, it all worked out and the following year, I bred her to a neighbor's registered paint quarter horse, hoping for a paint colt. When the colt was born, the only coloring on the colt was a perfect white diamond on his forehead and two white socks on his rear feet. I named him "Ace of Diamonds" because of the diamond on his forehead.

In late 2011, Ace sent me to the hospital emergency room with cracked ribs in my back, a torn hamstring, and ruptured blood vessel in my left leg. As the Native Americans, would say, "Horse go fast, Gil go fast, horse stop fast, Gil no stop fast." Actually, it was my own stupidity that caused the accident. I should have never been riding him without a saddle or bridle. It was a long recovery, but I finally mended. It took me three years to rehabilitate the hamstring, and the cracked ribs caused me pain for five years. I would not sleep lying down for two months; I could only sleep sitting up in a recliner. As I had learned for 26 years being a jogger, never surrender to the pain, always run through it, as I did in 1972 with my first appendicitis attack. Even after developing burning hammer toe and heal spurs, I would figure out a way to continue some type exercise. Surrender to the pain, and you risk losing your mobility, especially as you age. Several years later, I was plagued with a pinched sciatic nerve, which caused unbearable pain, restricting my mobility. To get past the pain, I would walk five miles a day, 10 miles on Sunday. Usually after about a mile, I could eliminate the pain, but that first mile was painful.

The Final Chapter

In the summer of 2004, just a few months after Lucia and I were separated, as my friends and co-workers learned that I was soon to be single, they started encouraging me to start looking for a replacement partner online. I figured it was too soon to start another relationship and I felt that I had little to offer to a perspective online partner considering the remote area that I lived in. One of my coworkers had worked with Lucia and I in El Paso. He would regularly encourage me to contact a lady that he knew in El Paso that was soon to be separated from her current husband and co-incidentally rode a motorcycle. I repeatedly told him I would not initiate contact with a lady that did not know me. I told him to ask the lady first to learn if she was interested in meeting someone so soon after her separation. In time, we did meet and began a casual "mending" relationship. As many newly separated individuals do, we began to associate with each other mainly to get and receive support, just two people struggling with contentious divorces. She too was being kicked to the curb by her husband of 20 years. She had discovered that her husband was searching a Russian Bride site, looking for her replacement. Soon after they separated, he began efforts to bring a prospective Russian bride to the U.S. He moved the Russian woman into his home before the divorce was even final. They were married the day after his divorce was final. Over several years, we bonded as "best friends" and the relationship blossomed into something meaningful.

I had never anticipated that she and I would share conservative values and goals. How she handled a significant event in her life caused me to develop a high degree of respect for her. She was married at age 15 to a 19-year Marine, but six months later, she became a widow when her Marine husband was killed in Vietnam. Initially, she went to live with her deceased husband's family on a farm in Minnesota. She contributed her military benefits to her in-laws for her upkeep. She also worked on the farm, feeding the animals during those cold Minnesota winters. She would eventually remarry and go back to school, eventually obtaining her undergraduate degree and three master's degrees. She and I would eventually marry after 10 years of riding together. Thirteen years later, we are still together.

In early 2007, my brother Eddie reestablished contact with the family. He supposedly had cleaned up his act and gotten off drugs, but now he drank every day. No one even knew how to contact him when our mother died to let him know. I have visited him in a couple times in California, where he lives with his African-American girlfriend. I thought it was a little unusual that after two Hispanic wives, he was now living with an African-American woman. He now had five grown children. He seemed to be on a quest to make things up to them, in his way, for the years he was not around. I do not know if that is possible.

He told me that he came home one evening and caught his

second wife and another girl in the shower together, so he just joined them. The three then participated in a threesome, which caused his wife to become jealous of her girlfriend having sex with Eddie. His wife finally left him for another woman, even though they had four children together. I am sure it probably had a lot to do with his drug use.

He admitted that for 17 years, he was living on the streets, collecting aluminum cans so he could use the money to buy meth. At first, I hit it off with his new girlfriend, but in time, I realized how much of a bigot she was. In an email exchange between us, I made the statement that I had read all the books that were written on the O.J. Simpson trial and I believed O.J. was guilty.

Her response was, "You hate black people." What a hell of a thing for someone that is living with my black brother to say. In another exchange, she was talking about issues that my brother had. I told her she should imagine how she would feel to be raised in a white family and not know how you got there until you were told by your older brother when you were 19 that a black man raped your white mother.

Her response was, "Gil, you have to stop carrying that around, and don't tell your brother that. Back in the old days, white men raped black women all the time." How could a woman excuse a man of any color raping a woman of any color? To me, I think that speaks to her not wanting my brother to acquire any resentment toward her race. We may have had acquired resentments toward blacks had we learned of the circumstance of his conception at a younger age, but instead, we were protected from that by him be-

ing in our family. I do not think she wants my brother to acknowledge that he is 50% white. I have not had any contact with her
since. That reinforced something I had learned many years ago;
you cannot say anything that may be construed as being critical of
a person of color unless you are a person of color. Their relationship did not last long after he lost his job. He would again distance
himself from the rest of the family, He did not even attend funeral
services for Sadie when she passed.

On April 24, 2007, I quit drinking, cold turkey. I was tired of
the hang-overs and the miserable mornings after. I spent the better
part of my life drinking to medicate stress, but it was only a temporary relief. I am the classic example of the phrase, "a man takes
a drink, a drink takes a drink, then the drink takes the man." I had
always told my ex-wives they never had to worry about me getting
involved with a woman when I was drinking. I would rather have
another beer. I did what I could to eliminate the stress in life by
avoiding things that might cause me stress, most of it is caused by
my own fretting personality. Finally having control of my own life
eliminated so much stress that can be caused by others. I had become estranged from my own family to eliminate the chaos, but by
marrying Lucia, I just brought another family's chaos into my life.

In February of 2012, on the heels of falling off Ace, I was diagnosed with prostate cancer. My first reaction was that it was the
end. I started getting my affairs in order, rethinking my will, finding homes for my nine animals, generally getting things in order.
The hardest part was trying to figure out how to tell my lady friend
that it would be best if she just moved on. After 43 radiation treat-

ments, I had my lab work done again, but my PSA was elevated to from 8.6 to 12, which was a shocker. The cancer doctor told me to go to the hospital immediately and have a bone scan and a CAT scan. He wanted to see if the cancer had "spread." Hearing the word "spread" shook me up. Waiting a week to get the results was stressful. There was no indication of any cancer, but it is something that may have to be revisited in the future. Ironically, in 2014, I learned that my chronic lymphocytic leukemia was in remission. My doctor could not explain what caused the remission. In fact, he said he had never heard of that before. I told him that I had no scientific proof, but when I was diagnosed with leukemia, I concocted an aloe vera cocktail, which I drink 12 ounces of daily. The cocktail consists of:

One half gallon of pure aloe vera juice
One liter of low sodium V8
One 15 oz can of asparagus
One cup of lemon juice (I puree a whole quartered lemon, peel and all)
Two tablespoons of minced garlic, all pureed together.
Two whole green chilis

Realizing I may have been given a second chance, I have started on my "bucket list" in earnest. My first adventure was a week-long visit to Ireland.

I just recently passed the 350,000-cumulative mile mark riding five different Harleys over the past 17 years. I have ridden them in all fifty states, including Alaska and Hawaii. I had to fly to Hawaii and rent a Harley there to tour the island. Fortunately, I have not had any accidents in those 340,000 miles, unless you count the Walmart parking lot senior moment. I was pulling into a parking place at Walmart. As I was stopping, the bike got off balance, causing me to drop the bike. When it fell over, it pinned my right foot to the ground. I was lying there on my back, with tears in my eyes, trying to kick that bike off me while people kept walking by, looking down at me with the expression, "You dumb shit, what are you doing down there?" I finally couldn't stand the pain anymore and begged some passerby to help get the bike off my foot. Ironically, Levi had had a similar experience, but he was not so fortunate.

Levi was riding back to Kentucky by himself and decided to pull off the interstate to check his map. He did the same thing I did. He didn't get his left foot down before the bike got off balance. He dropped the bike on his foot. Somehow, he kicked that 850-pound bike off his foot then somehow picked that bike up by himself with a broken ankle. I don't know if I could have done that. He got back on the bike and rode it down to the nearest Motel 6 to check in. He parked the bike out front of the office and limped into the lobby. There were other customers checking in, so he had to wait. Eventually, the pain from the broken ankle must have become too much to bear. He fainted in the lobby. Levi looks the part of a crusty old biker in his leather jacket and leather chaps, so he made quite the scene when he collapsed. Naturally, panic overcame the occupants of the lobby. They didn't know if he had a heart attack or what had happened, but someone called 911. The ambulance hauled him off to the emergency room, and at the hospital, they discovered his broken ankle. They wanted to put a cast on, but Levi would not have that. He would only allow them to put a temporary walking cast on him. He was going to go home. He had to lay up in the motel for three days. That in itself must have been as bad as the broken ankle for him. He then rented a small U-Haul truck, got someone to help him load the motorcycle in the back of the truck, and headed back to Yuma.

The Hard Way

Obviously, I have made some mistakes in my life. I did not live a perfect life. I would never suggest to anyone that I was a saint, and surely those that know me would laugh at such a suggestion. But I did live a life. I did not sit on the sidelines and watch others live their lives. I lived life the only way I knew how. I am about to start another chapter in my life, and I will continue to live it my way, but hopefully it will not be as hard as the past years. One of my wives described me as "painfully independent," and I would have to agree, but I owe that to my mother's "mother bird mentality"— you will have to fly from the nest on your own someday. I flew away and never looked back.

I believe that I may have been somewhat naive throughout my career to think that the users and takers, the bootlickers, or, as one of my supervisors put it, the "barracudas" could be avoided by just doing your job, expecting to be left alone. But in a law enforcement career, you draw attention to yourself just by making arrests and seizures. It is not always positive attention. Even Don Ware, who was a law enforcement icon, experienced the inter-office and intra-agencies jealousies that are so common in law enforcement. You are only as good as your last case.

If the measure of a man's success is a successful marriage, then

I may have failed. But I now might achieve that success, now that I have found someone with common goals and common values. If the measure of a man is how well the children he raised turned out, then I believe I have succeeded. My son graduated college with two degrees, speaks three languages beside English—Spanish, French and Russian—and is now an FBI agent assigned to the Counter Terrorism Center on the east coast. He married a smart, beautiful woman. They have a beautiful 13-year-old daughter. Both of Lucia's daughters graduated from college in three years, then obtained graduate degrees, one in law and the other in speech therapy. All three of them worked their way through college. Both daughters are married to very respectable young men and have five children between them.

I cannot take credit for their success. They have earned their success themselves. I do feel my conservative parenting, keeping them on the right path and guiding them in making the right decisions, have helped them along life's path. None of the children I have raised are just "gettin' by" like I did. If there is a formula for raising successful children, then I believe it starts with the word "vigilance." Always watch, always listen, and always guide. Yes, they thought I was a nag, a pain in the ass, and a strict old gringo, but I wanted to help them avoid some of the mistakes I had made. I believe their success speaks to my efforts. I believe that, like my mother, I pushed my children to be self-reliant. But the "prepare them to launch" mentality, as they say, is not always appreciated. It probably will not endear you to your children. Many of us want our children to do better than we did. I believe my children have done just that. Looking back at my life, it reads like a salacious TV soap opera.

Some might suggest that I have entered the winter of my life, but I tell them I am still in the autumn. The leaves on the trees are still brightly colored, the roads are clear, the sky is blue, and the sun is shining brightly. I am looking forward to tomorrow and Saturdays, but every day is a Saturday now.

Regrets, yes, I have a few. It is said that bad decisions make for great stories. I have a few of those also. Being hardheaded some-times leads to bad decisions. But I do not regret standing up for myself. Being taught your place in life at an early age tends to mold your personality. You appear to be good-natured, non-con-frontational, and quietly cooperative in most things. I have never been the loud and rowdy type, and I do not believe anyone thinks of me as confrontational. But I will stand my ground. The trait of quiet resolve is the only weapon of social resistance available to you. But occasionally, you must poke people in the eye to make your point.

I wish I'd had the courage to live a life true to myself, not the life others and society expected of me. As a law enforcement offi-cer, you are expected to live by certain standards, to live your life in a fish bowl, as they say, and over a lengthy career, you develop a professional demeanor, which you tend to carry into your per-sonal life—guarded emotions, calm coolness, vigilance or "situa-tional awareness," etc. Relating to others as a career law enforce-ment officer can be a double-edged sword. Some might thank you for your service, but others might offer cutting remarks, especially when they discover most of your career you spent putting narcotics violators in jail, some for life.

Some people wish that they did not work so hard. I don't have that regret. I enjoyed my law enforcement career. It was never like work to me. I went to work to entertain myself. I wish I'd had the courage to express my feelings more, but we are who we are. It is very difficult to shake the Tom Horn attitude. I have a belief that many of the silver-tongued people, the wordsmiths and bull-shitters, use that trait to sway others solely to achieve their own ends. I believe you can't judge a man by the words he speaks but rather by his deeds. I wish I had stayed in touch with my friends, especially my cousin Charlie and Don Ware. I wish that I knew for sure who my father was but, as Eddie has said, Tom raised us. I wish I knew more about the first 45 years of Tom's life. I wish I had a better relationship with my son and brother. My son has not visited me in 14 years. His wife of 16 years and their 13-year-old daughter have never visited me. During one of my visits to their house, I invited them to visit, but his wife's comment was, "You don't have any shopping." I told her that I would take them to one of the three neighboring towns to shop. Her response was, "But you do not have a Niemen Marcus." I did not have a response to that. I have extended the olive branch to both, but they seem too busy with their lives. I have not seen them in six years. I really wish I had let myself be happier, but becoming a worrier, a fretter, at an early age prevented that. But wishing for what might have been will not solve anything. Like the saying goes, "Wish in one shoe and urinate in the other and see which one fills up the quickest." If it is true that the secret to being happy is having a good sense of humor and a dirty mind, I should be happy.

One of life's mysteries is how I could have spent 29 years in Federal Law Enforcement, walking the straight and narrow, never even trying drugs or doing anyone any intentional harm, and yet still be remembered for the negative. I have only been riding the Harleys for the past 17 years, but I am now seen only as the old biker. I always tell people, you do not have to be a fat, greasy, tattooed drunk to ride a Harley. I have no tattoos and do not plan on getting any. When I first met my father-in-law-to-be, he told my lady friend that I was a "dangerous man." After a visit to my home, he told my lady friend that I was a "hidden man." I never did figure out what that meant. Twice my lady friend and I took motorcycle road trips to Springfield, Illinois, to visit her brother. On both trips, her brother made a point of seeing that we did not visit his home; he would meet with us away from his home. I got the impression that his wife did not want us bikers to be seen at her house. It is like the old joke about the guy that goes to church all his life and just before he dies, he commits an act of carnal knowledge with another man, and that is how he is remembered.

Before I retired, I noticed that the entitlement mentality was well rooted within the government ranks. It was no longer about achievement but what you were entitled to by the mere fact that you had obtained a government position. Many of those in law enforcement career employees are there solely for the government paycheck and the security of the government job. When I was promoted to Senior Agent, I was 42 years old and had 15 years of service. An agent had to do a significant case to be promoted to Senior Agent. When I was promoted to supervisor, I was 50 years old with 26 years of service. I watched as many of the entitled, the protégés, the bootlickers, and those with "connections," rose in the ranks with little or no achievement at all. When I retired, a young, 22-year-old new hire could start a career in the legacy U.S. Customs Office of Investigations, before it became Immigration and Customs Enforcement (ICE), and within five years become a senior agent automatically, making over $100,000 per year. Before I retired, there were attempts to deny some non-producing agents their automatic promotion to Senior Agent. However, it required such lengthy documentation and litigation, especially if the employee was considered a minority, that future attempts were eventually abandoned.

I have seen many in the government that have been taught at an early age, maybe unknowingly, that the system is stacked against them. Thus, when things do not get their way, they feel discriminated against. In one year after achieving the position of Senior Agent, the employee is then eligible for promotion to a management position. Each employee seems to believe that they are entitled to the positions or transfers to locations of their choice, which they have applied for. Denying them the position can lead to complaints of discrimination, no matter how unfounded. Such was the case with Lucia. In fact, the entitlement, petulant child mentality seems to be prevalent throughout our society today. I believe it is a cancer in our society that will not be stopped until the mentality is no longer sustainable or acceptable. Once a government entitlement program is created, it is next to impossible to abolish the program. I no longer envy the entitlement class. I feel pity for them, maybe even disgust. The Lord giveth and the Lord taketh away. The government giveth but the government cannot taketh away unless you pay taxes. The lord will prevail!

I believe that a large portion of disenfranchised Americans have conveniently acquired a victim mentality. They have been subtly convinced by nurturers, political groups, and government entities that they have been treated unfairly by the system, and thus are entitled to special consideration. Many of these so called "victims" are convinced by others they that need some type of a support group to protect them from further unfairness, i.e. unions, the NAACP, ethnic organizations, terrorist groups, etc. There seems to be a conscious effort to organize these victims, mainly to exploit them for political purposes. These groups intentionally engage in "Victim Pimping" so the victims will align themselves with the support group. The Democratic Party seems to prey on the "victims" by convincing them that they are the support group they need. Thus, they have created the "war on women," the "the war on black males," and discrimination against the 12 million illegal aliens and other minorities that supposedly are being treated unfairly.

My mother unknowingly, unintentionally, instilled that "victim" mentality in her children, but that was before the entitlement programs. "Poor people have poor ways," and poor people, the underclass, are not integrated into mainstream society. She used to say that "We are democrats because they are for the poor people."

Thus, the Republicans are for the rich people. And the poor people are victims of the rich. That "victim" mentality I think is what drove me into the deep feeling of despair at age 15, which caused me to contemplate suicide that summer of 1961. Had I not broken away from that stifling despair, at the least, I probably would have become an alcoholic.

My self-esteem was never nurtured by my parents. I had low self-esteem for most of my younger life. My mother unintentionally taught us to "know our place in life." Over the many years of being on my own and accomplishing things I never thought I could, I would nurture my own self-esteem and finally validate myself. I no longer have the "victim" mentality. Americans need to shed the "victim" mentality and the entitlement mentality, but I do not think it is possible. There will always be those that will exploit the "victim" mentality. Americans should be nurtured to believe that they are winners, not whiners.

Reflecting on my life, I have concluded that several choices, or lucky breaks, determined the path that I followed. Failing the draft pre-induction physical prevented me from being drafted into the Army, thus allowing me the second chance of choosing an alternative service, the United States Air Force. The insignificant choice of taking a typing class in my senior year of high school determined the career field I was trained in during my Air Force career. That career field led to my first government job. Taking the Air Traffic Control test opened the door to the Sky Marshal job, which in turn opened the door to a 29-year law enforcement career. Having the nerve to accept the law enforcement position led me to a career that suited my short attention span personality. I did not take to law enforcement initially, but quickly found that the variety of the job kept my interest.

Epilogue

"Don Cleo Ware: "Special Agent Don Ware began his career in law enforcement in 1967 with the Albuquerque Police Department in New Mexico. He then joined the Bureau of Narcotics and Dangerous Drugs" (BNDD), which later became the Drug Enforcement Administration (DEA), in 1973." After Don spent six months in the hospital, he returned to work, never losing his dedication to duty. Although Don qualified for full medical retirement, he instead chose to continue working for the DEA until his retirement in 1995. During the four years that Don and I worked together, he walked with a limp due to a hip replacement, and he always wore a corset to hold in his stomach. He had never had his stomach muscles reconnected. I had asked Don several times why he did not have another hip replacement and have his stomach muscles reconnected. He would always say, "he did not want to go back under the knife." I could sure understand that, considering all the medical treatments he had been through. "For his service, Special Agent Don Ware was awarded the DEA Medal of Valor and the DEA Purple Heart Award."7

Don Ware died on October 12, 2004, due to "complications during surgery," directly related to injuries received in the line of duty. Don died while under the surgeon's knife, something he had avoided for years. Don was memorialized on the National Law Enforcement Officers Memorial on May 12, 2011 and the DEA Wall of Honor on May 13, 2011.

On the Saturday afternoon that Don and I were chasing Bert's classic cars out of Las Vegas, Don paid me one of the highest compliments I could ever have asked for. As I was leaning out the window of Don's vehicle, flashing my badge at the semi-truck driver and Don honking his vehicle's horn, trying to get the truck driver to stop, Don said "Gil, you are one hell of a cop." I couldn't have been given a greater compliment from "one hell of a cop" himself.

After we indicted the Requiem to a Queen case, we had to have the main violator extradited from the Philippines, where he was hiding. Through Don's DEA contacts in the Philippines, we had Bert deported to Hawaii. The cowboy in me wanted to go to the Philippines and participate in the arrest, but Don preferred going to Hawaii. Bert was escorted to Hawaii by a Philippines Immigration Officer, where we arrested him. The Philippine Immigration Officer presented Don with a beautifully hand-carved, mahogany wood, ten-inch-high statue of a Game rooster. The cone on the head of the rooster was painted bright red. Don did not feel it was appropriate to accept the statue, so he gave it to me. I kept the rooster in my office for years. I had typed up a label, which I affixed to the base of the statue. It read 10 INCH ERECT WOODEN COCK WITH A RED HEAD. I would always tell people that Don gave me the 10-inch erect wooden cock with a red head.

Adolph Rivera: After a six-month struggle, Adolph was successful in his efforts to be reinstated after the disciplinary review board recommended his termination. It seems a female member of the review board disclosed the findings of the board to a coworker, thus violating Adolph's employee rights. He got his job back on a technicality. After being reinstated, he was transferred to the west coast as an assistant agent in charge. After his reinstatement, he sent a message to me through one of my subordinates: "Tell Gil I am still here." He always assumed I wrote the anonymous letter, not Lucia. Adolph never did obtain the position to which he aspired, Special Agent in Charge of a west coast office. He was forced into retirement on the last day of the month in which he turned 57, February 29, 2000. I retired three days later, March 3, at age 53. I was still standing when he retired.

Joe Bob: Joe Bob is a good man who found himself the ultimate victim of the Tucson Burn detail debacle. All the employees who were terminated got their jobs back with back pay, apart from one, and that employee was reinstated but he opted to return to work without back pay before the others got a settlement. Even J.R. did his penitence in Chicago and was transferred back to Texas. He is now in management with ICE himself. After Joe Bob did his penitence in New York City, he too transferred back to Texas, where he would retire. It was sad the way the Customs employees were treated because of two individuals stealing the marijuana from the smoldering pile. The then Commissioner of Customs, Ray (Popeye) Kelly, only cared about making an example of the employees, even though those employees had followed the same procedures that had been followed for years. Kelly only cared about the embarrassment that was caused to him as commissioner. All he accomplished was a great waste of the tax-payer money by forcing the government and the employees into lengthy litigation.

Speed Bump/Jabba the Hutt/Dr. Evil: After leaving Texas, he was assigned as Special Agent in Charge in Phoenix, Arizona, where he and then Governor Janet Napolitano would find themselves at odds. The irony would be that in 2009, Napolitano would become Secretary of Homeland Security, which has authority over Immigration and Customs Enforcement, Dr. Evil's agency. Supposedly, he was summoned to Washington D.C. before Napolitano was sworn in. It was suggested to Dr. Evil that it would be in his best interest to retire before Secretary Napolitano took office in 2009. Dr. Evil saw the wisdom in the suggestion and retired.

Mr. Player: Player continued to work at the contract job after his retirement, "the golden parachute," until it was abolished. Then he found himself doing background investigations for U.S. Border Patrol in 2007. I suspected that Player became aware of me reporting his involvement with Precious, but he never challenged me on it.

The female manager who ignored my anonymous letter about Player soon found herself force-transferred back to Washington D.C. As a manager, she had operational authority over a narcotics group that was regularly using an informant who was a member of a "death squad" for a drug organization in Juarez, Mexico. The controlling agent, as well as some managers, became aware of the informant's participation, but continued to utilize the productive informant, even after they learned of an audio tape in which the informant participated in the torture and murder of another suspected informant. Once the information came to light, the informant should have been deactivated and black-listed from use by all agencies. The agent in charge of the El Paso office at that time soon followed the female manager back to Washington D.C. over the same incident. Assignment to the Special Agent in Charge position in El Paso was a kiss of death to many managers over the years. Back in the 1970s, it was said that if you screwed up in U.S. Customs, you were sent to El Paso, Texas. Being sent to El Paso was like being sent to Siberia. After one of the training classes Lucia attended at the academy, the Assistant Commissioner stated to the class, "We would like to draw a line from Dallas to El Paso and give everything south of the line back to Mexico." If you screwed up in the FBI, you were sent to Fargo, North Dakota. The work load in a border office like El Paso lends itself to operational problems that managers must deal with daily, but many of the managers overplayed their new-found authority when dealing with the problems.

Mini-Me: Mini-Me retired and continued working in the "golden parachute" contract job until it was abolished. He became close friends with Player. He also began doing background investigation for U.S. Border Patrol. Just before he retired, he was removed from operational authority over staff and enforcement personnel and relegated to a building manager status. Ironically, I also did background investigations for Border Patrol during that period in the same town that Player and Mini-Me worked. I had occasional contact with both. Even then, Mini-Me tried creating problems with his tattletale style.

Adolph, Joe Bob, Dr. Evil, Player, and Mini-Me all eventually would learn what many of us learned under their authority—your attitude toward your job is greatly determined by the relationship you have with your immediate supervisor and those in positions of authority above you. What goes around comes around. They too found themselves, at times, "just gettin' by."

Post script:

In August 2014, I married my riding partner of 10 years. She and I were married in a Harley-themed wedding at the annual Sturgis Motorcycle Rally in Sturgis, South Dakota. Ol' Levi was best man. Guierllmo Juevo and Kent were groomsmen.

Mutt report:

In 2015, I submitted my DNA sample, along with my three younger female sibling's DNA samples, for comparison. The DNA comparison revealed that the samples do not support Tom being my father. The report states that there is 0.000001% probability that Tom is my father. The report states that I am 67% English, not Irish as I had always believed. It would appear that Mom lied to Tom and me all these years. I guess it could be possible she did not know herself. It is also possible that when the responsible party did not accept his responsibility, Mom found someone else to be a plausible substitute. I will never know who my father was.

References

(1) http://www.ci.exeter.ne.us/general.htm

(2) http://www.militarymuseum.org/ArbucklePOWCamp.html

(3) BraceroArchive.org/about

(4) http://murderpedia.org/male.T/t/tison-gary-gene.htm

(5) http://www.famous-detectives.com/j-j-armes.htm

(6) https://theunredacted.com/the-legend-of-golden-lily-yamashitas-gold/

(7) https://www.odmp.org/officer/20685-special-agent-don-cleo-ware

About the Author

Gil Andrews (pseudonym) is a 71-year-old first time author. Gil had a 40-year career with the Federal Government, 29 of those years in law enforcement. Most of his work involved narcotic cases on the Mexican border. Some of his high profile cases took unfortunate turns but were usually successfully completed. Gil is now retired and now lives in Southern New Mexico with his wife and six dogs.